W9-BNF-911

Religious Schools v. Children's Rights

Religious Schools v. Children's Rights

JAMES G. DWYER

CORNELL UNIVERSITY PRESS

ITHACA AND LONDON

First published 1998 by Cornell University Press

Printed in the United States of America

Cornell University Press strives to use environmentally responsible suppliers and materials to the fullest extent possible in the publishing of its books. Such materials include vegetable-based, low-VOC inks and acid-free papers that are also recycled, totally chlorine-free, or partly composed of nonwood fibers.

Cloth printing   10   9   8   7   6   5   4   3   2   1

Library of Congress Cataloging-in-Publication Data

Dwyer, James G.
    Religious schools v. children's rights / James G. Dwyer.
       p.   cm.
    Includes index.
    ISBN 0-8014-3426-2 (hardcover : alk. paper)
    1. Church schools—Law and legislation—United States.
    2. Religious education—Law and legislation—United States.
    3. Parent and child (Law)—United States.   I. Title.
    KF4124.D97   1998
    344.73'0796—dc21   98-14863

To my parents

Contents

Acknowledgments

I am very grateful to Debra Satz, Susan Okin, Tom Grey, and Michael Bratman for their encouragement and guidance in the early stages of creating this work and to the many people who took the time to read all or part of the manuscript and offer useful comments, especially Ned Foley, Stephen Gilles, Wendy Gordon, Sandy Levinson, Dick Markovits, Frances Olsen, Paul Roth, and Judith Jarvis Thomson. I am also grateful to the Chicago-Kent College of Law for its institutional support during the completion of this work.

Chapter 3 of the book is adapted from "Parents' Religion and Children's Welfare: Debunking the Doctrine of Parents' Rights," *California Law Review* 82 (1994): 1371–1447, and is reprinted with permission. © 1994 by California Law Review, Inc. Chapter 5 and the first part of Chapter 2 are adapted from "The Children We Abandon: Religious Exemptions to Child Welfare and Education Laws As Denials of Equal Protection to Children of Religious Objectors," *North Carolina Law Review* 74 (1996): 1321–1478, and are reprinted with permission. © 1996 by North Carolina Law Review Association.

Religious Schools v. Children's Rights

Introduction

Early in this century, there was widespread support in the United States for imposing substantial restrictions on religious schools. Several states passed laws prohibiting foreign language instruction in private schools, which severely hampered the operation of religious schools by immigrant communities, and one state went so far as to mandate that all children attend public schools. Proponents of universal common schooling emphasized its conduciveness to social cohesion and equal opportunity. They feared that schools not under state control promoted the insularity of religious and cultural minorities, inculcated improper values and beliefs, and failed to provide children with an adequate secular education.

In the 1920s, however, the Supreme Court issued a series of decisions that created for parents a constitutional right to send their children to a private school of their choosing, and to resist state-imposed restrictions on instruction in their children's schools. Since that time, religious schooling has flourished, becoming, for millions of parents in this country, an alternative to state-run education. Catholic schools have long been most prevalent, but in recent decades Fundamentalist Christian schools have exploded in number, and many other religious groups, including Orthodox Jews, Lutherans, Seventh Day Adventists, Jehovah's Witnesses, and Muslims, also operate their own schools. The existence of these schools is no longer controversial, and though political and ideological conflicts between religious minorities and the state persist, the methods and content of the education religious groups provide their children now receive little public attention. In fact, to the extent that religious schooling is the subject of political debate at all today, it is in the context of proposals for increased state subsidies for such schooling, such as through tuition voucher programs. These proposals have triggered outcries in some quarters about religious establishment and abandonment of public education but little public deliberation about whether religious schools provide an appropriate educational alternative for children, or whether increased regulation should accompany any new subsidies.

The pervasively uncritical attitude toward religious schooling in our society probably reflects, in part, a widespread assumption that states already oversee religious schools sufficiently to ensure that they provide an adequate education and do nothing to threaten the well-being of their pupils. The Supreme Court, in granting parents a right to opt out of public education, emphasized that states retain the authority to regulate all private schools to protect the states' interests in children's education. One might expect that states today would be motivated to regulate religious schools for many of the same reasons that motivated the universal public schooling movement. The truth of the matter, however, is that the states and the federal government have effectively relinquished all authority to oversee private schooling. As shown in the first chapter of this book, in contrast to the extensive regulatory scheme governing public schools in most states, there are virtually no constraints today on what religious schools teach or how they treat their students.

Though this fact may surprise many people, in itself it may not alarm anyone. Perhaps there is no reason for state officials to be looking over the shoulders of religious school operators. The fact that parents choose to pay for their children to attend a religious school rather than a public school might suggest that any such school must actually outperform public schools in order to survive. Indeed, there have been reports in the past that students in Catholic schools average slightly higher on standardized tests than do public school students. As it turns out, the schools themselves may have had little to do with the students' higher test scores, but more important, these tests reveal little about the quality of education and the treatment of children in Catholic schools and, of course, nothing about the experience of children in schools operated by other religious groups, which are generally ignored. Moreover, if one were to seek additional information, one would find that there is very little publicly available and that what is available is, at least from a secular perspective, cause for serious concern.

There has been only a handful of in-depth studies of Catholic and Fundamentalist Christian schools, most conducted in the early 1980s, and almost none of other types of religious schools in this country. The studies that have been done, however, paint a picture many people would find troubling. Most of Chapter 1 is devoted to summarizing and synthesizing the information these studies provide. To give just a hint of the kinds of concerns I discuss, consider that hundreds of thousands of children today attend a type of Fundamentalist Christian school that has *no* teachers. Students in these schools, from kindergarten onward, sit alone all day at individual work stations, completing Fundamentalist workbooks through the elementary and secondary years. The studies further reveal that Fundamentalist Christian schools of all kinds explicitly inculcate sexist views and aggressively discourage girls from pursuing any ambition in life other than serving a husband. Sexism, in more and less overt forms, has also afflicted children's schooling in other denominations, including Catholicism.

In this book, I consider whether "the state"—by which I mean federal, state, and/or local government entities—ought to regulate religious schools to a greater extent than at present to ensure that the content of instruction and the treatment of children in these schools is consistent with the temporal (i.e., secular, nonspiritual) interests of the children. This is a different question from whether, in some particular communities in this country today, the religious schools are better or worse for children in terms of safety and academic quality than the local public schools—a question parents might reasonably ask before deciding where to send their children, but one that should not determine a state's obligation to establish guidelines for instruction and treatment of children in religious schools. Regulation of religious schools will be the topical focus of a broader analysis of the state's role in child rearing and the state's obligation to protect and promote the well-being of children. I will also touch upon the topic of medical care for children and on the religious objections some parents have to their children's receiving such care; this is an area that raises legal and philosophical questions analogous to those arising in connection with state oversight of nonpublic schooling.

I approach these questions in a novel way that I believe to be more appropriate than the current standard approaches. The great bulk of legal and philosophical writing to date on the topic of state control over child rearing in religious contexts has mirrored judicial treatment of parent-state conflicts (described in Chapter 2) in pitting the interests and rights of parents and religious communities against societal interests and in trumpeting the liberal values of toleration and pluralism. Remarkably little attention is given to the interests and rights of individual children in these situations or to what children are owed as a matter of justice, despite the fact that it is quite clearly children themselves who have the most at stake in their upbringing. In Chapters 3 and 4 I show why the adult-centered approaches that have dominated discourse in this area—focusing on the rights of parents and communities and/or on the rights of the state or the needs of a liberal democratic society—are all improper. I endeavor in these chapters to show that the only *rights* we should recognize in the law governing child rearing are rights of children themselves, and that state policy regarding education—public and private—and other aspects of child rearing should be based on the interests of children.

The book's central purpose is thus to demonstrate the need for a new theoretical and legal approach to resolving parent-state conflicts over child rearing, and it uses the particular context of state regulation of religious schooling to illustrate the debates and conclusions that this approach entails. In this context, the clash of values is particularly intense, parental interests appear particularly strong, and thwarting parental preferences seems particularly at odds with our self-conception as a tolerant society. Accordingly, this context presents perhaps the greatest challenge to a child-centered position; a convincing argument here will have even greater force when applied to other child-rearing situations.

After deconstructing the prevailing, adult-centered modes of addressing conflicts over state regulation of child-rearing practices, I present an alternative framework for analyzing what state policy toward religious schooling and other religious child-rearing practices should be, one in which children alone—not their parents, not religious communities, and not the state—have rights. With respect to the role of parents in children's lives, I draw an important distinction between enjoying the *privilege* of occupying a certain position and of having presumptive authority to make certain decisions or provisional freedom to act within one's own discretion, on the one hand, and having a *right* to occupy a position, to make decisions, or to act as one chooses, on the other. Parents should have presumptive authority to make many decisions on behalf of their children and considerable discretion in how they govern their children's lives, but that is because this is best for children, not because parents are entitled to it.

How much parental authority and freedom are best for children is an empirical question, one I address in Chapters 5 and 6 in the context of religious schooling. In doing so, I diverge from most liberal writing about child-rearing conflicts, not only by rejecting the parents' rights/state interests paradigm, but also by not giving priority of place to moral autonomy. I do not assume that moral autonomy (i.e., informed, independent, and reflective judgment as to what is "good") is intrinsically valuable, nor do I make much of its instrumental value. I believe it is less important for every individual to have arrived at his or her beliefs about religion and morality in a certain way than for children as well as adults to be free to think and speak as they choose without coercion and to develop general higher-order reasoning skills (whether or not they apply this capacity to religious beliefs). It is these skills that allow all children to occupy careers and fulfill other ambitions for which their native talents and abilities are suited. Thus, in Chapters 5 and 6, I show that certain formal and substantive rights that all children should have in connection with their education create an obligation on the part of the state to ensure that children who attend religious schools are not subjected to harmful practices, such as those that deny them basic liberties, and that they receive an education that fosters higher-order thinking skills and provides a robust knowledge base. The state has this obligation not because fulfilling it serves our society as a whole (though it may well do so) but because it is best for each individual child and is what each child deserves.

The reader will no doubt already have numerous questions about the assumptions on which this analysis rests: Why is a secular perspective the correct one from which to analyze religious school practices? Even from a secular perspective, who decides what children's interests are? Who has ultimate authority over children's upbringing anyway? What significance should children's own religious beliefs and preferences regarding their schooling have? What about the fundamental right to religious freedom guaranteed in the Constitution? Wouldn't universally applying majoritarian child-rearing norms create a homogeneous population and thereby make us all worse off? I will address these and many other important questions in the course of the book and will urge a new way of thinking about them. I intend to show that by recognizing and treating children as persons distinct from their parents, rather than as mere appendages or property of their parents or as mere means to the furtherance of societal aims, we reach conclusions about how the law

should govern children's lives that are much different from the conclusions courts and most commentators have reached. These conclusions
would require significantly greater restrictions on parents' freedom than
presently exist, particularly with respect to children's education.

People familiar with past battles over regulating religious schools
know that parental opposition within some religious groups—most notably Fundamentalist Christians—has matched, in vehemence if not in
numbers, opposition to public school desegregation. Some may argue
that enforcing any substantial regulations of religious schools would in
some cases be so difficult and traumatic for all parties involved, including the children in the schools, that states should not make the attempt
but should instead resign themselves to the fact that it is simply not
possible to secure for all children what they are owed as a matter of justice. In my view, however, there are many untried strategies for generating acceptance of school regulations among those most adamantly opposed. The desegregation struggle provides valuable lessons as to the
better and worse approaches to accomplishing what our law and morality tell us is the right outcome.

Though I discuss some possible strategies in the conclusion of the
book, working out these practicalities is not one of my goals. Even if in-
surmountable practical obstacles were likely in the case of all types of
religious schools—and not only or primarily Fundamentalist Christian
schools—it would still be important to undertake the legal and theoretical analysis. We should know what the right outcome is so that even if
we cannot accomplish it, we know what our aim is and what we have
sacrificed when we settle for compromises. Moreover, those who would
oppose increased regulation of religious schools are not impervious to
popular beliefs about their practices; their opposition in the past has no
doubt been fueled by the legal doctrine and widespread belief that parents are entitled to raise their children as they see fit. Should a majority
in this country come to adopt what I will argue is the proper view of parenting—that it is a privilege rather than a right—and gain a proper understanding of the rights of children in connection with their education,
this might dampen the objections of adults in minority religious groups
that have in the past opposed state oversight of their child-rearing practices, thereby allowing states to move closer to an ideal regime of religious school regulation.

1 Catholic and Fundamentalist Schooling Today

I begin by describing the regulatory environment in which religious schools operate today and then explain what it is about certain religious schools that might be harmful to children. Because parents and church school administrators have been able to prevent outsiders, including state regulators, from investigating their schools, it is difficult for anyone, including state regulators, to draw definite conclusions about the quality of religious schooling. Yet, as will be seen, what little evidence there is should motivate state regulators to seek more information and should put the burden on proponents of religious schools to demonstrate that they provide an adequate education and do not harm children in any way.

Most of the available information concerns practices in Fundamentalist and Catholic schools; consequently I will focus on these denominations. My judgment about the particular ways in which some forms of religious schooling might be harmful to children has been informed by my own conservative religious upbringing and by my early experience in elementary and secondary Catholic schools. This experience may allow me special insight into the situation of children born into conservative religious communities, but in my description of Catholic schools I have relied as much as possible on the few published studies available.

The Regulatory Environment

Public schools in this country are extensively regulated. All states require, for example, that public schools hire only teachers possessing
state-awarded credentials, and they prescribe specific training—ordinarily at least a bachelor's degree in education—and examinations as prerequisites to obtaining credentials.[1] Many states also require that public
school teachers periodically receive supplementary training and evaluation and that teachers whose work is unsatisfactory undergo special re-
medial training and reassessment or be dismissed. These requirements
reflect a legislative judgment that the educational needs of children are
likely to be fulfilled only by teachers with proper preparation under appropriate supervision, and that the quality of teacher training bears a
close relation to the cognitive development of students.

In addition to controlling who teaches in public schools, states typically also exercise substantial control over the content of that instruction. They mandate that public schools teach certain subjects, follow
specific curricular guidelines, use particular textbooks and other instructional materials, and regularly administer standardized tests and
other evaluative devices. Some states also dictate minimum requirements for progress to higher grades and for a high school diploma. State
and local school officials regularly inspect public schools to ensure their
compliance with these directives.

California is one state that has undertaken to control public education quite extensively. The state requires that all public schools teach—
in addition to core subjects such as English, mathematics, social studies, sciences, fine arts, health, and physical education—"programs in
ethics and civic values" that (1) teach children to value "[h]uman individuality, dignity, and worth," "[f]reedom and autonomy," "the common good," and "[e]quality of opportunity," and (2) foster in children
self-respect, cooperativeness, and "critical thinking skills necessary for
sound judgment in matters of ethical conduct and civic responsibility."
The critical thinking skills public schools are to foster include the abilities "to recognize when a claim is reasonable . . . in view of the relevant
evidence and supporting arguments" and "to understand and entertain
the reasons for points of view other than one's own."[2] California's education code further requires that, in adopting textbooks for use in public schools, the state board of education select "materials that illustrate
diverse points of view, represent cultural pluralism, and provide a broad

spectrum of knowledge, information, and technology-based materials."[3] These provisions reflect a legislative judgment that children must develop habits of cooperativeness and critical thinking in order to thrive as adults in the pluralistic social and business environment of contemporary mainstream America.

Other California statutes require that middle schools and high schools provide instruction in AIDS prevention, including information about "the failure and success rates of condoms and other contraceptives in preventing sexually transmitted HIV infection."[4] Public school students must also take, in either seventh or eighth grade, a course in parenting skills designed to teach them about child development, nutrition, effective parenting strategies, child abuse prevention, personal relationships, how to promote self-esteem in children, and family health. Requiring instruction about sexually transmitted diseases reflects the state's judgment that this is the best means of helping children to avoid them. Learning to be successful future parents benefits the students as well as the children they will have and society as a whole, since failing as a parent not only harms the child but also causes the parent to suffer.

One particularly important type of public school regulation is the prohibition against sex discrimination and sexist teaching in elementary and secondary schools. In this area, the U.S. Congress—which historically has left regulation of the internal practices of schools to state and local government—has been sufficiently concerned to enact federal legislation prohibiting a practice it perceives to be harmful and providing funding for programs designed to eradicate it. Title IX of the Education Amendments of 1972 forbids sex discrimination of any kind against any pupils in schools that receive direct or indirect financial assistance from the federal government. Although most claims under Title IX have challenged exclusion of female students from certain school activities or programs or unequal distribution of school resources among programs for girls and boys, the language of the statute is broad enough to encompass sexist teaching and other forms of unequal treatment of boys and girls in the classroom and in academic and career counseling. It states: "No person in the United States shall, on the basis of sex, be excluded from participation in, be denied the benefits of, or be subjected to discrimination under any education program or activity receiving Federal financial assistance. . . ."[5] Pursuant to the Women's Educational Equity Act, Congress has since 1988 been providing financial support to programs that train teachers to avoid gender bias, develop nonsexist curricular materials, encourage female students to take advanced math and science courses, provide leadership training for female students, and otherwise promote female students' self-esteem.[6]

Numerous states have also passed legislation prohibiting sex discrimination and sex bias in education. These are partly redundant of the federal legislation, but in many cases they serve to clarify and/or extend the mandate. State prohibitions take two forms. First, they proscribe inequities in the availability of classes and extracurricular activities (most often athletic programs) for male and female students. Second, some explicitly proscribe giving instruction or career counseling in a sexist manner and prohibit the use of sexist instructional materials. The state of Washington, for example, has mandated that public schools "eliminate sex discrimination . . . in textbooks and instructional materials used by students," and that counseling and guidance personnel "stress access to all career and vocational opportunities to students without regard to sex."[7] Some states go beyond such prohibitions to require that teachers act affirmatively to counteract sexism, particularly by promoting the self-esteem of female students. Illinois, for example, requires that all public elementary and secondary schools include in their curriculum a unit of instruction on the history of women in America, including "a study of women's struggles to . . . be treated equally as they strive to earn and occupy positions of merit in our society."[8]

These statutory provisions regarding sexism in schools rest on a legislative judgment that sexist education and denial of equal opportunity based on gender are harmful to female students. Voluminous research supports this judgment. Even subtle forms of discrimination and bias in curriculum, teaching methods and language, and teacher interactions with students result in diminished self-esteem, inhibited cognitive development, passivity, reduced aspirations, and lower achievement on the part of female students. Many female students suffer psychological and material harm and great frustration because they are discouraged from pursuing any interests that are nontraditional, have fewer opportunities than boys for challenging pursuits, and receive fewer rewards for achieving in traditionally male-dominated domains, such as athletics and science. These harms afflict females not only while they are in school but throughout their lives.[9]

In stark contrast to this extensive regulation and oversight of public schools, state regulation of private schools—particularly religious schools—is minimal or nonexistent. Some states have a two-tier system of regulation, making state accreditation for private schools optional and then restricting the scope of most regulations to accredited schools. These states typically require of nonaccredited schools only that they annually file an enrollment and attendance report and a statement that they are teaching the core academic subjects and are operating for a certain number of days each year. Other states require that all religious schools receive state approval or accreditation, but they limit the scope of any substantial regulations to public schools, imposing on private schools only the same minimal requirements that nonaccredited schools must meet in states where accreditation is optional. Moreover, many states in practice simply do not enforce their regulations against religious schools, particularly if a school manifests resistance.

Perhaps most important, very few states require that teachers in religious schools possess a state-issued credential, receive any particular training, or undergo any evaluations. Twenty-three states repealed existing teacher certification requirements for religious schools in the 1980s. Some states attempt to monitor the quality of education in private schools by mandating that they periodically administer one or more standardized tests to their students and report the grades to state officials. However, they do not condition continued operation of the schools on students' reaching certain levels of achievement, and in any event, such tests are notoriously superficial and indicative of only a very narrow type of skill—rote memorization—that an authoritarian education may promote at the expense of other important capacities, such as critical and creative thinking. This testing requirement therefore provides little or no protection against inadequate schooling.[10]

With respect to antisexism measures, neither Title IX nor any of the state laws prohibiting sexist schooling apply universally. Title IX, after setting forth its prohibition in very broad terms, specifically exempts from its coverage any "educational institution which is controlled by a religious organization to the extent the application of this part would not be consistent with the religious tenets of such organization." Most analogous state statutes are written to apply in the first instance only to public schools, but in at least two states, California and Kentucky, they mirror the federal legislation. They set forth an antidiscrimination mandate applicable to public schools and to any private schools that receive state financial aid or enroll any students who receive state or federal aid, but then they specifically exempt from the mandate schools that operate on the basis of sexist religious beliefs.[11] Thus, religious schools are explicitly singled out at the federal, and in some jurisdictions state, level to enjoy special license to engage in sexist educational practices and instruction. In contrast, Title VII, the federal law that prohibits sex discrimination in the employment practices of private entities receiving federal financial assistance, does not exempt religious organizations. Thus, ironically, adult employees of a religious school, who are able to leave and find work elsewhere if they are mistreated, enjoy statutory protection against sexist treatment by the school, while the children in the school, who are not able to leave, receive no protection.

In addition to leaving religious schools virtually unregulated, nearly all states allow parents to "home-school" their children instead of sending them to a public or private school. Over half the states enacted new legislation in the 1980s permitting parents to choose this option. An estimated one million children in this country are in home schools today, most of them children of Fundamentalist Christians. These parents typically choose to home-school because of religious opposition to the content and manner of instruction in the increasingly secular public schools, though opposition to court-ordered racial desegregation of public schools has also played a major role in the exponential growth of home schooling and of Fundamentalist Christian day schools in recent decades. Regulation of home schooling is, on average, slightly greater than that of religious schools. Most states require official approval of one or more aspects of the schooling that parents intend to provide. The prerequisites for approval, however, generally involve little more than filing with the state a description of the course of study and periodically administering a standardized test. Not a single state today requires that children in home schools receive instruction from a state-certified teacher if the parents object on religious grounds to such a requirement, as Christian Fundamentalists uniformly do. At most, states may require that the teacher in a "religious home school" have a certain level of education, usually a high school diploma or G.E.D. Over half of home-schooling parents have no more than a high school diploma. Some states also require that home-schooled children achieve certain scores on standardized tests or attain certain grade levels by a certain age, as a condition for continued excusal from attendance at a regular school. Home-schooling parents may be able to avoid even these minimal requirements, however, by "affiliating" with a local church school that is not subject to them.[12]

In sum, the clear picture that emerges from a review of education laws is that the states and the federal government have abandoned children in religious schools. Such schools operate with virtually no outside constraints on who teaches, what they teach, how they teach, and how they govern children's lives during school hours. One might hope that the parents and administrators who support and operate these schools care sufficiently about their children's well-being to ensure that they receive the best possible education and suffer no harm, and that the children would therefore have no need for state oversight. The dilemma, of course, is that the religious beliefs of some groups of adults, in conjunction with other factors, such as social class, lead them to adopt views about what is best for their children that differ significantly from the views of most people in our society.

The state's responsibility for the situation of children in religious schools is not limited, however, to its failure to oversee the practices of such schools. In addition, the federal and state governments affirmatively support these schools with substantial subsidies.[13] For example, all religious schools (except those with racially discriminatory admissions policies) and their sponsoring churches enjoy tax-exempt status, freeing them from income and property taxes and making tax-deductible any contributions from the public. Most states also offer religious schools many services, such as transportation of students or textbook loans, and direct payments to reimburse the costs of legally mandated services. Though some schools refuse some of the proffered forms of aid, most religious schools take full advantage of the state's financial assistance. The state thus clearly and affirmatively supports religious schooling without imposing any significant restrictions on the form that such schooling takes, and so is deeply implicated in the situation of children who receive that form of schooling.

Inside Religious Schools

Catholic and Fundamentalist Christian (hereafter "Fundamentalist") church-run day schools rank first and second, respectively, among religious schools in this country in number of students and together account for the great majority of all American children in religious schools. They also represent theological positions that, to different degrees, sanction an authoritarian and repressive approach to education and the relative isolation of children from the world outside the religious community. Schools operated by some other religious groups, such as Orthodox Jews and Muslims, may have characteristics similar to those of Catholic and Fundamentalist schools, but there is so little published information about their practices that it is not possible for outsiders to form much of an impression of what goes on inside them.

The source materials on which the following presentation principally relies, ethnographic studies and personal testimonies, provide a holistic and textured view of the development and well-being of children in these schools. They reveal what life is actually like for these children—what they learn, how they learn, what skills and habits they acquire, how they develop psychologically and emotionally, and whether they are happy. Scores on standardized tests do not tell us much, if anything, about these important issues.

Despite the virtues of the source materials used here, though, the empirical presentation is necessarily incomplete. Compared with the volume of literature on public education, discussion and research of religious schools in this country is slight, in large part because conservative religious groups, particularly Fundamentalists, are strongly resistant to scrutiny of their practices by outsiders—especially state education officials. Nevertheless, because there are several good published accounts of Fundamentalist schools that paint a consistent portrait, it is possible to proceed with some confidence in describing these schools.[14] Studies of Catholic schools are fewer and less representative, all done by persons who are themselves Catholic and supporters of Catholic education, and most of them are dated, having been based on observations in the early 1980s.[15] There simply have not been any objective, in-depth studies of "typical" Catholic schools in recent years (Anthony Bryk's much-touted 1993 study, *Catholic Schools and the Common Good*, focused on a few schools predetermined to be the best academically among Catholic schools; and it aimed only to discover their virtues). This is unfortunate, since many people believe the character of Catholic schooling has changed significantly over the past twenty years. The studies I must rely on do, however, provide some insight into the practices of typical Catholic schools in the not-too-distant past, sufficient to show, at a minimum, the need for more extensive, current, and nonpartisan research. In addition to these ethnographic studies, a recently published collection of personal testimonies by adults who received their education in Catholic schools helps to fill out the picture.

The existing evidence supports the empirical hypothesis that the methods and content of instruction intrinsic to the religious mission of Catholic and Fundamentalist schools affect the students in several harmful ways. First, these schools infringe children's basic liberties by imposing excessive restrictions on students' intellectual and physical freedom and fostering excessive repression of desires and inclinations. Second, they fail to promote, and in fact actively discourage, children's development of the generalized capacity for independent and informed critical thinking (i.e., "intellectual autonomy"). Third, they foster in students dogmatic, inflexible modes of thought and expression and, at least in the case of Fundamentalist schools, an intolerance for persons who hold viewpoints different from their own. Fourth, these schools have adverse psychological effects for many students, including diminished self-esteem, extreme anxiety, and pronounced and sometimes lifelong anger and resentment.

I do not mean to imply that any of these schools is all bad, lacking any positive attributes, nor do I intend an evaluative comparison with public schools. Even if, from a secular perspective, many of these schools have certain strengths, such as a sense of community or high degree of faculty commitment, it is still necessary to consider whether the state should eradicate any practices that are, on the whole, harmful to children. No one would dispute, I assume, that even if a school were in every other respect an exemplar of mainstream educational standards, if it branded students with hot irons the state would have an obligation to prevent that practice.

In assessing whether particular practices are harmful, I adopt the perspective of the state, since the question at hand is whether the state should prevent certain practices in light of the evidence available to it. Adopting this perspective restricts the scope of relevant considerations. Specifically, it requires taking into account only the effects of school practices on children's *temporal* (i.e., secular, worldly) well-being, because in our liberal society the premise of state abstention from religious debates means that the state may not assume to be true any beliefs about children's spiritual interests—whether they have any or wherein they lie. Thus, the analysis below will not incorporate claims parents might make about the nature and importance of their children's religious needs, which parents might believe outweigh any conflicting temporal interests. I will address in subsequent chapters what legal effect, if any, should be given to parents' religiously based preferences regarding their children's upbringing and to parents' beliefs about their children's temporal interests.

AN OVERVIEW OF RELIGIOUS SCHOOLING

Roughly one-tenth of the 52 million school-aged children in this country attend religious schools. Half of this one-tenth, around 2.6 million children, attend Catholic schools.[16] The second largest religious school enrollment is in conservative Christian schools, most of which are Fundamentalist. Because many Fundamentalist schools refuse to submit reports to the state, outside observers, including state officials, have only the vaguest idea of how many children are attending these schools.[17] It is widely accepted, though, that Fundamentalist schooling has been the fastest-growing segment of formal education in this country over the past twenty-five years. A reasonable estimate might be that 1.5 million children, or approximately 30 percent of children attending religious schools today, are in Fundamentalist schools.[18]

The two types of schools on which this chapter focuses thus together enroll somewhere in the neighborhood of four million students, or 80 percent of all religious school pupils and 8 percent of all school-aged children in America. I address Fundamentalist schools first in each of the sections below because in each of the aspects considered their practices appear more extreme than those of Catholic schools.

Fundamentalist Christian Schools

Christian fundamentalism is a conservative religious movement that arose early in this century among members of various Protestant denominations that were united by the aim of maintaining traditional interpretations of the Bible and what its adherents believed to be the fundamental doctrines of the Christian faith.[19] The Fundamentalist movement was in large part a reaction to the emergence of a liberal Protestant theology that endeavored to recast Christian teachings in light of modern scientific and historic thought. Harold Bloom describes Christian Fundamentalism today as dogmatically anti-intellectual. Fundamentalists profess strict and unquestioning adherence to a list of core principles, the Fundamentals, which include belief in the inerrancy of the Bible, the premillennial second coming of Christ, and Christ's atonement through his suffering for the sins of all those who are "saved" or "born again." Bloom asserts that despite their insistence on the inerrancy of the Bible, Fundamentalists actually manifest great ignorance of the Bible and substitute for a close reading of it the highly subjective polemic of poorly educated ministers, who use the Bible simply as a totem with which to impress upon their congregation the transcendent authority of their preachings.[20]

According to Bloom, the sociopolitical world view that Fundamentalists share involves "racism, antifeminism, anti-intellectualism, and plutocratic politics." They advocate segregation of the races, traditional subordinate roles for women, and noninteraction with those who do not conform to the Fundamentalist ideal—in particular, nonwhites, Catholics, Jews, atheists, feminists, intellectuals, and liberals. And while insisting on their own constitutional (and God-given) right to exercise their religion and raise their children without state interference, they do not value religious freedom or diversity more generally but rather wish for America to become a Christian theocracy. Consistent with this political outlook, they discourage independent thinking about religious belief and other matters among their members, and instead demand conformity to the "clear" commands of the Bible; Biblical inerrancy is for Fundamentalists "an unconscious metaphor for the repression of all individuality."[21] For Fundamentalists, the principal battleground for the hegemony of this public and private orthodoxy is children's schooling.

Fundamentalist schools operate in secrecy and in isolation from the larger communities in which they lie because of a suspicion that outsiders will try to interfere with their religious mission—as by state regulation of educational content and selection of teachers—and because of a determination to shield their children from the influences of the secular world. Almost all children in these schools are white and most are from lower-class or lower-middle-class families.[22] There are two basic types of Fundamentalist schools, with much variation among individual schools within the two categories.

At last count, roughly one-third of the students in Fundamentalist schools attended "self-paced curriculum" schools, such as Accelerated Christian Education (A.C.E.) schools. These are small, often one-room, K through 12 schools with an average total population of thirty-five to seventy students. Their "teacherless" curriculum consists of a packaged set of work booklets that the schools purchase from a Christian publishing house. The second type of Fundamentalist school is structurally more similar to a public school, with children at different grade levels in different classrooms receiving instruction from teachers that integrates oral presentation and discussion with reading of texts.

In an A.C.E. school, students spend their days alone at individual workstations, or "offices," silently completing workbooks that assign "low-level cognitive tasks, mostly consisting of association and recall activities" or "rote memory techniques."[23] Some A.C.E. schools supplement the packaged materials with their own writing assignments, "since the canned curriculum concentrates on regurgitation of information rather than on creative thinking."[24] But the creators of the A.C.E. curriculum have purposefully omitted "speculative methodologies, such as laboratory and field work, group activities, inquiry learning and research investigations."[25] In these schools, an adult supervisor, whose training generally consists only of reading a manual supplied by the curriculum publisher, and who typically has no education herself beyond the twelfth grade, is present to answer questions about the reading and to authorize trips to the bathroom, but otherwise students have no interaction with other persons during "instruction" time.

The A.C.E. curriculum, written by graduates of Bible colleges, teaches the usual core academic subjects but always with a heavy ideological overlay, interweaving religious and political commentary with "factual" information. The materials offer accounts of historical events, scientific findings, and the political or religious views of other persons and groups that mainstream scholars deem to be severely distorted and often simply inaccurate.[26] Everything the students learn about the natural universe, for example, must be consistent with creationism, rather than evolution, and with a biblical dating of the age of the earth. The inconsistency with standard scientific and historical beliefs does not trouble those in the A.C.E. fold because their philosophy gives priority to producing Christians rather than fostering academic achievement. A teacher's manual states: "The people who have prepared this book have tried consistently to put the word of God first and science second."[27] One A.C.E. official admitted that, more generally, "the ACE curriculum is not 'on about' education in the sense in which most educators would understand the term," or "concerned with academic schooling," but rather "is a Christian 'character training program which turns out Christian leaders.'"[28] The curriculum also omits discussion of many important current and historical events and figures deemed controversial.

Apart from the structural similarity between the non-self-paced Fundamentalist schools and public schools, the former present a striking contrast to the latter, in educational philosophy, course content, and social atmosphere. All the teachers in these Fundamentalist schools are born-again Christians, the schools use Christian textbooks for all subjects, and interactions between teachers and students have a pervasively religious tone. Like the A.C.E. materials, the curricular materials these schools use teach the same basic subjects public schools offer but are pervaded with conservative religious and political messages and distorted or false views of history, science, and American society. For example, they portray the defeat of the Spanish Armada as a divinely ordained victory of Protestantism over Catholicism, the framers of the Constitution as theocrats, the Civil War as an effort by the South to preserve its Protestant identity, slavery as consistent with the Bible, and Western imperialism as a good way of spreading the gospel.

Catholic Schools

Catholicism, like Fundamentalism, is a Christian faith with a strong strain of dogmatism. Catholics repose their faith not in an inerrant Bible but in the divinely inspired wisdom and, on some subjects, infallibility of the pope, whose pronouncements on theology, liturgy, social and personal morality, and children's education are authoritative and set the tone for the church worldwide. Catholic theology emphasizes the spirit more than the letter of biblical teachings, and interpretation of this spirit and its application to the real world come to the believer from the top of the clerical hierarchy, the pope, down through cardinals, bishops, and parish priests. The current pope's moral instructions to the clergy and laity are notoriously conservative: only men may become priests; abortion, contraception, and nonprocreative sexual relations, including homosexuality, are sinful; and remarriage after divorce is impermissible.

American Catholics today place less emphasis on the moral teachings of the pope than they did before the Second Vatican Council of the early 1960s, and clergy do not seek control over the personal lives of church members to the extent that Fundamentalist preachers do. From the pulpit, priests emphasize development of Christlike virtues—for example, charitable works, love for others, and self-denial—and participation in the life of the local church more than strict obedience to the church's behavioral code, though they certainly do not neglect the latter altogether. This recent liberalization, though, is less evident in Catholic schools than in community worship. In the schools, where the church has greater opportunity to shape minds, it appears to take a more aggressive approach to controlling individual thought and behavior in its effort to produce new Catholics receptive and obedient to the Church's moral doctrines.

Schools administered by the local diocese, rather than by independent religious orders, constitute nine-tenths of all Catholic schools. My discussion of Catholic schools in this book is limited to these diocesan schools, which are generally more conservative than those operated by independent orders, such as the Jesuits.[29] The clerical makeup of the faculty in diocesan schools has declined considerably over the past few decades as the number of active priests and nuns has fallen, with recent figures showing only 8.5 percent of faculty in Catholic elementary schools and 12 percent of faculty in Catholic high schools to be clergy. The student population is somewhat more diverse than that in Fundamentalist schools; nationally, roughly 13 percent come from non-Catholic families and 24 percent belong to racial minorities. Minority and non-Catholic enrollment is concentrated, however, in urban areas; in suburban and rural areas, nearly all Catholic school students are white and come from Catholic families.

Certain general points of contrast between Catholic and Fundamentalist schools stand out. Though inculcation of religious doctrine is a central mission of Catholic schools, during most instructional periods the primary focus is on academic progress and preparation for success in the secular world. In addition, although religious symbolism is pervasive and teachers may inject ideological messages into some academic lessons, Catholic schools generally use the same textbooks for core subjects that public schools use, and they teach mainstream views on most secular topics.

Evidence of Harm

The concerns identified below relate not only to the developmental interests of children—that is, to the kinds of adults students will become—but also to their experience of life as children. We tend to think of children's schooling only or primarily in terms of their preparation for adulthood, but it is certainly important to them now to be able to act on their preferences and desires and to express who they are as five-year-olds, ten-year-olds, or sixteen-year-olds. Respect for children's personhood requires that adults take this into account as well when presuming to determine what their lives will be like.

Infringement of Personal Liberty

Fortunately, neither Fundamentalist nor Catholic schools impose such restrictions on children's freedom as to shock the conscience; there are no shackles or whippings. One might therefore respond to claims of excessive restrictions by saying that the children in these schools simply have it a little tougher than other children; they will eventually grow up and be able to control their own lives, so there is no need to worry. Later chapters of this book will argue, however, that some justification beyond "it's not so bad," "they'll grow out of it," or "it's up to the parents" should be required before the state tolerates any infringements of children's liberties that it would not tolerate in the case of adults.

Physical Liberty

Fundamentalist school administrators rigorously enforce strict codes of conduct and dress that apply to students' lives outside school as well as to their time in school.

Fundamentalists adhere to a puritanical belief in the corruptness of the body and the utter depravity of human nature; as the director of Christian Schools International, the largest Christian school association in this country, has stated: "If you believe that your students came into this world with human nature that is morally good, your view is in direct contradiction to the teachings of God's Word, which says 'The heart is deceitful above all things, and desperately wicked.'"[30]

With this view of children in mind, Fundamentalist schools endeavor to suppress students' physical expressiveness in general and condemn many specific behaviors that, from a secular perspective, are not intrinsically harmful to students so as to warrant a complete prohibition: dating (in some schools even standing too close to, touching, or speaking at any length with, a member of the opposite sex), dancing, watching television or going to the movies, and listening to nonreligious music. It is also in part because of this philosophy that A.C.E. schools confine students to individual workstations for most of the day, without providing opportunities for physical expression or interaction with other students apart from short recesses.

Fundamentalist school administrators and teachers monitor compliance with codes of conduct outside school by admonishing parents to supervise their children closely and by imposing peer reporting requirements. One observer remarked about a Fundamentalist high school "the extraordinarily consistent effort [the school] directs to the total control of students whatever the time or place."[31] Administrators punish deviance not only with demerits, suspensions, and expulsion, but also with paddlings; Fundamentalist educators uniformly support corporal punishment, claiming biblical authority such as Proverbs 23:14: "Thou shalt beat him with the rod and shalt deliver his soul from hell." In fact, they recommend starting it with infants; a manual for parents states: "'When the child is too young to use a switch, paddle or belt, a couple of swift swats with the hand on the thigh or bare bottom, laying the child down and hastily walking out of the room, showing total rejection is effective. . . . The cradle is the place to lick the teenage problem.'"[32]

Fundamentalists particularly condemn as sinful any sexuality outside the context of heterosexual marriage. Some schools do not discuss sexuality explicitly, hoping by "ignoring the libido . . . to bury sexual feelings which they feel are unbecoming to anyone,"[33] and instead impress on children the more abstract notion that human beings have depraved natures that must be repressed. For example, one study found a teacher instructing her pupils that "satisfying self is a sin."[34] Other schools do include a form of sex education in their curriculum that consists of simply condemning in absolute terms any behavior, outside marriage, that would stimulate or satisfy sexual desire, including dancing, hugging, and holding hands.

Most older Fundamentalist school students, like adolescents everywhere, do assert some independence by, for example, watching television or listening to rock music when they can avoid detection. However, because they internalize the threat of adult punishment and divine retribution for infractions of the strict codes of behavior, they are likely to repress, to a greater degree than any mainstream child development expert would regard as healthy, significant aspects of their physical and social natures.

Catholic schools also impose strict norms of conduct in an authoritarian manner, though the proscribed behaviors appear limited primarily to unruliness and playfulness during school hours. Teachers cannot be faulted for prohibiting unruliness, but stifling all spontaneous amusement inside the school's walls, even if not disruptive, is not necessary to accomplish pedagogical aims and makes school less enjoyable for children. Gary Schwartz, who studied an all-female high school, Mother of God, found that the nuns at the school treated all playfulness, humor, and spontaneity as signs of disrespect and lawlessness.[35] Perceiving themselves to be carrying out divine will led them to react in an extreme fashion to even minor deviance. Similarly, Peter McLaren's study of a Toronto middle school, St. Ryan, revealed that teachers had "a tendency to view 'playing' as anti-Catholic" and "pathological"[36] and emotional displays as antisocial. Faculty pronouncements, presented with an air of unopposable, divine authority, instilled a strict work ethic and discouraged individual expressiveness: "While teachers obviously did not go so far as to proclaim themselves a type of educational National Guard or Christian militia, blessings nevertheless took the form of an invisible truncheon used to symbolically club students into line—to dragoon them into an agreed-upon sense of propriety and respect for classroom law and order."[37] McLaren concluded that "at a fundamental level, the schooling that I witnessed was oppressive."[38] These authoritarian restrictions on behavior and expression produced not only compliance but also pain: "Students 'wore' the hegemonic culture of the school in their very beings: in their wrinkled brows, in their tense musculature, in the impulsive way they reacted to their peers, and in the stoic way they responded to punishment. . . . In addition, there was the pain of 'keeping things to oneself' . . . [and] strong debilitating feelings of enchainment."[39]

Though Catholic schools do not impose such radical restrictions on interactions between boys and girls, they do strongly promote denial of natural, especially sexual, inclinations. McLaren found at St. Ryan "a distinct eros-denying quality about school life, as if students were discarnate beings, unsullied by the taint of living flesh."[40] Denigration of the flesh was a pervasive motif in moral instruction. This repression of natural desires stays with Catholic school students long after they leave school, even if they later renounce the theological underpinnings of this self-denial. Female students in particular appear to internalize the messages of self-abnegation and the sinfulness of sex, reinforced by study of the lives of Christ's mother, Mary, and other women figures in the Bible and by the example of nun teachers. They find themselves unable as adults to act on desires, to take control of their sexual/reproductive lives, or to leave abusive marriages. In a recent survey of women ex-Catholics who attended Catholic schools from the 1950s through the 1980s, Joanna Meehl found that many had endured lifetime struggles with their sexuality, unable to enjoy it freely because of feelings that it is somehow wrong to experience physical pleasure. One stated: "'If I ever had strong urges and desires, . . . I certainly buried them deep enough so that they stayed repressed for many years. Any hint of sexual feelings left me with feelings of great shame.'"[41] Some had put up with many years of physical and mental abuse by husbands, unable to shake the attitude that they should deny their own needs and quietly accept whatever suffering befell them.

What treatment of sexuality in school is most conducive to students' well-being has been the subject of heated debate in the context of public school health education. How one comes down on the issue depends in part on one's view of what motivates adolescents, but it also depends on the normative preconceptions one has regarding the appropriateness of physical interaction among unmarried persons and, in particular, adolescents. The question I address in subsequent chapters is whether parents' religious views about sexuality should dictate the normative framework in which the empirical issues are discussed, or whether instead assumptions about appropriate levels of physical affection between consenting adolescents should be determined solely by reference to their temporal interests, such as their educational needs, career opportunities, and physical and psychological health.

Freedom of Thought and Expression

Studies of Fundamentalist schools uniformly support the conclusion that they severely repress children's freedom of thought and expression. Since Fundamentalists claim biblical authority for nearly every belief they hold—whether it be scientific, political, historical, or moral—and since the Bible is for them absolutely and literally true in all respects, all beliefs are unquestionable. Students in these schools are therefore not permitted to question what they are taught on any subject or to express any opinion contrary to the orthodox views that teachers, school administrators, and pastors aggressively impress upon them. To do so would constitute rebellion, a grave sin warranting harsh punishment by God. In the Fundamentalist view of human nature, children are innately inclined to rebellion and immorality; as one pastor told a reporter, "[Y]ou don't have to teach a child to lie. They lie from the time they're babies. They cry when they're not wet, but just want to be picked up."[42] Accordingly, absolute truths must be forced upon students without opportunity for reflection

In addition to suppressing dissent, these schools stifle self-expression and independent inquiry more generally. Students in many schools are prohibited from displaying non-Christian messages—including such things as a peace symbol or an expression of support for a sports team—on a button or book cover, or from reading, even outside instruction periods, magazines or books that might be inconsistent with Fundamentalist teachings. Moreover, sharing personal concerns or experiences other than those that involve being saved or witnessing Christ's presence in their lives is virtually taboo, since it signifies an inordinate concern with the self. Children in A.C.E. schools do not even have opportunities for expression of any kind, since they must work silently at their desks throughout most of the day completing workbooks. Needless to say, students in all Fundamentalist schools are compelled to receive religious instruction and to participate in religious activities.

Catholic schools appear somewhat less repressive of student's minds; not all personal opinion and assertiveness manifest sinful pride. However, the studies suggest that when self-expression means disagreeing with a teacher on any subject or questioning the reason for some school rule or moral doctrine, condemnation is forthcoming. With respect to religious teachings, expression of mere doubts or concerns is likely to trigger censure. Catholic high school and elementary school students are not given the option of not receiving religious instruction or declining to participate in religious activities; they are effectively compelled to be adherents to and practitioners of Catholicism. Moreover, neither religious instruction nor liturgies appear to allow for self-expression; McLaren found school masses to be "perfunctory instructional rite[s]" in which "the priest 'lectured' to the students about their inadequacies."[43] This climate, McLaren perceived, "was the path to apathy, passionlessness, and emotional and spiritual emptiness."[44]

Though children certainly benefit from learning self-control and appropriate respect for authority, forbidding any and all disagreement with what is taught is a restriction on freedom of expression that cannot be justified in terms of children's developmental interests or classroom decorum. And foreclosing individual opinion on religious matters cannot, from a secular perspective, be necessary to ensure children's healthy development.

There is evidence that these severe restrictions on children's mental lives affect their liberty not only in school but also long after graduation. They internalize sanctions against free thought and expression to such a degree that those who later develop some inclination to question, privately and/or interpersonally, the religious, political, or social beliefs that their schools taught them find that psychological barriers prevent them from doing so. Meehl's study found many of her subjects laboring under these constraints: "To begin to have questions, even doubts, about the Catholic church . . . is a frightening thing. . . . Such imbedded teachings are powerful, as is the guilt they inspire when a Catholic questions the church. To question is to disobey."[45] One respondent wrote: "The Catholic church had created such tight bonds to keep you under their control, we lost the freedom to think and grow up. The church kept us forever children, obedient out of fear, which they tried to convince us was love."[46] Likewise, in interviews with graduates of Bethany Baptist Academy, Alan Peshkin found that many expressed continuing fear of divine punishment should they ever question their religious beliefs.[47]

Political Liberty

There is a more attenuated connection between Fundamentalist schooling and students' political liberties. The connection is indirect because it has to do principally with effects on students' capacities for exercising political rights as adults, rather than with immediate restrictions on behavior. Today Fundamentalists are one of the most politically active constituencies in the country; thus children in Fundamentalist schools are likely to learn—by example if not by explicit instruction—that political participation is important. However, half of the children in these schools are explicitly discouraged from becoming involved in political life. The Fundamentalist creed includes rigid views concerning the roles of men and women, and the role of women is to stay home and devote themselves to caring for the family. Their schools therefore teach that only men should become involved in public life, run for elected office, or even express views about matters beyond home life.

A.C.E. materials explicitly teach that men are the leaders of the community and family, whereas women are to obey and serve them. Students reading these materials learn to oppose equal rights for, and assertiveness in, women. In other Fundamentalist schools, teachers openly tell their students that a woman must submit to a subordinate, obedient role in the home; if she does not, "the doors are wide open to Satan."[48] In these schools, everyday life also reflects sex stereotypes and conditions female students not to exercise political liberty. For example, Alan Peshkin found in his study of a Fundamentalist high school, Bethany Baptist Academy, that girls were not permitted to hold the office of class president and could serve in lower offices only if teachers did not deem any boys qualified. By such means, these schools prepare female students for lives of subordination rather than leadership, inhibiting their exercise of constitutionally guaranteed political rights as adults. Boys and girls at Bethany Baptist uniformly accepted the biblically mandated precept that only males should assume leadership positions in school, in the home, and in the outside world.[49]

Sexism also afflicts Catholic schooling but in less overt and less severe forms. Catholic theology and church hierarchy are patriarchal, and this must convey to girls the message that they occupy a subordinate position in life. In addition, some Catholic educators have themselves recognized that textbooks and other instructional materials used for religious instruction in Catholic schools convey sex stereotypes that promote the subordination of women. Discrimination in opportunities within school, on the other hand, appears less prevalent today than it was twenty years ago; boys and girls now enjoy equal opportunities, at least formally, to be class officers, altar servers, and crossing guards—all highly prized positions. Moreover, since most Catholic school teachers *and* administrators are women, students benefit from seeing women in positions of authority. That the schools are ultimately under the control of the parish or diocesan (male) clergy, though, undoubtedly detracts from this salutary influence.

Educational Deprivation

Mainstream educators assume that children today should acquire in school certain skills as well as a certain body of information. As reflected in the school regulations and standards of many states, the skills include—in addition to the timeless reading, writing, and arithmetic basics—scientific methods, analytic and synthetic reasoning, and an ability to compare objectively the rationality of alternative conclusions about the world and the benefits of alternative courses of action. These skills are deemed necessary if one is to participate successfully in social policy making, carry out most occupations in the modern world, and structure one's own life in a way that will best take advantage of one's native talents and abilities and result in a sense of personal fulfillment. These skills develop gradually over time, if at all, and require encouragement, practice, and a wealth of knowledge about the world. The information regarded as important includes knowledge of our society's cultural heritage, system of government, and political history; basic scientific principles and contemporary applications; and an understanding of the lives and perspectives of the various cultural groups a person is likely to encounter in mainstream American life. Without these skills and information, a person's opportunities in life for employment, socialization, political participation, and other forms of self-fulfillment are severely constrained.

As previously noted, all states in this country require that public schools hire only state-certified teachers. This reflects a legislative judgment that competent teaching is a prerequisite to children's acquiring the essential skills and information and that completion of certain training is, in general, necessary to being a competent teacher. Even if only the first of these propositions—that children need competent teachers to receive an adequate education—is true, Fundamentalist A.C.E. schools clearly fail to provide an adequate education, for they do not have teachers at all. Moreover, A.C.E. curricular materials do not, and are not intended to, provide the higher-order skills, or even much of the information, identified above. In fact, these schools endeavor to thwart the development of intellectual skills and to provide very limited and distorted information: "[T]he intent of those using A.C.E. materials is to control the thoughts and articulations of students and to censor the kinds of information they are exposed to."[50] These materials impress on students the view that there is no need to search after truth oneself because the Bible provides answers to all questions. To be a good Christian means to conform to prescribed behaviors, to obey authority without hesitation, and to accept all the religious, moral, and social views that the curriculum presents as truth, without question or discussion. Thus, for example, the A.C.E. materials do not teach or provide practice in scientific methods but instead teach biblical doctrine concerning the natural world. Even one long-time Christian educator admitted that with the A.C.E. curriculum "'the exchange of ideas is almost altogether lacking, [and] the necessity of articulating what it is you think you've been taught . . . has been eliminated.'"[51] Educators in A.C.E. schools manifest little or no interest in the personal thoughts and feelings of the children in response to what they learn.[52] Their focus is on breaking the individual's independent will.

Non–A.C.E. Fundamentalist schools do employ teachers, but these are rarely state-certified. Those who have attended college at all have generally attended only Bible colleges. School administrators choose teachers first and foremost on the basis of their religious beliefs and dedication to creating future Fundamentalists. There is therefore no reason to believe that these teachers satisfy any secular criteria of competence or that they are capable of imparting the skills and information described above. In fact, even if they are capable, the philosophy of these schools is opposed to their doing so.

The observed pedagogical approach of teachers and school administrators in these schools reflects a clear hostility to independent, critical thinking on any significant issues and to competing viewpoints. They reject learning strategies that many public schools use, such as emphasis on the reasoning process. "Rather than expose their students to all sorts of ideas and teach them to analyze their validity and weigh their merits, they prefer to censor the curriculum strictly and protect their children from conflicting, confusing thoughts."[53] Learning in these Fundamentalist schools is not a search for one's own views; it is acceptance of the word of God and rote memorization of what teachers and textbooks say. Understanding is neither necessary nor valuable. Peshkin found that

Bethany Baptist Academy "rejects the notion that students benefit by dealing with alternative perspectives of ideology, interpretation, and policy. Choice, doubt, suspended judgment, evidence—these are excluded from its pedagogical arsenal. . . . To search for that which already is known, is to give credence to a vain intellectualism which vitiates the integrity of an inerrant Bible."[54] Textbooks, too, convey a decidedly anti-intellectual attitude: "In subtle and not-so-subtle ways, students are warned against pursuing the life of the mind."[55]

Moreover, "church and school consciously, unapologetically work to restrict their students' cognitive associations 'in order to avoid contact with people, books and ideas, and social, religious, and political events that would threaten the validity of one's belief system.'"[56] Teachers and textbooks "present only very one-sided views of history, geography, literature, and science,"[57] predicated upon religious doctrine. If they present differing views at all, it is only to denounce or ridicule them. This is true not only of religion and politics, but also of history, science, and literature. All views are evaluated by reference to religious orthodoxy rather than by the standards accepted in the respective fields. For example, great American poets like Robert Frost, Carl Sandburg, and Emily Dickinson are disparaged solely because they did not conform to the Fundamentalist notion of Christianity. The schools also screen all library materials to ensure consistency with Fundamentalist doctrine.

At the high school level, teachers in Fundamentalist schools may allow some discussion of differing points of view on moral and social issues to avoid the appearance of brainwashing, but the Fundamentalist position on such matters "will never be taught as though it might be open to question; above all, when teachers have pronounced what is true, students may not question the teachers' authority to do so. For the essence of the proper student response to authority is submission, total and unqualified. . . ."[58] Some high schools encourage male students to go on to college but only to a Christian college of which Fundamentalists approve; they believe they have failed if a student chooses to attend a nonsectarian university.[59]

Even some Fundamentalists have complained that "too many fundamentalist schools have atmospheres that stifle individual thought and development."[60] Proponents of religious education in other denominations level the same criticism against Fundamentalist schools. For example, Peter Deboer writes that "too often Christian schools have been the 'last thing anyone would point to as a pedagogical model.' Too often they have been 'unlovingly and oppressively authoritarian,' they have 'stifled creativity and individuality,' have been 'racist,' have treated students merely as animals 'rather than as a human being who, made in God's image, is capable of free and responsible action.'"[61]

These schools are not completely successful in their mission of producing unquestioning, conforming adult Fundamentalists, but interviews with children of Fundamentalists when they reach high school reveal that the schools are highly successful in this regard at least up to that age. Seventy-five percent of students at Bethany Baptist believed it not important for them to learn to question authority; by contrast, 44 percent of students at the public high school in the same community believed this. Ninety-three percent of students at Bethany Baptist said they fully accepted the school's theological positions.[62] Conformity regarding social issues was also apparent. For example, students strongly opposed interracial marriage, mirroring the official stance of the school. Seventy-one percent of Bethany students said that libraries should not contain books written by Communists, and 84 percent believed that homosexuals should not have the same rights as other people. In addition, "neither male nor female students contest the subordinate role of women. They believe it is God-ordained."[63] Notably, the students' alignment with orthodox Fundamentalist views was significantly stronger than that of their parents, indicating that the views are, at least in part, the result of the children's schooling and not simply of their family background.[64]

Susan Rose, who studied several Fundamentalist schools in New York State, points to the probable lifelong consequences for children who receive this kind of schooling: "by purifying the curriculum, they are also simplifying the curriculum in ways that may make it difficult for their children to be able to question and evaluate ideas that they may be exposed to later on."[65] Rose surmised that, for the working class or agricultural communities in which most Fundamentalist schools spring up, habituation to conformity is adaptive to the social position that adults in the students' community expect them to adopt. The schools reproduce a class of obedient, unquestioning adults who will assume subordinate positions in factories or "stay down on the farm." Parents and teachers "do not expect their children to revolutionize society or to become distinctive individuals in their own right."[66] For persons consigned to such a station in life, self-exploration, self-expression, intellectual curiosity, and understanding may not be necessary or even useful. The problem, of course, is that training children to fill very limited roles in life severely constrains their powers and opportunities. Education theorists have predicted, and studies have confirmed, that a Fundamentalist upbringing retards educational attainment and diminishes educational aspirations and that students in Fundamentalist schools would have great difficulty coping in mainstream institutions of higher learning, having been "denied access to the basic and accepted concepts, issues and knowledge" on which advanced study depends.[67] In addition, thwarting children's intellectual autonomy and limiting their awareness and understanding of the outside world may pose a threat to their self-esteem when they discover that much of American society thinks poorly of people who lack the capacity for independent thought and reasoned expression, and a lack of self-esteem may further impair their ability to pursue careers outside their local community.

Catholic schools also employ many teachers who are not state-certified, but that is becoming increasingly less common as the supply of certified teachers increases and positions in public schools become scarcer. Because Catholic school administrators value state certification in applicants for teaching positions as an indication of competence, they would probably agree that teachers lacking certification are in general likely to be less competent teachers. They would probably also agree that their teachers are, on the whole, less well trained than they would be if the schools had greater resources and could afford to pay salaries comparable to those in public schools. On the other hand, they would contend that their teachers have the compensating virtue of a higher than normal degree of commitment because of their religious motivation for teaching, and some studies of Catholic schools bear out this claim.

The relevant question from the state's perspective, with respect to the competence of teachers in Catholic schools, is thus whether a higher degree of commitment can make up for lesser training. The answer depends on what it is the teachers are committed to; if it is to fostering the kinds of intellectual skills and imparting the kinds of information previously identified as important, the answer may be yes. The available evidence suggests, however, that Catholic schools are also quite authoritarian in their approach to teaching. They, too, are committed to inducing acceptance of received beliefs without question or critical reflection. Catholics do accept and teach mainstream views on secular subjects, but they do not appear to encourage questioning or rational deliberation about any beliefs or values. It is difficult to draw general conclusions, however, because discussion of pedagogical approach in published studies of Catholic schools relates primarily to moral instruction, which may be anomalous.

For example, Peter McLaren found that St. Ryan Middle School effectively precluded independent thought regarding the moral views imposed upon students: "the prayers and religion classes defined a distinct cosmology for the students which—given the daily repetitiveness and formality of the rituals—the students were powerless to reject."[68] The system of rewards at St. Ryan, always based on students' being good Catholics, tended to produce "passive, pliable, straightforward, predictable" children.[69] My experience in elementary school was the same and for all subjects; at no time were my classmates and I encouraged to develop habits of independent and critical thinking on any subject matter, and in fact this was discouraged, in explicit and implicit ways, as reflective of sinful pride and dangerous to our spiritual health.

At least one study suggests that an aura of unquestionableness continues to surround school administration and instruction in Catholic high schools. Gary Schwartz found at Mother of God High School that rules governing student life were not even explained to students, let alone negotiated. Nuns passed peremptory judgments on the students' behavior without discussion. Moral instruction was sermonic rather than discursive. The nuns feared "the threat of pluralism, of seeing another normative code as having equal validity to one's own, with the consequent inability to defend one's principles as those worthy of respect."[70] Closing off discussion of competing views obviated such a defense. Schwartz found that even though some students expressed resentment at the authoritarian nature of their schooling, they nevertheless continued to adhere without questioning to the core Catholic beliefs that their school and family inculcated.[71]

In sum, the methods of instruction in both Fundamentalist and Catholic schools appear to thwart rather than foster development of higher-order intellectual skills and in that sense to work an educational deprivation for children whose parents place them in those schools. As noted earlier, the standardized tests to which supporters of Catholic schools typically point as evidence that they are doing at least as well as public schools measure not critical thinking or the ability to synthesize information but rote learning and mechanical application of formulas, which authoritarian schooling may be particularly adept at promoting and which are of very limited utility in today's world. In addition, as many critics of studies claiming superior Catholic school performance have pointed out, these studies generally fail to control for critical variables extrinsic to the quality of education provided, such as parental commitment to children's education and the fact that Catholic schools are able to select their students and exclude those with serious problems.[72]

Fundamentalist schools raise an additional serious concern because they appear to deny their students important knowledge about the world, providing "information" about our society and its history and about the natural universe that is at best distorted. This aspect of Fundamentalist schooling led one observer to remark that "by non-Christian school standards these children are cognitively handicapped."[73] Though the performance of Fundamentalist school students on standardized tests has received little attention, one study suggests that they do not do particularly well at even the limited tasks these tests measure. It showed students in a large Florida school over a three-year period achieving average combined math and verbal SAT scores of 726 out of 1600 points, or 170 points below the national average.[74]

Fostering Intolerance and Dogmatism

Studies of Fundamentalist schools suggest that they concertedly and effectively promote intolerance of other religions and ways of life. Simply restricting students' awareness to a single point of view and presenting it as absolutely and universally true can undermine respect for the civil liberties of persons who do not share that view.[75] Such a lack of respect for others and their rights must be even greater where schools also aggressively disparage competing views and persons who hold them, as Fundamentalist schools appear to do.

Fundamentalists condemn any religious creed not based on the assumption of biblical inerrancy. They reject the liberal value of religious toleration, believing this attitude to be simply a disguised moral relativism. The Pledge of Allegiance to the Christian Flag, which students in Fundamentalist schools recite each day, expresses a commitment to "life and liberty for all who believe."[76] Fundamentalist teachers and textbooks present simplistic and negative characterizations of other cultures and belief systems. For example, one textbook suggests that the founder of Islam, Muhammad, was actually the devil, stating that "while Muhammad used many biblical terms in his teaching, he distorted biblical truth. Satan often uses this tactic to deceive people—he dresses error in the clothes of truth."[77] A grammar book asks students to diagram the sentence "India is a crowded land of heathen people."[78] A.C.E. materials teach that other religions enslave people so only "Christians" (by which they mean only fundamentalist Christians) are free. These schools "have no tradition, nor do they feel any need, to give sympathetic attention to the beliefs and opinions of any group outside the fundamentalist fold."[79] Even one Fundamentalist pastor bemoaned that the prevailing attitude of the Christian school movement is that of a "militant, judgmental people."[80]

The two principal targets of Fundamentalist invective are Catholics and secular humanists. Catholicism is dangerous because it is a fraudulent Christianity insofar as it elevates church tradition and the pronouncements of the pope to a status equal to that of scripture. Secular humanism, on the other hand, is a conspiracy to extinguish all Christianity. Humanist attitudes of personal freedom, moral skepticism, and primary reliance on man's knowledge, rather than God's revelation, are evil and dangerous. Teachers and textbooks in these schools also categorically condemn people who adopt "alternative" lifestyles—homosexuality, heterosexual cohabitation outside marriage, and departures from clear, traditional gender roles within a marriage.

The evidence suggests that Fundamentalist schools further engender mistrust of non-Fundamentalists by instructing their students that Christians should keep themselves separate from the unsaved. Because humans are inherently corrupt and sinful beings, to be saved they must become totally immersed in Christian teaching and remain separate from the evil forces at work in the non-Christian world. One commentator describes the Fundamentalist attitude as a "siege mentality," under which "all other religious groups are evil and must be held at bay."[81] The schools take this principle to extreme lengths. Students are not to form friendships with persons who are not born-again Christians, and dating such persons is strictly taboo. Administrators have dismissed teachers for marrying non-Fundamentalists. Schools that have sports programs participate in competition only with other Fundamentalist schools. Peshkin reports that officials at Bethany Baptist Academy canceled all future basketball games with another school, against whom it had played for three years, when they learned that the other school was Catholic.[82] In addition, Fundamentalists espouse a doctrinal position against racial mixing—for example, in marriage or even friendships—claiming as authority the book of Genesis, which, they say, recounts how God "deliberately scattered the races across the face of the earth because he did not want them to be united."[83]

Fundamentalist intolerance of difference also manifests itself in advocacy of Christianizing the public sphere—specifically, government and the public schools. "The kind of government preferred by [Fundamentalist curriculum] authors is a theocracy, or at best a very limited democracy which restrains various activities considered immoral and represses the cultural and religious values of those who are not conservative Protestants."[84] Fundamentalists favor prayer and Bible reading in public schools, and they vote only for born-again Christians and other candidates they believe will legislate Christian values.

The results of this chauvinistic training are unsurprising. Peshkin found that the great majority of students at Bethany Baptist believed that theirs was the only true religion, were quick to denigrate non-Fundamentalist beliefs, and did not regard religious pluralism as a good thing.[85] Indeed, how could characterizing Catholics and Jews as "enslaved" and refusing even to play basketball with them fail to induce an unaccepting attitude toward these groups? Peshkin concluded that Fundamentalist schools produce a social element likely to engage in religious persecution should it ever possess sufficient political power. After spending a year at Bethany, Peshkin, who is Jewish, observed: "I confess to seeing Bethany's doctrinal yardstick poised like a guillotine to lop off dissenting heads, mine and others. . . . I confess to worrying that true believers may dismiss my precious right to dissent as the arrogance of non-believers, an impediment in the path of Truth. Can those who know God and have his blessing be far from concluding that I must be constrained for my own good and that of the righteous brethren who live in his will?"[86] Albert Menendez also concluded, from his study of Fundamentalist school curricula, that these schools are "intent on creating a generation of adults with a mindset that can only be harmful to democratic freedoms and to interfaith harmony."[87]

In addition to developing an intolerant disposition, children who receive a Fundamentalist education are also likely to become quite dogmatic and inflexible. In learning that all Fundamentalist beliefs are absolutely and unquestionably true, that all inconsistent views are not only false but the work of the devil, and that the only proper basis upon which to reason about public policies is by reference to the Bible, as interpreted by Fundamentalists, these students are likely to become incapable of reasoned and respectful dialogue with non-Fundamentalists on matters of disagreement. Peshkin concluded that Bethany Baptist promoted intransigence and inclined students toward heated and irresolvable conflict with persons holding different beliefs:

> Placing God behind one's cause turns causes into crusades. When one's beliefs admit of no uncertainty, one thereby bars debate, bargaining, and compromise. . . . I do not see how Bethany's ideal of Christian schooling from kindergarten through college can avoid promoting intransigence, since students neither learn the habit of compromise nor grasp its neces-

sity in a diverse, complex society. Furthermore, I do not see students learning that dissent and compromise are critical attributes of healthy democracies, rather than unwelcome guests in the house of orthodoxy, the sort who ungratefully take your food, molest your children, and set fire to the upstairs bedroom.[88]

Catholic schools also present their faith as the one true understanding of the world and humanity's place in it and do little to foster genuine respect for other faiths, but they do not appear to breed intolerance. At the elementary level, there is the kind of isolation from persons of other faiths that characterizes Fundamentalist schools—for example, engaging in interscholastic activities only with other Catholic schools. In high school, though students do engage in interscholastic activities with non-Catholic schools, principally in athletics, and may be encouraged to participate in civic activities, where they are likely to interact with non-Catholics to some degree, the focus of their life remains the insular Catholic environment of the school. Moreover, the world-religions course that students typically take in eleventh grade offers only a cursory and patronizing treatment of other religions. As one Catholic high school teacher acknowledged, the comparative religion course "is really a way of getting them to look at Catholic doctrine. It's what used to be called apologetics."[89] However, Catholic clergy and teachers generally do not denigrate people of other faiths or prohibit interaction with them. In fact, Catholic moral teaching emphasizes sincere love for others, including one's enemies, rather than condemnation of those who have different beliefs. Moreover, in recent decades, parishes and dioceses have to an increasing degree organized ecumenical activities with members of other Christian faiths, at least for their adult members.

The result of Catholic schooling in this regard seems not to be intolerance toward non-Catholics but rather a psychological barrier—fear and insecurity—to interaction with members of other religious groups or with nonreligious persons, simply because students' isolation from and unfamiliarity with such persons makes them appear alien. In addition, the authoritarian nature of Catholic schooling and the rigidity of Catholic moral teaching appear to produce adolescents and adults who are dogmatic in their opinions and confrontational rather than conciliatory with persons who disagree with them.[90]

One might think that the costs of Fundamentalist intolerance and of Fundamentalist and Catholic dogmatism fall entirely on the rest of society, and work no harm to the children in which they are instilled. For these children, there may actually be psychological benefits from receiving authoritarian, chauvinistic indoctrination. An unshakable conviction in the absolute truth of one's beliefs and the superiority of one's way of life may provide psychological comfort. In contrast, uncertainty about the answers to important moral and theological questions, or about the virtues of one's lifestyle, might cause a person appreciable anxiety.

However, there is good reason to believe that children trained to be intolerant or dogmatic also suffer as a result. Antagonism toward others and an inability to discuss matters of shared concern in a peaceful, open-minded way are antithetical to personal well-being in at least three ways: First, hostility is simply an unpleasant internal state, a mixture of anger, disapproval, and fear. Second, hostility and close-mindedness divide an individual from other people and therefore cut off opportunities for rewarding interactions and relationships. They also tend to produce a like response in others, causing the hostile person to come under attack and thereby suffer additional fear and anxiety. This has clearly happened to Fundamentalists, who have complained bitterly in recent years of being abused by the media and shut out of political discourse, and it undoubtedly occurs on the individual level as well in interactions between Fundamentalists and non-Fundamentalists. Third, intolerant or dogmatic individuals are unlikely to succeed in environments that require constructive interaction with a heterogeneous group of people and thus are likely to enjoy fewer educational and career opportunities than persons who are able to operate fluently in such environments. In my experience, these costs far outweigh any benefits from an unshakable conviction in the unique validity of one's beliefs.

Psychological Harm

Finally, there are two principally psychological consequences of religious school practices that warrant separate discussion—lowered self-esteem and severe anxiety and resentment.

Damage to Self-Esteem

There is substantial evidence that both Fundamentalist schools and Catholic schools engage in practices that threaten children's self-esteem. First, both teach children that they are sinful and must meet extremely high standards of virtue in order to merit approval. Fundamentalist pastors and teachers inculcate in children a self-image of insignificance, powerlessness, and sinfulness as humans, and teach them that they have worth only as submissive, completely dependent children of God.[91] One researcher observed teachers instructing students that "man is a worm" and that until they are "saved," they are the devil's children. Laboring under extreme restrictions, expectations, and admonitions, all carrying the weight of parental, community, and divine authority, Fundamentalist school students must suffer a loss of self-esteem when they inevitably fail, accepting their teachers' view that they are essentially depraved, deeply flawed beings. Students in Fundamentalist schools punished for departing from the strict codes of conduct report feeling belittled and rejected by their teachers.[92] Moreover, Fundamentalists teach children that they deserve no credit for their positive qualities or accomplishments; any good is the work of God alone.

Catholic schooling, too, is marked by constant reminders of human sinfulness, unworthiness, and insignificance. Meehl writes: "The church attempts to instill a sense of sin in every Catholic individual—even children as young as five years old—in catechism classes. The emphasis is on why you're born evil, how you sin daily, and how, if you don't confess and repent, you'll never go to heaven or be worthy of God." One respondent in her survey wrote: "I was caught in a web of never-ending self-examination, in which every thought and feeling was questioned, denied, and repressed as 'evil.'"[93] McLaren found at St. Ryan that religious "symbols and religious instruction focused preponderantly on self-denial, on endurance, and on one's individual faults and inadequacies."[94] As a result, students experienced diminished self-image and "frequent—and sometimes intolerable—feelings of guilt." McLaren also observed that the most common tactic St. Ryan teachers used to control their students was to embarrass them. I recall that humiliation was also the principal, and for some teachers the only, means used to produce compliance at the schools I attended.

Children who suffer this attack on their self-esteem in school may never overcome it. Even those who as adults leave the Catholic Church report spending many years, even entire lifetimes, trying to overcome feelings of guilt and unworthiness. Meehl refers to this problem as "'Catholic shrapnel'—the damage of thinking of yourself as 'bad' goes deep, causes grave injury, and takes a lifetime to work itself out, if ever."[95] One recent Catholic school graduate who participated in Meehl's study expressed anger about the denigration to which she was subjected: "'It is criminal . . . to mold a child to believe he is inherently evil. It stifles spontaneity, creativity, self-esteem, trust, and love for one's self."[96]

Female students in both Fundamentalist and Catholic schools suffer the additional threat to their self-image of being taught, explicitly or implicitly, that they are, by virtue of their gender, inferior human beings. As noted earlier, Fundamentalist schools deliberately and systematically inculcate in their students the belief that females are inferior to males, that a woman's only purpose in life is to serve a husband and raise children, and that only men should pursue careers outside the home, become active in public affairs and leaders of their community, or even assert opinions about matters beyond home life. To think otherwise is sinful: "sexual equality denies God's word."[97] School practices such as excluding female students from athletics and student government also condition them to regard themselves as inferior. In addition, Fundamentalist schools communicate sexist views through their unequal treatment of male and female employees, typically giving greater salary and benefits to males.

Sexism in Catholic schools has also damaged female students' self-esteem. Almost all the women in Joanna Meehl's survey reported a diminished sense of self-worth, both as children and as adults, as a result of their teachers' treating them as less worthy, less competent persons. They received explicit and implicit messages that boys were superior, that girls were not expected to succeed academically, that it was unladylike to be assertive, and that a woman's proper role in life was one of domestic subservience—in short, that women "are supposed to be quiet, naive, nameless people who are only good for having children."[98] A survey of Catholic school students in the early 1980s also indicated that these schools fostered traditional, stereotypical attitudes regarding women's role in society; students were more likely than either Catholics or non-Catholics in public schools to disapprove of a mother with young children working outside the home.[99]

The women in Meehl's study also reported being daily reminded in school of the patriarchal nature of church authority. They saw their teachers who were nuns act obsequiously toward priests and were taught that the highest calling they could follow was this same life as a cloistered, self-abnegating handmaiden to the male clergy. Some of the women described the exclusion of girls from altar service—like priesthood, a special privilege imbued with sacred significance—as "a profound and hurtful revelation about their church."[100] The church's denial of procreative freedom to women, the blatant sexism of the Bible itself (for example, the passage "Wives, obey your husbands" is read each year on the Feast of the Holy Family), and church teachings that, as these women understood them, portray female sexuality as evil (for example, that menstruation and the pain of childbirth are divine punishment of women for Eve's sin of tempting Adam with the apple) also deeply affected their self-image. Many reported continuing experiences of depression and anger in reaction to the recognition that they could have accomplished more in their lives if they had not been conditioned to take a less challenging and less fulfilling path.

As noted earlier, there are indications that sexism is less a problem today in Catholic schools than it was ten or fifteen years ago. Unfortunately, any significant widespread change in Catholic schools' treatment of female students has not been documented. Some up-to-date, independent research of Catholic schools would be very useful and might exonerate the church to some degree on this count. However, there are also indications that the problem persists. For example, an organization of American Catholic women recently expressed continued concern about sexist messages in the textbooks that Catholic schools use, especially for religious instruction. In addition, there has been no shift in church doctrine regarding the exclusion of women from the priesthood, the preferred role of women in the family, or women's control over their bodies.

Excessive Anxiety and Resentment

The narrowness and rigidity of Fundamentalist education may entail the benefit of providing students with an ideologically and socially safe environment (so long as they are content to conform). These students need not yet confront the fact of difference in the world, question or defend their beliefs and way of life, or struggle with ethical questions. In addition, because most Fundamentalist schools provide a more intimate environment than the typical public school, students are unlikely to experience alienation from anonymity.

At the same time, though, Fundamentalist moral instruction appears to impose an enormous psychological burden on children. The studies indicate that children in Fundamentalist schools are under great pressure to conform to the extremely restrictive Fundamentalist mold and, because of the school's intimacy, are under constant surveillance, their every move watched for signs of deviance. They are asked at an early age to become "born again"—a transformative experience witnessing Christ's presence in one's life—usually in the second, third, or fourth grade but sometimes even in the preschool years, and they are frequently reminded that children who do not become born again, or "saved," face eternal damnation.[101] The Fundamentalist creed also includes the belief that Christ's second coming, and thus the end of the world, is imminent and that final judgment will occur at that time. Students learn that the success of liberals in politics, feminist incursions into the family, and humanist corruption of public education are all signs that the end is near, making spiritual rebirth and unquestioning obedience all the more urgent.[102] It is not surprising, then, that the studies of Fundamentalist schools show students to be greatly preoccupied with concerns about their sinfulness.

In addition, students who at some point develop an inclination to question what they are taught or to strive for some other way of life, or who simply have desires inconsistent with the strict moral code, experience intense internal conflict and fear. Peshkin observed that the students at Bethany Baptist were under extraordinary pressure to adopt habits of thought and action that were often incongruent with their own self-perception and inclinations. As a consequence of the prohibition on many normal social activities—dating, dancing, listening to non-Christian music—many children felt constantly torn between desire and conscience, believing that they should not do many things that felt natural for them to do and that many of their peers at other schools were permitted to do.[103]

Fundamentalist pastors and teachers in fact consciously strive to impose guilt, shame, and fear of the Lord on children to ensure compliance. One teacher at Bethany Baptist told his students about a man "whose refusal to heed God's call to the mission field led to his young wife's death, his girlfriend's rape, and his own brains being blown out."[104] Peshkin's conversations with students revealed that they took such admonitions to heart. They feared God's wrath should they commit any infractions of the conduct code, and they attributed great tragedies in people's lives to their sinfulness. One female student stated: "If you do something wrong, then God's going to hurt you, either by hurting someone, like killing someone that you are real close to, or something like that. I found that out because not too long ago John Briggs, he used to go to our school, he got killed. We were really close friends. . . . I feel that the Lord was punishing John and teaching others through that. I've heard things about him and his girlfriend and I thought, "Well, if I'm not careful, then that is probably what could happen to me.'"[105] Because Fundamentalist educators couple this moral haranguing with a message of divine love, children are likely to develop mixed feelings about the God who watches closely over them, as they might about a harshly judgmental parent whom they dare not displease. Persons who later in life do reject the Fundamentalist belief system express intense anger at the great emotional and psychological burden imposed by this kind of treatment.[106]

Catholic schools, too, may provide a more intimate environment than the typical public school but at the same time engender great anxiety in children by their moral teachings. The evidence suggests that the notion of sin and divine retribution for it is a pervasive motif: teachers frequently remind students that chronic sinners burn in hell for eternity, and catechism workbooks and filmstrips present terrifying images of hell and the devil. The women in Meehl's survey recalled constant warnings that God would punish them for their sins, and many were traumatized by it. One women stated: "The guilt I experienced in my childhood was incredible. I feel denied a childhood by my preoccupation with sinning and [obtaining] a priest's forgiveness."[107] Though teachers also speak of the rewards of eternal life in heaven with God and departed loved ones, their tendency to treat even very minor deviance as sinful and common childhood misbehavior such as swearing, fighting, and lying as moral outrages leads many children to conclude that this happy prospect does not await them.

A means of redemption is available for young Catholic sinners—the practice of confession—and it is a complete redemption provided one performs the prescribed penance; thus it may help to relieve children's anxiety, at least for a short time. However, the act itself can be extremely intimidating and anxiety-producing. I recall quite vividly, beginning in first grade, processing solemnly with my classmates to the dimly lit church, then kneeling in the pews praying, waiting for my turn to enter the dark confessional box. Inside, I knelt, recited a prayer in which I apologized for offending God, and whispered my sins through a black screen to the unseen priest beyond. When I had finished, I waited for the priest to utter a few words of admonition and dispense a penance, which was to recite certain prayers a prescribed number of times. Though this ritual was primarily just embarrassing by the time I reached secondary school, in the early elementary grades it was quite frightening. At first it was a struggle to sort through my past behaviors and identify some sins to confess, and not having something to say in the confession box was itself cause for fear ("I've been good" was not an acceptable report). After a few years of catechism and regular confession, however, I became quite adept at finding fault with myself and had to deal only with the anxiety of disclosing my faults to the priest in the intimidating environment of the confessional. The women in Meehl's study similarly spent their childhoods "examin[ing] our consciences ad nauseam. We kept trying and trying to find things that we had done that were bad and that we could confess."[108]

In high school, the anxiety continues and is often accompanied by resentment of authority, as adolescents' growing need to assert their independence fails to be recognized. Schwartz found in the high school he studied that turning all behavioral issues into moral ones and espousing the belief that young people are incapable of moral independence frequently led to escalation of minor conflicts into major disputes, eliciting strong emotional reactions from persons in authority and attendant anxiety and resentment in students.[109] The lack of respectful discussion of moral issues, in Schwartz's view, diminished the quality of life and education at the school: "The language that would enable the generations to communicate their feelings about what really gives pleasure to being in school together is almost completely missing at Mother of God. There is a joyless quality to the way authority insures that its voice is heard and removes whatever warmth it feels for those for whom it is responsible."[110] A study of students in Catholic middle and senior high schools has shown that they score "significantly higher on depression, hostility, and dysphoria, and significantly lower on positive affect and overall positive mood" than their public school counterparts.[111]

Many persons educated in Catholic schools who ultimately free themselves intellectually find the process of doing so very difficult and express pronounced resentment and anger toward Catholicism. Meehl's study, for example, is replete with expressions of continuing deep-seated anger and indignation about what the women perceived as abuse inflicted on them by Catholic schools. One woman expressed anger about "how many years of thinking and learning I lost." Another wrote: "The thing that makes me angriest . . . is the thought that I might have been a better, different, more self-assured person if I hadn't been subjected to the shame, guilt, and humiliation they dealt out to me for twelve years."[112] Many of the women had been in counseling or psychotherapy for years to try to deal with their resentment.

Finally, an additional cause of continued suffering for many disaffected graduates of Catholic schools is that they were never given a forum or a language for discussion of personal beliefs and desires, moral uncertainties, and fears about the future with others, particularly with members of their parents' generation.[113] Because neither their teachers nor their parents engaged them in free and mutually respectful dialogue about matters of faith and conscience, independence generally means radical separation, a total breach in the lines of communication on these issues. Because no alternatives to the Catholic creed and rules of conduct are ever seriously entertained, when Catholic school graduates depart from that faith or lifestyle, there is no longer a common ground on which they can stand with teachers, parents, relatives, or friends who remain in the faith, to converse about what means the most to them in their lives.

Conclusion

I have covered quite a bit of ground, but it is important to bring together and examine all the available evidence of harmful practices in religious schools so that we can understand what interests of children are being sacrificed by the failure to regulate these schools. Let me briefly summarize the general conclusions. The evidence suggests that both Fundamentalist and Catholic diocesan schools, to varying degrees, infringe the personal liberties of students, fail to develop in students important cognitive skills and/or to provide them with an adequate knowledge base, promote intolerance and/or dogmatism, undermine students' self-esteem, and engender excessive anxiety and resentment in students. The effects of these practices often continue long after graduation, causing former students to suffer throughout much of their adult lives. Catholic schools appear somewhat less threatening on each count and may be improving. Nevertheless, both types of schools appear to constitute a sufficient threat to these aspects of children's well-being that some form of additional regulation would, on the whole, benefit the children in them.

As noted at the outset, these conclusions are necessarily provisional, given the relative paucity of available information about religious schools. However, since the existing evidence uniformly supports the conclusions, the burden of proof should rest on those who would dispute them. It also bears repeating that the relevant question is not whether any particular religious schools are, on the whole, better or worse than other types of schools. A finding that just one specific practice of some religious schools is harmful to children should itself be sufficient to trigger inquiry into whether the state should act to protect the children.

2 The Constitutional Backdrop

As we have seen in Chapter 1, there is substantial evidence that the pedagogical practices of many religious schools are harmful to children. Other types of practices involving conflicts between parents' religious beliefs and mainstream norms regarding children's welfare include the refusal of parents in some religious groups to allow their children to receive immunizations that would prevent disease or to receive medical care to treat diseases or injuries after children incur them. In these contexts as well, the same basic question arises: Must the state defer to the religious preferences of parents or may it act to protect what it regards as a child's temporal interests?

The answer to this question depends greatly on what analytical framework one applies in considering it. This chapter describes the approach that has dominated judicial decision making, political deliberation, and academic discourse in this area—the parents' rights approach, which attributes to parents plenary rights to raise their children as they see fit and requires a showing of severe harm to children before the state may restrict parents' child-rearing freedom. This presentation should make clear that the state always has acted, and in fact must act, in these situations at the ultimate level of deciding who is to have presumptive legal authority over particular aspects of children's lives. It is the state that confers on parents rights to control certain child-rearing matters, to the exclusion of all other persons, private or public, who might wish to exercise such control. A society in which there were no laws governing the custody and upbringing of children would be one in which chaos reigned, with parents having no security in their relationships with children. Thus, the notion that the state can, and according to some should, abstain from "intervention" in the family is ludicrous. The question that must be faced is why the state has chosen the particular allocation of legal authority over children's lives that now prevails.

Though states have never attempted to regulate religious schools to any appreciable degree, there have been several court battles between Fundamentalists and state education officials over private school regulations. In some cases Fundamentalist school operators have refused to comply with even the most minimal requirements, such as merely requesting approval or providing attendance reports, claiming that their faith does not allow them to recognize *any* state authority over their schools. Though state officials have often simply looked the other way in these situations, lacking the political will or resources to engage religious groups in prolonged conflict,[1] occasionally they have pressed these schools to comply and the schools have responded by judicially challenging the state's authority. The courts' decisions in these cases reveal that the principal legal obstacle to an increase in state regulation of religious schools would be the well-established legal doctrine that parents possess a fundamental right under the Due Process Clause of the Fourteenth Amendment and the Free Exercise Clause of the First Amendment of the United States Constitution to direct the upbringing of their children as they see fit, largely free from state interference. The scholarly community has almost unanimously supported and adopted this doctrine; disagreement among scholars and criticism of judicial decisions center principally on the proper scope and weight of parental rights, rather than on the appropriateness of parents' having child-rearing rights at all.

Several Supreme Court decisions dealing with parent-state conflicts over child rearing have established the prevailing legal framework. Though most of these decisions involved situations quite different from that of Fundamentalists struggling to avoid state oversight of their schools, they determined the way in which lower courts now must analyze all such conflicts. To explain precisely what these seminal Supreme Court decisions did, it is useful to lay some terminological groundwork. In the following discussion, I draw upon the distinction between a "right" and a "privilege," a distinction that is often blurred in common discourse. In his seminal work on the naming of legal relations,[2] Wesley Hohfeld urged the legal community to confine its use of the term "right" to what he called "claims," which entail corresponding duties in other persons—duties either of noninterference (corresponding to a negative claim) or of assistance (corresponding to a positive claim) owed to the holder of the claim or right. Thus, a parent has a "negative claim," or "negative right," against the state with respect to a given action when the state is under a duty to the parent not to interfere with the parent's performing that action. A parent would have a "positive right" against the state if the state were under a duty to the parent to provide some form of assistance.

In contrast, a "privilege" is simply the legal freedom to engage in a given activity, or in other words, the absence of any duty on the part of the privilege holder *not* to engage in that activity. Unlike a right, a privilege does not entail a duty of noninterference or assistance by another party to the holder of the privilege. If, for example, I allow my neighbor to borrow my shovel, she then enjoys a privilege to take and use it; she is no longer under a duty to me *not* to take and use my shovel. However, this privilege does not itself entail any claim against me should I interfere in her use of the shovel—for example, by taking it away from her or insisting, under threat of my taking it away, that she not use it in certain ways—because it does not entail any duty of noninterference on my part. Thus, parents would enjoy only a child-rearing *privilege* if the law merely *permitted* them to raise a child and did not bestow *on them* any claim against interference by the state or other third parties in their doing so—that is, if no one owed a duty *to the parents* (as opposed to, say, the child) not to interfere with their child-rearing practices.[3]

The Supreme Court's Creation of a Parental Free Exercise Right

In a series of decisions in the 1920s, the Supreme Court invalidated several state laws and regulations pertaining to private schooling. *Meyer v. Nebraska*[4] invalidated a Nebraska law prohibiting instruction in a foreign language. *Pierce v. Society of Sisters*[5] invalidated Oregon's prohibition of private schooling altogether, and *Farrington v. Tokushige*[6] invalidated a Hawaii law that prohibited foreign-language day schools and effectively placed after-school foreign language programs under nearly complete state control. The Court based each of these decisions partly on a conclusion that the Due Process Clauses of the Fifth Amendment (governing federal action) and Fourteenth Amendment (governing states' actions) grant parents a right to direct their children's upbringing. The Court held that state action materially interfering with this right must bear a reasonable relation to a legitimate state purpose—that is, it must have a "rational basis"—and found in each case that the state laws did not satisfy this requirement.

In 1944, the Supreme Court addressed for the first time a parental challenge to state action that coupled a Fourteenth Amendment parental rights claim with a First Amendment Free Exercise Clause claim. In *Prince v. Massachusetts*[7] the state of Massachusetts had prosecuted a woman under a statute prohibiting parents or guardians from directing or permitting their children to sell publications in public places. Mrs. Prince, a Jehovah's Witness, had permitted her niece, who was under her guardianship, to join her in distributing religious literature at night in the streets of Brockton. The Court in *Prince* understood the case as involving a burden on the religious free exercise rights of Mrs. Prince, which it interpreted to include the right to give children religious training and "to encourage them in the practice of religious belief." The Court ultimately held, however, that the burden was constitutionally permissible. A state's authority to restrict parents' freedom in child rearing by means reasonably related to legitimate state ends, the Court stated, "is not nullified merely because the parent grounds his claim to control the child's course of conduct on religion or conscience. . . . The right to practice religion freely does not include liberty to expose the community or the child to communicable disease or the latter to ill health or death." The Court went on to state with rhetorical flourish: "Parents may be free to become martyrs themselves. But it does not follow they are free, in identical circumstances, to make martyrs of their children before they have reached the age of full and legal discretion when they can make that choice for themselves."

At the same time, however, the Court limited its holding in *Prince* by indicating that the Free Exercise Clause might in some situations serve parents as an additional shield against state-imposed restrictions on child rearing, extending beyond the protection that the Fourteenth Amendment affords. This higher shield, the Court suggested, might be effective even in some situations that threaten the health and welfare of the children: "Our ruling does not extend beyond the facts the case presents. We neither lay the foundation 'for any [that is, every] state intervention in the indoctrination and participation of children in religion' which may be done 'in the name of their health and welfare' nor give warrant for 'every limitation on their religious training and activities.'" Further, there is no hint in the *Prince* opinion that children have a right to protection from harms to which parents might subject them in acting on their religious beliefs. Instead, the Court treated the danger to the child's welfare only as a public policy concern, as a threat to society's interest in "the healthy, well-rounded growth of young people into full maturity as citizens," rather than as a threat to the interests of the child herself. The lesson of *Prince*, therefore, is that the Free Exercise Clause protects parents' efforts to indoctrinate their children and to include them in various religious practices so long as they do not expose them to very grave dangers.

In 1972, the Supreme Court rendered the most important decision to date relating to parents' right of control over children's upbringing. In *Wisconsin v. Yoder*[8] the Court made explicit that the Free Exercise Clause confers a more extensive parental right to control children's lives than does the Fourteenth Amendment Due Process Clause. Henceforth, a state wishing to restrict religiously motivated child-rearing practices would have to pass a "strict scrutiny" test: it would have to demonstrate a state interest in the restriction that was not only legitimate but also compelling, and would have to show that no less restrictive means were available to protect that interest. Showing merely that a challenged regulation was a rational means of furthering a legitimate objective would not be sufficient when religion was involved. This decision has received much attention for the test of constitutionality it established for parental free exercise cases, but the precise nature of the claims advanced or of the Court's treatment of these claims has not received close analysis. I provide such an analysis here because it is revealing of the Court's attitude toward the children involved.

In *Yoder*, Amish parents claimed that Wisconsin's compulsory school attendance law, which required parents to ensure that their children attended a public or private school until the age of sixteen, violated their right to practice their religion freely. The Amish parents had sent their children to public schools through the eighth grade but refused to allow them to attend any high school, public or private, for the additional two years that the law required. The parents contended that their faith required them to raise their children for "life in a church community separate and apart from the world and worldly influence." Attendance at a regular high school, they argued, would expose their children to worldly influences during the critical adolescent stage of development and to "higher learning [which] tends to develop values they reject as influences that alienate man from God." These values included "intellectual and scientific accomplishments, self-distinction, competitiveness, worldly success, and social life with other students." The parents' free exercise claim thus had two components: (1) that no one, including their children, had a positive right to the parents' assistance in ensuring that the children attend school (in other words, that they held a *privilege* not to act themselves to get their children to school), and (2) that they also possessed a *right* to train their children at home to become Amish adults, free from interference (in other words, that the state had a duty *to the parents* not to frustrate their preferences regarding the life their children would lead by taking the children out of their homes during the day to attend school).

The Court first had to determine whether the compulsory attendance law encroached upon any "*legitimate* claims to the free exercise of religion." Its analysis of the burdens that the Wisconsin law imposed on the Amish parents reveals that the Court accepted both components of the parents' objection to that law as "legitimate claims" to personal religious freedom. The Court found that "the Wisconsin law affirmatively compels [the parents], under threat of criminal sanction, to perform acts undeniably at odds with fundamental tenets of their religious beliefs." Though it is not clear to which acts the Court was referring, one might understand them to be the actions that would have been involved in the parents' enrolling their adolescent children in a school—for example, going to the school to fill out paperwork. To require such actions would be to deny the parents the privilege they sought, the first component of their claim identified above.

However, the true burden on the Amish parents was clearly that the compulsory school attendance law would have denied them the ability to indoctrinate their children at home in the Amish faith without competing influences. It would not have satisfied the Amish parents if the state had relieved them of all duties to act, if the parents merely had to forbear from preventing the children from leaving the house to go to school each day. Thus, the Court's ultimate holding turned on an assessment of whether the state's interest in the children's education "is so great that it is paramount to the undisputed claims of [Amish parents] that their mode of preparing their youth for Amish life . . . is an essential part of their religious belief and practice." The Court therefore also treated as a legitimate claim to the free exercise of religion the second component of the Amish parents' claim—the assertion of a right to control the lives of their children, entailing a duty owed by the state to the parents not to interfere in the parents' direction of their children's lives.

In analyzing the burden on religious freedom, the Court in *Yoder* also referred repeatedly to the encroachments of modern society on the

Amish way of life and to the danger of extinction that the community faced. In doing so, the Court came close to suggesting that the Amish community as a whole possessed a corporate legal right against state action tending to undermine its survival. The community could survive only if it remained set apart and free from government intrusion into the way the children of its members were raised: "[C]ompulsory school attendance to age 16 for Amish children carries with it a very real threat of undermining the Amish community and religious practice as they exist today; they must either abandon belief and be assimilated into society at large, or be forced to migrate to some other and more tolerant region." Since the Wisconsin law could not conceivably have coerced the Amish *parents* into assimilating into society at large, and since the Court stated that the children's religious liberty was not at issue, this concern about the survival of Amish culture also provides further evidence that the Court viewed state restrictions on the parents' efforts to control the minds and lives of their children as an impermissible burden on a *parental* right to religious freedom.

The Court in *Yoder* thus recognized a very peculiar sort of right. It firmly established that the Free Exercise Clause protects more than an individual's freedom of thought and *self*-determining religious conduct and more than an individual's freedom from state-imposed duties to take actions inconsistent with his or her beliefs. Under *Yoder*, the Free Exercise Clause also protects a right to control the lives and minds of certain other persons—the children in one's custody, to keep them to oneself, isolated from outside influences, and to make of them the type of persons one wants them to be in light of one's own religious beliefs. This right entails a duty that the state and other third parties owe to parents not to interfere with what the parents wish to do. Parental entitlement is thus clearly the moral focus of the *Yoder* decision, and that entitlement is said to include not just self-determination but also a form of "other-determination." The *Yoder* decision also implicitly recognized as a legitimate element of parents' free exercise protection a power to waive their children's positive rights to government benefits, such as a state-provided education, on no basis other than their religiously motivated desire to do so. What is best for children or what children deserve in terms of their education was thus clearly subordinated to parental preferences and in fact had no place in the Court's moral and legal reasoning.

After determining that the Wisconsin law burdened the parents' free exercise rights, the Court balanced the parental interest these rights protect against the state's interest in requiring school attendance. The

parental interest the Court treated as fundamental and therefore possessing the greatest weight given to any interests in constitutional adju-
dication. The Court construed the state's interest as an interest in ensuring that children can one day meet "the duties of citizenship" and
that they will not become "burdens on society because of educational
shortcomings." In other words, it focused on the diffuse interest the
rest of society has in not having to support poorly educated, non-self-
sufficient persons rather than on an interest in fulfilling a moral responsibility to protect vulnerable members of society. In deciding whether
this state interest was sufficient to justify the compulsory school attendance law, the Court took the important step of interpreting the Free
Exercise Clause as increasing the state's burden of justification beyond
that arising from the Fourteenth Amendment Due Process Clause for
imposing constraints on parental control over children's lives. Henceforth, "when the interests of parenthood are combined with a free exercise claim . . . , more than merely a 'reasonable relation to some purpose within the competency of the State' is required." Rather, state
officials would have to show that the State had an interest "of the highest order . . . not otherwise served" in applying its regulations, however
reasonable those regulations might be as a means of securing an appropriate education or other important benefits for children.

Wisconsin officials did argue in *Yoder* that granting Amish parents an
exemption from the school attendance law would fail to recognize the
positive rights of the children to a secondary school education. However, the Court reinterpreted this argument as one positing negative
rights of children to be free from grievous harm. It then placed the burden on the state to demonstrate the likelihood of such harm and found
that the state had not met this burden. The state also failed to show that
exempting the Amish would result in harm to "the public safety, peace,
order, or welfare." Therefore, the Court held that the state had not provided sufficient basis for overriding the religious rights of the parents,
and it awarded the Amish community an exemption from compulsory
school attendance laws that it enjoys to this day.

The majority opinion in *Yoder* further indicated that the free exercise
right of parents to control their children's lives also trumps any conflicting preferences of the children. Even if the children in this case had
wanted to attend school, granting the state authority to enforce the
wishes of the children or to protect what the State deemed to be the
best interests of the children "would, of course, call into question traditional concepts of parental control over the religious upbringing and

education of their minor children" and "would give rise to grave questions of religious freedom." The Court thereby suggested that parental free exercise rights can operate to defeat the religious liberty of children themselves. In dissent, Justice Douglas took issue with this aspect of the majority's opinion, stating that the proper result would have been to give the children involved the choice of whether or not to go to school. Justice Douglas, however, appeared to overlook the psychological harm that could have resulted from placing these children in the position of having to make such a momentous decision, as well as the fact that thirteen-year-olds, particularly those who have spent their entire lives in an insular, illiberal religious community, are probably not capable of making an informed, rational decision about whether they should go to school.

In sum, these Supreme Court decisions regarding child rearing established an interpretation of a constitutional right that, as will be seen in the next chapter, is unique—one that attributes to some persons a right to engage in conduct and make decisions aimed at controlling not their own lives but the lives of other human beings. Hereafter, I use the term "self-determining behavior" to denote actions and decisions concerning solely or primarily one's own person, property, and life course, and "other-determining behavior" for decisions and actions directed primarily at others, including efforts to control the person, property, or life course of another. Examples of self-determining behavior include wearing religiously symbolic clothing, abstaining from eating meat on certain holy days, going to temple, and ingesting sacramental drugs. Although any such behavior might indirectly affect people other than the actor, it generally does not constitute an effort by the actor to control the life of another or to decide what another person will do. Precise lines between the two types of conduct may be difficult to draw, but it is quite clear that, under *Yoder*, the free exercise right of parents protects conduct that is quintessentially other-determining. This right requires courts to weigh the parents' supposedly fundamental interest in fulfilling their religious aspirations through their children against the state's interest in ensuring that children do not suffer grievous harm or become dependent on public assistance as adults. None of the Supreme Court decisions considered whether children have or should have a legal right to protection from parental conduct that is antithetical to their temporal interests or an immunity from others' waiving their positive rights to state-proffered benefits, such as a right to attend school. In essence, the Supreme Court has consistently treated children as nonconsenting instruments for the furtherance of the ends of parents or the ends of the larger society, rather than as persons with distinct interests and rights that the law must respect.

It is important to recognize that the parental free exercise right established in these cases is *not* a by-product of parents' legal responsibility for the welfare of children. Instead, it rests solely on the religious beliefs of parents and the tradition of granting parents dominion over their children. In fact, insofar as this right gives parents the legal authority to treat their children in ways contrary to statutes and regulations designed to protect children's interests, the parental free exercise right amounts to an entitlement to act in ways *contrary* to the normal legal responsibilities of parents.

Interpretation of the Right by Lower Courts

Though these Supreme Court decisions established the conceptual framework for resolving parent-state conflicts over child rearing, they provided little specific guidance as to the permissible scope of state restrictions on the child-rearing practices of parents or their proxies, such as religious schools. One might think that if parents possess a right to withhold all education from their children (at least after a certain age), they must also possess a right to operate a school for their children more or less free from state regulation. However, the Court in *Yoder* hinted that its holding was limited, by emphasizing the uniqueness of the situation before it: the Amish community was isolated from the rest of society and had survived in this unassimilated condition for centuries. Moreover, the *Yoder* Court in dictum reaffirmed the states' power "to impose reasonable regulations for the control and duration of basic education."

Nevertheless, subsequent lower court rulings have consistently invoked *Yoder* in substantially different factual situations to advance the position that the Free Exercise Clause guarantees parents an extensive right to control the minds and bodies of their children. In many of these cases, the courts have found that because the parents involved were not members of an insular and threatened religious community, the state regulations did not impose on parents' religious freedom a burden as severe as that at issue in *Yoder*, and/or that the states' interests were sufficiently compelling to override the parents' free exercise right.[9] However, in other cases, courts have invalidated state efforts to promote the well-being of children as violations of parents' free exercise rights.[10] Even when lower courts have sided with the state, they have ignored or mini-mized the rights and interests of children and advanced an interpretation of free exercise rights that effectively treats children as nonconsenting in-struments or means to the achievement of the parents' ends rather than as ends in themselves. I do not mean by this to suggest that *parents* in the situations that the courts have addressed had wholly self-regarding motives or took an instrumental view of their children. Rather, the point is that *courts* take an instrumental view of children insofar as they are willing to sacrifice what *they* view as the interests of children in or-der to satisfy the desires of parents or when they simply fail to consider the children's interests.

Because the states have never attempted to go very far to control the nature and content of instruction in private schools, lower courts have not had occasion to define the outer limits of permissible state regula-tion. Moreover, the decisions they have rendered on this issue do not provide unambiguous indications of how receptive courts are to parental challenges to school regulations. Thus it is difficult to determine pre-cisely which types of state regulations of religious schools are constitu-tionally permissible according to the prevailing judicial interpretation of parents' rights. There are a few exceptions, however. State and federal courts have almost uniformly held that requiring all private schools to receive state approval, in and of itself—that is, apart from the particular content of the approval criteria—is constitutionally permissible, as are requirements that all private school teachers be state-certified, that all schools give instruction in certain core subjects, and that all schools re-port attendance information.[11] Courts have also consistently held that states may require all parents, other than the Amish and very similar groups, to send their children to school and so may deny parents the op-portunity to home-school.[12] Notably, these decisions have rejected par-ents' religious objections only after subjecting the regulations at issue to heightened scrutiny, and many have suggested that only such minimal regulations are permissible.

For example, a 1985 Iowa Supreme Court decision, *Johnson v. Charles City Community School Board*,[13] affirmed the extensive child-rearing authority and freedom of parents under the Free Exercise Clause while holding constitutionally permissible a state law requiring that all school teachers possess state certification and submit periodic attendance re-ports to the state. The court agreed with the state that this law consti-tuted only a minimal interference in the affairs of the school but cau-tioned: "We agree with plaintiffs' contention that the religious freedoms guaranteed them under the first amendment entitle them to educate their children at the private religious school they have established. The same guarantees accord them the right to operate the school with minimal necessary supervision by the state." In upholding the regulation, the court emphasized that the legislation at issue would not prevent the school from selecting Fundamentalist Christian teachers or from teaching required subjects "in its own way"—that is, permeating all curricular materials with biblical convictions, presenting all subjects only from a biblical point of view, teaching sexist beliefs, and requiring all parents of students, as well as all teachers, supervisors, and assistants, to agree with the church's doctrinal position. Whether such schooling was on the whole conducive to the students' well-being, let alone whether it was the best available educational alternative for them, was not of concern to the court.

Similarly, in *New Life Baptist Church Academy v. Town of East Longmeadow*,[14] the First Circuit Court of Appeals upheld a state approval requirement for private schools over Fundamentalist school operators' objections that their faith opposed any form of state judgment of their practices and that standardized testing was an adequate and less restrictive means for ensuring that children received an adequate education. Writing for the court, Judge (now Supreme Court Justice) Breyer manifested unusual sensitivity to the educational needs of children. He expressed great skepticism about the value of standardized tests as an indication of the quality of instruction, pointing out that such tests do not measure many critical aspects of an adequate education, such as the development of intellectual skills and inculcation of "the values of civic participation." At the same time, however, Judge Breyer emphasized that the approval process would not in any way "threaten interference with religious practices, prayer, or religious teaching" or involve "approval or disapproval of any religious matter." He thereby implied that state regulation must be limited to evaluation of the formal characteristics of religious schools, such as the subjects taught and the training of teachers, and may not include evaluation of the specific content and methods of instruction.

In the few cases in which parents have challenged more extensive and substantive regulations, they were successful. For example, the trial court in *Johnson v. Charles City Community School Board*[15] held that a statutory requirement that schools use a nonsexist approach to instruction could not constitutionally be applied to a religious school whose religious tenets conflicted with such an approach. Since the state did not appeal this ruling, higher courts never addressed the conflict. In the most important decision in favor of parents in a school regulation case, *State v. Whisner*,[16] the Ohio Supreme Court held that a regulation allocating in detail instructional time for required subjects violated the federal Constitution because it would interfere with "'rights of conscience' by requiring a set amount of time to be devoted to subjects which, by their very nature, may not easily lend themselves to the teaching of religious principles (e.g., mathematics)." The court also struck down Ohio's requirement that all activities of a nonpublic school conform to policies adopted by the board of education and that such a school "cooperate with elements of the community in which it exists." The combined effect of the state's regulations, the court contended, would be to "repose power in the state Department of Education to control the essential elements of non-public education in this state," and thereby to "eradicate the distinction between public and non-public education."

The import of the *Whisner* decision, which the courts of many other jurisdictions have cited favorably, is unclear. It might stand for the proposition that state regulation becomes excessive only when it entirely eviscerates the distinctively religious quality of church schools. Under that interpretation, a state arguably would be free to impose much greater regulations on religious schools than any state presently does and perhaps even to subject religious schools to *all* the statutory regulations that states currently impose on public schools. On the other hand, one might read the *Whisner* decision to declare that any mandates directly interfering to any degree with the religious purposes of a church school are impermissible. In that case, the holding might prevent a state from attempting to prevent any of the harms discussed in Chapter 1, since they all arise out of the religious mission of the schools. This latter interpretation is more consistent with the tenor of the decisions of the Iowa Supreme Court in *Charles City* and the First Circuit Court of Appeals in *New Life Baptist* and with the reluctance courts have shown in other contexts, discussed below, to interfere with the internal practices of religious groups absent a showing of severe harm.

Decisions regarding home schooling support the conclusion that lower courts have interpreted *Yoder* as giving parents more expansive rights over their children's education when they are motivated by religion. For example, in 1993 the Supreme Court of Michigan held in companion cases that Michigan's teacher certification requirement for home schools violated the rights of parents who objected to the requirement on religious grounds but not the rights of parents who objected on nonreligious grounds.[17]

Finally, the law regarding parental authority in medical contexts provides further, and perhaps clearer, evidence that parents possess a right to cause their children harm when their religious beliefs direct them to do so.[18] Nearly all states provide an exemption in their child neglect laws for parents who fail to secure medical care for sick children because they object to particular forms of medical treatment on religious grounds. Courts sometimes order medical care for children despite parents' religious objections but only when a child is in imminent danger of death or grievous injury. Neither a likelihood of harm that is not imminent nor imminent danger of a less-than-grievous permanent injury (e.g., a disfigurement that is not life-threatening but may cause persistent discomfort and/or embarrassment) or great pain is sufficient to support court-ordered treatment. Significantly, the courts' reluctance to override parents' wishes arises not from concern that forced treatment might be more traumatic for the child than the threatened injury, but rather from deference to the religious interests of the parents.

In addition, all states exempt parents with religious objections from compulsory child immunization laws, and many also exempt such parents from laws requiring testing of children for diseases or sensory deficits. Because these exemptions have in some states implicitly or explicitly applied only to particular religious denominations, they have been challenged on equal protection grounds by parents who had religious objections to medical care for their children but who did not belong to a favored denomination. Decisions in these cases manifest clearly a judicial and social indifference to the distinct personhood and interests of children and extreme deference to the religious desires of parents. For example, in *Dalli v. Board of Education*,[19] Massachusetts's highest state court struck down such an exemption in the state's child vaccination law and encouraged the plaintiff parent as well as parents who had previously enjoyed the exemption to petition the state legislature for a broader exemption. The court described the original exemption as "an appropriate mark of deference to the sincere religious beliefs of the few which at the same time created a minimal hazard to the health of the many," and it noted medical evidence that there was no real danger to public health if only a small number of children remained at risk of contracting the contagious diseases. The court failed even to consider that the danger to the religious parent's unvaccinated child might itself be a compelling reason for eliminating any exemptions, or that children who do not receive the vaccination because their parents adhere to certain religious beliefs are themselves denied equal protection of the law.

The concept of parental rights in fact reigns supreme throughout most of family law; it determines the rules for protecting children from abuse and neglect, for placing children in foster care or freeing them for adoption, for granting a noncustodial parent visitation with a child, and in some situations for establishing custody of a child—for example, in the highly publicized "botched adoption" cases: Baby Richard, Baby Jessica, and others. In most states, the single area of the law governing child rearing in which it is not controlling is in deciding child custody disputes between biological parents, where the equal rights of two parents cancel each other and so do not provide a basis for resolution. In those cases, courts fall back on the interests of the child as a means of resolving the competing claims. In contrast, in a number of other countries today, including neighboring Canada, courts decide most matters regarding child rearing based on a "best-interests" standard.[20]

Conclusion

Courts have consistently interpreted the Free Exercise Clause of the First Amendment as guaranteeing parents a right to control the mental and physical lives of their children. This right is not always decisive, but only a compelling state interest can override it. In some contexts, courts have found the state's interest in protecting children's welfare to be compelling, but few decisions have even suggested that children themselves might have rights that should override or limit parents' rights. The Supreme Court's decision in *Wisconsin v. Yoder*, in fact, casts doubt on the viability of such a claim in educational contexts. The constitutional limits of state regulation of religious schools have not been tested, but the language of many judicial holdings suggests that regulations reaching the content of instruction, such as requiring exposure to competing world views, training in critical thinking, and elimination of sexist messages from instruction and curricular materials, would not survive a parental free exercise challenge even though they might be necessary to promote important interests of children in these schools.

It is important to recognize that the debate in cases involving religiously motivated child rearing is *not* over whether parents or state officials know what education or medical care is best for children in a temporal sense. Fundamentalists do not claim to know better than state education officials what knowledge or cognitive skills children need to prepare for a broad range of careers in mainstream society. They claim that their children's salvation is more important than, and perhaps even incompatible with, success in mainstream society. Similarly, Jehovah's Witnesses and Christian Scientists do not disagree with mainstream medical professionals about the best medical strategies for treating seriously ill or injured children. Rather, they argue that their children will be better off spiritually if they do not receive blood transfusions or, in the case of Christian Scientists, any kind of medical treatment. Some religious groups also claim that prayer is more likely than medical care to cure a child because the child will get well only if it is God's will, but that is neither an argument about the best medical care nor an argument that the state can accept as true or even reasonable. It is a mistake, therefore, to understand these situations as asking who is in a better position to know what is best for a child; rather, the question is whether the parents' religious beliefs should override secular beliefs about what is best for children.

Adults do not, of course, enjoy rights of control over the education or medical care of children who are not in their legal custody, regardless of their religious beliefs. The Seventh Circuit's decision in *Palmer v. Board of Education of the City of Chicago*[21] is instructive in this regard. A public school teacher who was a Jehovah's Witness demanded the right not to implement aspects of "the prescribed curriculum concerning patriotic matters" that conflicted with her religious principles. In rejecting her claim, the court intimated that the teacher's free exercise rights extended only to her self-determining behavior: "Plaintiff's right to her own religious views and practices remains unfettered, but she has no constitutional right to require others to submit to her views and to forego a portion of their education they would otherwise be entitled to enjoy." If the Supreme Court had applied this same principle to the parents in *Yoder*, its analysis would have been much different and the state of Wisconsin might have prevailed. Instead, currently the law grants parents a unique right to require that the lives of certain other persons— their children—conform to their religious views, even if that means the children must "forego a portion of their education [that] they would otherwise be entitled to enjoy."

I note finally that the Supreme Court's interpretation of the Free Exercise Clause took a sharp turn toward a nonaccommodation position in

1990 with *Employment Division v. Smith*,[22] which upheld denial of un-
employment compensation to Native Americans who were fired for ingesting the sacramental drug peyote in violation of Oregon law. This decision established the principle that facially neutral and generally
applicable laws that incidentally burden religious practice do not violate
the Free Exercise Clause, a principle with which *Yoder* and other parental
free exercise decisions are plainly inconsistent. However, with no rational explanation, the *Smith* court excepted from this general rule laws
that also burden some other constitutional right, such as the substantive due process right of parents to direct the upbringing of their children. Thus, ironically, after *Smith*, adults can no longer claim a religious
exemption from generally applicable laws intended to prevent them
from harming themselves but can still claim a religious exemption from
generally applicable laws intended to prevent them from harming their
children.

3 Why Parents' Rights Are Wrong

Legal scholars and political theorists, like the courts and legislatures, uniformly accept the notion of parents' rights and typically address child-rearing issues such as state control over education within a theoretical framework that has this concept at its core. Even those who advocate greater protection for children's welfare assume that parents should have rights with respect to the raising of their children; they would simply narrow the scope of those rights. Most discussion of parental child-rearing rights centers on how extensive they should be, how to balance them against state interests or children's interests, who should have them (for example, biological parents or "psychological parents"), and in what situations the people who have them should lose them.

In this chapter, I depart from these debates over the scope, balancing, and assignment of parental rights to ask at a more fundamental level what it means to say that individuals have rights as parents, and whether this is a legitimate claim. These questions pertain very broadly to legal treatment of the parent-child relationship in all contexts, rather than just in the context of religious schooling. I want to challenge not just the state's toleration of specific practices in religious schools but the entire way of thinking about child rearing in our society. Answering these general questions will lead to conclusions about *how*, conceptually, we should think about regulation of religious schools, as well as about the legal rules that apply to other aspects of child rearing, and I will carry these conclusions over in the latter part of the book to a discussion of *what*, in practical terms, we should think about regulation of religious schools. To answer these general questions, I first examine the basic concept of individual rights, as reflected in areas of the law other than that governing parents' rearing of children in their custody. Doing so reveals certain principles in American law and morality, relating to the nature and purpose of rights and limits on the notion of moral entitlement, that are patently inconsistent with parents having child-rearing *rights*, rather than simply being *permitted* to carry out parental duties and make certain decisions on a child's behalf in accordance with rights of the child. Specifically, the law in non-child-rearing contexts bespeaks an inherent limitation on the permissible scope of individual rights, confining them in principle to protection of a rightholder's personal integrity and *self-determination*. Outside the context of child rearing, the law and public morality categorically reject the notion that any individual is ever *entitled* to control the life of another person, free from outside interference, no matter how intimate the relationship between them.

The incongruity between these otherwise universal principles and the doctrine of parents' rights requires us to identify other moral or legal principles that explain and legitimize this anomalous set of rights. We ought to be able to identify unique and morally relevant features of parent-child relationships that justify treating children in a way that we deem inappropriate with respect to adults. The few writers who have paused to consider why parents should have *any* rights in connection with raising their children have all identified one or more justifications they believed to be sufficient. These typically fall into one of three categories, based on the interests they invoke: (1) children's interests in having an intimate, secure relationship with their parents and in receiving care from those who know them best and care most about them; (2) parents' interests in intimate relationships with their children and in molding a new life in accordance with their ideals; and (3) society's interests in pluralism and in the family as an essential building block of democratic culture. These writers have not, however, subjected their proposed justifications to rigorous analysis. I therefore do so in the second part of this chapter.

This analysis shows that all of the proffered justifications for parents' rights, as well as any others that I can conceive, are actually untenable. Absent some as yet unarticulated rationale that stands up to scrutiny, the conclusion is therefore inescapable that the very notion of parental rights is illegitimate, regardless of what content one gives to those rights.

What alternative is there? I propose that courts substitute for current doctrine governing disputes over child rearing a legal framework that makes children's rights the basis of decision making and that confers on parents simply a child-rearing *privilege* limited in its scope to actions and decisions not inconsistent with children's temporal interests. A parental privilege would legally *permit* certain adults to act as parents— that is, to form an intimate relationship with a child and to perform child-rearing functions such as housing, feeding, clothing, bathing, instructing, and disciplining—with respect to a particular child—but it would not accord those adults any legal claims of their own against state efforts to restrict their child-rearing practices or decision-making authority. Importantly, however, the legal regime I propose would accord such claims to children; children would possess a right against any state interference with their parents' child-rearing practices or choices that would not, on the whole, improve the children's well-being, and parents would be authorized to act as agents for their children and assert the children's rights against any inappropriate state action. From a moral perspective, a parental privilege would not convey or reflect a sense of entitlement to direct a child's life. Instead it would reflect a view of parenthood as a benefit enjoyed contingent upon fulfillment of attendant responsibilities, like other fiduciary positions such as a trustee or attorney.

It is important to recognize at the outset what this alternative legal regime would *not*, in and of itself, entail. First, it would not mean doing away with the institution of the family in favor of collectivized child rearing or abrogating all parental authority. It would simply shift the focus of inquiry, in defining the bounds of parental and state authority over child rearing, to the well-being of children. Since children have an important interest in enjoying an intimate relationship with parents, free from undue intrusion by persons who are not members of the family, and in parents' making those decisions that they are in the best position to make consistently with the children's temporal interests, the law should continue to protect family integrity and parental discretion, by ascribing to children a right against unwarranted intrusion and a right that their parents have presumptive authority over many aspects of their lives. Second, eliminating parental rights would not entail the "liberation" of children from all parental governance and discipline. Children require some governance and discipline for their healthy development; thus it would be senseless and improper to attribute to them rights against all forms of parental control or to exclude appropriate discipline from the scope of duties parents owe to their children. What the particular rights of children vis à vis their parents and the state should be is a matter for separate inquiry, which I take up in Chapters 5 and 6.

Finally, eliminating parents' child-rearing rights would not mean that adults who happen to be parents would no longer have any rights whatsoever. They would retain the self-determining rights that adults in general possess—for example, rights to choose their career, to travel, to change residence, and to leave a marriage. Exercising such self-determining rights may sometimes have negative effects on children, and there may be instances in which those effects would be so great that the law should discourage, and perhaps even prohibit, certain self-determining choices by parents. In some situations, there may be a clash of rights within a family and the law might sometimes decide in favor of the children's rights and other times in favor of the adults' self-determining rights. Analysis of such situations of conflicting rights is beyond the scope of this book. My purpose is rather to establish that parental child-rearing rights—the other-determining rights parents alone enjoy to effectuate their preferences regarding how a child's life will proceed, which are distinct from the self-determining rights all competent adults enjoy—are illegitimate.

What eliminating parents' rights *would* entail is a complete change in the conceptual framework courts use to analyze conflicts between parents and the community over child rearing, including education. Rather than balancing parents' rights against societal interests in the care and education of children, as presently occurs, judges would decide these conflicts on the basis of children's welfare interests. Thus, to determine when state-imposed restrictions on parents child-rearing practices or discretion are warranted, courts would require a showing not that parents have inflicted grievous harm on a child but that the benefits to the child of restricting the parents outweigh any costs to the child of intruding upon family life (for example, the anxiety such intrusion can produce among parents and children and the demoralizing effect it can have on parents, both of which can be detrimental to children). Some past cases that have rebuffed state efforts to restrict parents, decided on the basis of parents' rights, might have yielded the same practical outcome when analyzed within this alternative legal framework. They would have done so, however, because it was best for the children, not because the parents were entitled to that result. Many cases, however, would have had different outcomes.[1] The approach I propose would likely alter to a substantial degree the limits of parental freedom and authority and the boundaries of permissible state action. In particular, as

Chapters 5 and 6 show, it would require substantially greater state control over the content and methods of instruction in religious schools, to a degree that courts would be unlikely to approve under a parents' rights approach.

Before proceeding to the analysis, a few additional points about methodology and starting assumptions warrant mention. First, this chapter treats interests and rights as attaching to individuals rather than to relationships as unitary entities. This is consistent with the way in which courts typically interpret rights and construe interests in the context of parent-state conflicts over child rearing, as well as in other contexts involving intimate relationships, such as marriage. It is also the most sensible approach, given the undeniable fact that a parent and a child are two nonidentical persons whose interests at any point in their relationship may differ and even conflict. Treating "the family" as an indivisible unit is misleading and suspect; "reference to the family's interests or 'familial objectives' is all too likely to serve as a cover for the parents' interests precisely in those cases in which the latter conflict with those of the child." [2] The individual-oriented approach to discussing interests and rights, however, in no way denies that the interests of parent and child are ordinarily consistent with one another and are, in fact, largely interdependent. Nor is it inconsistent with the belief that familial relationships constitute a large part of the identity of young children.

Second, the most objectionable aspect of the courts' construction of parents' rights is their extension of these rights in some cases to entitle parents to treat children in ways contrary to the children's temporal interests. One might suppose that arguing for elimination of parents' rights is overkill, and that it should satisfy any advocate for children to narrow the scope of parental rights so that they do not conflict with children's interests. However, there are two problems that simply legislating a narrower scope for parental rights would not cure. First, inherent in the concept of a right is a notion of entitlement, [3] and I believe it morally improper to apply this notion to child rearing. Eradicating it from our understanding of parenting might make parents more cognizant of their responsibilities to children and also clear the way for people to take a more active interest in the lives of children not "their own," both of which would, I believe, benefit children a great deal. Second, because of the rhetorical power of parental claims to child-rearing rights, judges would be unlikely in practice to contain those rights within the bounds of children's welfare. Parents' rights claims would continue to distract judges (and everyone else) from the interests of children, because they inevitably direct attention to the interests and desires of parents themselves.

Finally, and perhaps most important, the analysis of this and all subsequent chapters begins with the basic assumption that children are persons and that morally they are equal persons. This means that they are entitled to all that the notion of respect for persons entails, in particular, a right to be treated as ends in themselves, rather than as mere means to the fulfillment of others' ends, and a right to have their interests considered equally with interests of other persons in the formation of laws and social policy.[4] I take children's equal personhood to be an uncontroversial, even though not universally recognized or effectuated, principle. Some Kantian moral philosophers predicate personhood on autonomy, an approach seeming to suggest that children are not persons or are less than full persons and so not deserving of equal respect. These philosophers attempt to avoid this implication, however, by extending their theory to make the *potential* for becoming autonomous also a predicate for personhood.[5] In my view, any basis for attributing personhood is arbitrary, so the most I can do is show the implications of believing that children are persons rather than objects to be treated as property, as I think most people do believe.

The Limits of Rights in Non-Child-Rearing Contexts

As a general rule, our legal system does not recognize or bestow on individuals rights to control the lives of other persons. In fact, there is an in-principle limitation on legal rights that confines them to protection of a rightholder's personal integrity and *self*-determining behaviors. It is a violation of this principle, a conceptual error even, to construe an individual's rights as including control over the life of another human being; anyone who does so misunderstands the nature and purpose of rights in our legal culture. A corollary of this principle, which I will refer to as the Limited Rights Principle, is that no individual is *entitled* to use another, nonconsenting person as an instrument to advance his own interests, free from interference by the state or other third parties. Underlying the Limited Rights Principle is a strong moral sense that we would fail to respect the personhood of an individual, even if incompetent, were we to say that someone else is *entitled* to determine the course of his or her life. Also underlying is a belief that the desire of one person to control another's life is not a fundamental interest that cries out for satisfaction.

In considering whether the Limited Rights Principle is in fact a controlling precept in our legal system, keep in mind the distinction between a right and a privilege explained in Chapter 2. The law does in some circumstances *permit* certain individuals to direct important aspects of the life of another adult who cannot act or make decisions on his own behalf. The law authorizes these individuals to act as agents in order to advance the interests of the incompetent adult, even if the latter is incapable of consenting to being represented. However, the law does not accord any individuals a *right* to direct the life of another adult, such that they would have legal grounds for complaint on *their own* behalf if someone interfered with their efforts to direct the other person's life.

The Limited Rights Principle also presupposes a distinction between a right to control another person's life and a right to demand particular, limited action or forbearance by another person in order to protect one's own person, property, and self-determining interests. As discussed further below, rights of property, of contract, or of any other kind in non-child-rearing contexts, while they may limit the freedom of others to some extent, never amount to plenary power over another person such that the rightholder could be said to be controlling that other person's life. Moreover, no rights outside the child-rearing context rest on a moral notion of entitlement to control another person simply for the sake of exercising such control—that is, abstracted from any particular objectives that such control might serve. Rather, rights generally rest on a notion of entitlement to promote certain self-determining objectives, such as protecting the integrity of one's own person and property and determining the direction of one's own life (e.g., one's own occupation, one's own health care, the investment of one's own property).

That no one has a *right* to control the life of another adult may seem self-evident. Nevertheless, demonstrating that this is a governing principle of law is made difficult by the absence of clear judicial statements to that effect. One also searches in vain for explicit statements on the subject in the writings of legal theorists and political philosophers. The silence might be attributable to the self-evident nature of the proposition, or it might be a consequence of the fact that, outside the context of child rearing, people simply do not claim a right to direct the lives of others, and thus the issue does not arise. The fact that people do not make such claims may itself reflect a common understanding that the scope of individual rights is inherently limited to control over one's own life.

THE RHETORIC OF RIGHTS

Though judicial opinions frequently address the content and purpose of specific rights, they rarely enunciate any theory of what a right, in general, is. However, the language the Supreme Court has used to define particular constitutional rights is consistent with, and so provides indirect support for, the proposition that, as a general rule, our legal system does not confer on individuals rights to control the lives of other persons. For example, the Court has described the religious liberty that the Free Exercise Clause protects as "the right of every person to freely choose *his own* course" with respect to religious training, teaching, and observance;[6] as "rights to one's own religious opinion";[7] and as a person's liberty "to worship God according to the dictates of his own conscience."[8] The Court has never suggested, except in child-rearing cases, that the Free Exercise Clause entitles any individual to force others to worship God according to the dictates of his or her conscience, or otherwise to control the life of other persons in accordance with the dictates of that individual's religion.

Not surprisingly, none of the free exercise cases that the Court has considered has involved any such claim. If a plaintiff ever asserted a right to compel another adult (or someone else's children) to go to the plaintiff's church, to receive religious training of the plaintiff's choice, or to forgo medical treatment proscribed by the plaintiff's religion, any court would summarily dismiss the claim, regardless of how passionately the plaintiff felt that he must indoctrinate the other person or prevent the religiously objectionable medical treatment. Imagine, for example, an elderly person confined to a wheelchair, under the care of an adult offspring who has converted to a religion other than that of his upbringing and who demands the right to wheel the parent off to religious gatherings for indoctrination into the faith or the right to refuse medical care that the parent needs because it conflicts with the offspring's faith. Courts would dismiss such claims even if the parent had no opinions or preferences regarding religion at the time and even if the parent were not sufficiently competent to express an objection. Moreover, courts would not find that state action preventing a plaintiff from forcing another adult into conformity with the dictates of the plaintiff's religion burdened the plaintiff's constitutionally protected religious liberty and then go on to consider whether compelling state interests outweighed this burden (and would not have done so even before *Employment Division v. Smith*). They would instead simply deny that the type of right that the plaintiff demands even exists. They would accuse the plaintiff of misunderstanding the nature of the right of religious freedom.

The one type of free exercise case courts have addressed that does involve one person claiming a religiously grounded right to control the life of another adult to a significant degree is that in which a spouse has raised a religious objection to a state's granting a civil divorce to the other spouse. This kind of claim falls far short of demanding a right to dictate the religious training or medical care of another person, and courts have uniformly and summarily dismissed such claims. For example, in *Sharma v. Sharma*,[9] a Kansas state court rejected outright a free exercise challenge to a civil divorce, reasoning that civil divorce in no way impaired the plaintiff spouse's religious freedom, even though her religion—Hinduism—did not allow divorce. The court emphasized that the civil divorce did not interfere in any recognizable way with the wife's practice of Hinduism and that the wife remained free to take any view of the relationship she liked. This decision stands in sharp contrast to *Yoder*, where the Supreme Court failed to recognize that compulsory school attendance for the children of Amish adults would not restrict what the parents' could believe or the parents' ability to be Amish. In *Yoder*, the Court implicitly held that an impediment to fulfilling religiously imposed familial obligations is a legitimate basis for finding a free exercise burden, while *Sharma* and the other decisions of its kind have rejected that notion without hesitation in the context of relationships between adults.

In construing the First Amendment Free Speech Clause, the Supreme Court has similarly spoken in terms suggesting that it views the protected right as limited in scope to the rightholder's sphere of personal autonomy. The Free Speech Clause protects the "right of *self-*determination in matters that touch individual opinion and personal attitude,"[10] and embodies the "concept of '*individual* freedom of mind.'"[11] Significantly, the Free Speech Clause also protects "the right not to be compelled" to support the dissemination of the personal and political views of others."[12] One could readily find numerous other examples of the Supreme Court's interpreting rights as protective of self-determination. The Due Process Clauses of the Fifth and Fourteenth Amendments protect the right of the individual "to plan *his own* affairs" and "to shape *his own* life as he thinks best."[13] The Court has described the right to make medical decisions as "the right of every individual to the possession and control of *his own* person" and "to determine what shall be done with *his own* body,"[14] and as a guarantee of "physical freedom and *self*-determination."[15] In the abortion context, members of the Court have described the rule of law that *Roe v. Wade* and its progeny established as "a woman's fundamental right to self-determination"[16] and as "the right to define *one's own* concept of existence, of meaning, of the universe, and of the mystery of human life[17] resting on "'the moral fact that a person belongs to himself and not to others nor to society as a whole.'"[18]

Though it would be extremely difficult, if not impossible, to prove the nonexistence of any counterexamples (I consider several possible ones below), the passages above provide a clear sense that courts consistently interpret rights in nonparenting contexts as protections of individual integrity and self-determination. In fact, it may be that even in the parenting context judges do not understand themselves to be creating other-determining rights and that the reason they uphold rights that are in fact of that nature is that they fail to perceive children as persons separate from their parents. Support for this conclusion may be found in a statement by Justice Douglas, which other justices and lower court judges have frequently cited, that appears to treat child rearing as simply another facet of an adult's control over his or her own life. He once asserted that the term "liberty" in the Fourteenth Amendment signifies "freedom of choice in the basic decisions of one's life respecting marriage, divorce, procreation, contraception, and the education and upbringing of children."[19]

SUPPORTING DOCTRINES AND POSSIBLE COUNTEREXAMPLES

More direct support for the Limited Rights Principle comes from areas of law in which controlling precedents deny individuals rights to engage in other-determining behavior. The Thirteenth Amendment's prohibition of slavery and involuntary servitude is the strongest and most obvious embodiment of the principle that no person should have a right to control the life of another person. The Supreme Court has interpreted this constitutional provision as proscribing not merely the formal institution of slavery but also all the "badges and incidents" of slavery, including any "state of bondage" or "control by which the personal service of one man is disposed of or coerced for another's benefit."[20] In one case, the Court defined slavery as "'the state of entire subjection of one person to the will of another.'"[21] Parental control over the lives of children certainly differs in important respects from the institution of slavery, but it nevertheless can manifest some of the "badges and incidents" of slavery, particularly "when a parent perverts this coercive authority by systematically abusing and degrading his ward—treating his child not as a person but as a chattel, acting as if he had title over the child rather than a trusteeship on behalf of the child."[22]

Developments in the law governing marital relations in the last forty years are also revealing. Under older common-law rules of marriage, husbands held rights of "consortium" with respect to their wives, which included rights to a wife's services in the home and to sexual intercourse with her and the right to direct the family's affairs. Wives were under a correlative duty to submit to the husband's governance.[23] Moreover, wives were unable to sue their husbands, even for such harmful conduct as rape. These common-law rights of husbands, though they might appear to be other-determining and thus to present a historical counterexample to the Limited Rights Principle, actually rested on an assumption that women agreed when they married to give up their separate identities and, in essence, to become the property of their husbands.[24] Thus, in controlling his wife, a man was simply exercising control over his own person or property. Moreover, when this common-law view of wives as property or as lacking a separate identity fell out of favor, courts dismantled husbands' traditional instruments of control over their wives. No-fault divorce laws have made it much easier for a woman to exit from a marital relationship, and wives have obtained greater control over their bodies while in a marriage as a result of growing legislative and judicial hostility to marital exemptions in rape laws,[25] improved legal protection against other forms of spousal abuse, and Supreme Court decisions establishing rights to obtain and use contraceptives and to have an abortion without a husband's consent.[26]

Husbands and wives still enjoy by law some measure of control over each other, and the reality of the respective economic power of women and men today translates into inequity in the degree of de facto control that husbands and wives generally hold over one another. Nevertheless, the formal, de jure rights and privileges that husbands now possess with respect to their wives by virtue of the marriage contract do not amount to plenary control over the wives' lives, are no different from the rights and privileges that wives enjoy with respect to their husbands, and are predicated upon both parties' voluntary consent. In other contract situations as well, it is true that the parties exert by right some measure of control over one another, but the legality of the contract depends critically upon the consent of the parties and upon mutuality of consideration and courts will not enforce contractual rights so extensive as to give one person plenary control over the life of another. In sharp contrast, parents' rights under the Fourteenth Amendment Due Process Clause and the First Amendment Free Exercise Clause *do* amount to legally sanctioned domination of one group of persons over the lives of other individuals who today are regarded, in law and public morality, as persons.[27] The courts have not predicated recognition of parental rights on any real or even hypothetical contract—that is, on imputed consent or receipt of reciprocal consideration by the child. Rather, as with rights of slavery and traditional rights of consortium, parental rights rest on an assumption of ownership and on a failure to respect the personhood of the individuals who are the objects of those rights.

The subjection of African-Americans and wives to the legal control of other persons was also sometimes defended as necessary because those under subjection were believed to be naturally suited to governance by others. This supposed justification lost its force with the recognition that the innate capacities of women and African-Americans are equal to those of white males. There are, however, other groups of persons who unquestionably *are* less capable of furthering their own interests, and one might think that genuine incompetence constitutes a legitimate basis for giving some individuals rights to govern the lives of such persons. Children at birth certainly fall into the category of persons lacking self-governing capacities, and they gain competence only gradually over the course of many years. However, some adults fall into this category as well, and if one's incompetence were sufficient reason to give another person the right to determine the course of one's life, these adults, too, would have someone deciding by right what would happen to them, and we would find counterexamples to the Limited Rights Principle in the law relating to incompetent adults. This turns out, however, not to be the case.

In *Cruzan v. Director, Missouri Department of Health*,[28] the Supreme Court considered the case of a woman in a persistent vegetative state whose parents wished to have the hospital remove her life-support system. Missouri, like many other states, permits a surrogate to make various medical decisions on behalf of a patient in a persistent vegetative state but merely as a spokesperson for the patient herself. For his choice of treatment to be effective, the surrogate must show by clear and convincing evidence that the choice conforms to the wishes of the patient before she became incompetent. Thus, the surrogate, in effect, advances and effectuates the rights of the patient herself to decide on her medical treatment because she cannot exercise these rights directly. The surrogate does not exercise any right of his own to decide what the hospital will do with the patient. The Missouri Supreme Court had held that Nancy Cruzan's parents had not provided clear and convincing evidence that their daughter would have wished to have hydration and nutrition withdrawn if she were ever in such a condition and so had upheld the hospital's denial of the parents' request.

The parents in *Cruzan* insisted that Missouri should accept the judgment of close family members regarding the treatment of an incompetent patient, even in the absence of sufficient evidence that their own views matched those of the patient. The Supreme Court rejected the suggestion that the parents possessed a right to decide what would happen to their adult daughter: "[W]e do not think the Due Process Clause requires the State to repose judgment on these matters with anyone but the patient herself." The Court recognized that close family members will generally have very strong feelings about what happens to the patient in such situations, but also that these feelings may not be entirely disinterested and that "there is no automatic assurance that the view of close family members will necessarily be the same as the patient's would have been had she been confronted with the prospect of her situation while competent."

Nowhere in *Cruzan* does the Court hint that family members would possess a right to make decisions for an incompetent adult patient if the decision were less momentous than one involving life and death. Nor does the Court suggest that it would be appropriate to balance parents' free exercise rights against a patient's interests or preferences if parents were to have religious objections to artificial life support for their son or daughter, and it is inconceivable that the Court would ever seriously entertain such a notion. Rather, *Cruzan* stands for the bald proposition that no one is *entitled* to make decisions for an incompetent adult patient. The Court held that in the absence of sufficient evidence as to what the patient herself would want, the state permissibly elected to act on its own presumption that the patient would wish to continue to live. The state was not required even to consider the preferences of close family members. New Jersey's highest court took the same approach in deciding the fate of Karen Ann Quinlan in the mid 1970s, rejecting her parents' claim that they had a right, based on their religious beliefs, to decide whether artificial life support would continue.[29] The court ultimately decided that it would "*permit* the guardian and family of Karen to render their best judgment" (emphasis added) as to what *her* "putative decision" would have been in the circumstances, emphasizing that the only person with rights in the matter was Karen Quinlan herself. The court refused to "recognize an independent parental right of religious freedom" where the incompetent offspring is of majority age, deeming the Free Exercise Clause to be simply "inapplicable" in such cases despite the religious basis of the parents' wishes; their claim of impingement of their religious beliefs, the court stated, "does not reflect a constitutional question."

These decisions, with their focus on the integrity and distinct personhood of the incompetent adult offspring whose fate was being decided, stand in sharp contrast to decisions under the Due Process Clause and the Free Exercise Clause upholding parents' rights to determine the life course of their minor offspring. In *Yoder*, for example, the Court expressed indifference to the children's wishes, going so far as to suggest that the parents' preferences for the children's future would outweigh any contrary preferences of the children themselves. In *Pierce v. Society of Sisters*, the Court treated the children's interests even more cursorily and gave no consideration to what rights children themselves might have with respect to education. Neither *Yoder* nor *Pierce* manifests any concern that parents' preferences regarding the children's education might not be entirely disinterested.

Of course, the situation of an adult who was competent but has become incompetent is distinguishable from that of a child who is not and has never been competent, since it is often possible in the former case, but not the latter, to refer to rational, informed preferences of the now incompetent person as a basis for decision (putting aside conceptual and practical difficulties with doing so). It is therefore useful to examine judicial and legislative treatment of the role of parents in decision making for mentally retarded adults. Like young children, many mentally retarded adults whose medical treatment or residential placement is contested have never formed or expressed informed, rational opinions regarding their situation. Though some legislatures have authorized parents to *participate* in the decision-making process regarding institutionalization or medical treatment of adult mentally retarded offspring, they have not granted parents a right to *make* these decisions. For example, at issue in *Heller v. Doe*[30] was a Kentucky statute that gave guardians and immediate family members party standing in proceedings for institutional commitment of mentally retarded adults but did not give any family member's views dispositive weight or presumptive authority in those proceedings. The question before the Supreme Court was whether the statute went *too far* in granting this limited right of participation. The Supreme Court found the statute constitutional because it was consistent with mentally retarded adults' due process rights, reasoning that even though guardians and family members might have interests adverse to those of the person facing commitment and even though their participation might increase the likelihood of commitment, their party status would not alter the focus of the proceedings on the welfare of the retarded adult or increase the risk of an erroneous decision. Thus, the Court treated the beliefs and desires of the parents as subordinate to the rights and interests of the incompetent adult.

In cases involving proposed medical treatment for mentally retarded adults, courts have used a substituted-judgment procedure, similar to that at issue in *Cruzan*, in which they attempt to discern what the incompetent person's decision would be if he were competent. This approach allows parental input but does not confer on parents a right to make decisions for their adult offspring or even treat them as legal parties to the proceedings. Thus, the law ensures parents of mentally retarded adults some role in the important decisions of the offspring's lives because this is conducive to their offspring's welfare, but their authority is much more limited than that which parents exercise over minor children and clearly does not amount to a presumptive right to decide for their adult offspring. This is so even though many mentally retarded adults have lesser capacities and are more dependent than even young children.

The Limited Rights Principle is thus manifest even in situations that are distinguishable from the parent-minor offspring situation only by virtue of the nominal age of the offspring, which does not in itself have any moral or practical significance. Even though many mentally retarded adults need to be under someone else's care and guidance and cannot make informed, rational decisions about their living situation or medical care, the law reflects a belief that it would be improper to accord someone else a *right* to make those decisions, that it would fail to respect them as persons to say that someone else is *entitled* to determine the course of their lives, and that the simple fact that they are human beings means that they have rights that dictate what others may or may not do to them. One might even find it ironic, particularly if one believes (as I do not) that rationality or autonomy is the basis of human worth, that persons who never will be autonomous appear to receive greater respect in law and public policy than do persons who have the potential to become autonomous.

Before considering possible justifications for the anomaly of according child-rearing rights to parents, there are two additional areas of the law that suggest potential counterexamples to the Limited Rights Principle. First, the abortion rights of pregnant women might appear at first glance to be rights to control—indeed to destroy—the life of another person. Of course, the "person" at issue here would be a child, so the right could be seen as an extension of parents' rights over their minor children, rather than as a contradiction of the claim that parents' rights are the sole exception to the Limited Rights Principle. However, since the Supreme Court in *Roe v. Wade* declared that a fetus is not a person, the abortion right the Court created is actually not a right to control the life of another person. The Court did not have to face the question whether a person could appropriately possess a right to decide that another person will die or whether an unborn child could appropriately possess a positive right to "use" of another person's body for nine months—both of which might be viewed as other-determining rights of the kind that would offend the Limited Rights Principle. In dictum, the Court intimated that if the fetus *were* a person, its rights would be controlling on the abortion question.[31] A number of commentators have objected, however, that even if the fetus were a person, according it a right to life would amount to unjustifiably using the pregnant woman as an instrument to further the interests of another person.[32] Thus, under the assumption that the fetus is a person—an assumption many people hold—abortion would pose an inevitable and intractable clash of rights, and the rights of either party would have grave other-determining side effects. However, attributing rights to one or the other party in that case actually would not run afoul of the Limited Rights Principle, because the rights would be, in their purpose and primary effect, self-determining and/or self-protective ones for the rightholder. The woman's rights would protect her ability to control her body and her freedom to pursue various paths in life that might be closed off by carrying a child to term. The fetus's right would protect his or her life.

In fact, it is very revealing, in considering the reach of the Limited Rights Principle, to examine the rhetoric that surrounds the pro-life/pro-choice struggle. Pro-life activists who seek to disrupt the activities of abortion clinics do not claim that the Free Exercise Clause or the Due Process Clause grants them a right to control pregnant women's lives. Rather, they claim a right of self-expression and, as justification for their more disruptive activities, claim (unsuccessfully) to act as agents for the unborn child, asserting the child's right to life.[33] Thus, even though abortion evokes the strongest feelings about how other people should act and offends fundamental principles within some religious belief systems, even the most fanatical participants in the pro-life movement accept a distinction between what their religious beliefs entitle them to do to themselves and their children and what their beliefs entitle them to do to other adults. They appear to understand that their constitutional right to freedom of religion simply does not include a right to determine what a pregnant woman does with her body, no matter how desperately they might wish to do so and no matter how benevolent their motivation (which for some pro-life activists includes genuine concern for the pregnant woman's salvation as well as for the life of her unborn children). For their part, pro-choice advocates do not claim that women have a right to kill another human being, but rather champion a woman's right to decide what will happen to her own body.

The final area of law that suggests a possible counterexample to the Limited Rights Principle is, interestingly, the one that imposes duties on parents in connection with child rearing. It is not clear to whom those duties run; children are the immediate beneficiaries, suggesting that the duties run to them, but legal action to enforce the duties is typically brought by the state on its own behalf, suggesting that the duties run to society as a whole. Assuming for the moment that the duties run to the benefited children, it would appear that children possess, vis à vis their parents, not only negative rights against grievous harm but also positive rights to ongoing care and support: food, clothing, shelter, supervision, medical care, etc. These rights can effectively limit parents' life choices and dictate a large part of what they must do on a daily basis.

There are, however, at least two reasons why children's claims on their parents do not constitute a counterexample to the Limited Rights Principle. First and most important, the adults who bear the duties corresponding to children's positive rights have, as far as the law is concerned, undertaken these duties voluntarily. Those adults who do not wish to shoulder the obligations of parenthood are legally free not to conceive children, to abort a fetus before the stage of viability, or to give up a child for adoption or care by the state. The positive rights of children therefore do not operate against nonconsenting persons. It is true that even after they no longer wish to fulfill their role, parents often continue to bear some duties relating to their children in the form of support obligations. However, to the extent those duties are viewed as owed to the child, rather than to the larger society that would otherwise have to support the child, it is because when persons initially choose to parent a child, they are deemed to have knowingly created a reliance interest on the part of the child and therefore are assumed implicitly and voluntarily to have accepted the condition that they may not thereafter abandon certain duties owed to the child. Second, the self-imposed constraints of parenthood are quite different in purpose and effect from the control that parents are currently entitled to wield over their nonconsenting children. The purpose and primary effect of a child's claims on her parents are to protect and promote the child's interests, in her own physical and cognitive development and, ultimately, her self-determination, not to restrict parents' life options. Thus, for example, children have no right to decide which faith their parents will adopt, what schooling their parents will receive, where and whether their parents will work, or what medical treatment their parents will undergo.

Thus, parents' child-rearing rights remain the sole exception to the general rule that rights in our legal system are limited to self-determining safeguards, choices, and activities. As noted above, this general rule rests in part on a moral belief that deeming an individual a fit subject for rights of control residing in others fails to respect the personhood of that individual. There is an understandable tendency, given ingrained social attitudes about children, to say that the parent-child relationship is unique and that this uniqueness is all the explanation needed for treating children in a way we deem unacceptable with respect to any category of adults. Whether the parent-child relationship is significantly different from the relationship between a prent and a severely mentally disabled adult offspring is debatable. More important, though, uniqueness is not itself a legal or moral reason for decision making. For any unique characteristics of the parent-child relationship to justify giving child-rearing rights to parents, they must have legal and moral significance.

Supposed Justifications for Parents' Rights

Justifications for parental rights voiced in scholarly writings and in popular discourse fall into three categories, according to the interests on which they rely: the interests of children, the interests of parents, and the interests of society. Before considering each of these categories, it is necessary to address the one justification on which the courts have principally relied, which does not fall into any of these categories. As shown in Chapter 2, the only special feature of the parent-child relationship to which the Supreme Court has pointed as a basis for according rights of parental control protection under either the Free Exercise Clause or the Due Process Clause is simply that parents have traditionally held such control.

That some practice or rule has a long tradition does not, of course, mean that it is in *anyone's* interest. A tradition might persist even though on the whole it diminishes the well-being of all concerned parties, including those who appear to be its beneficiaries. That a practice or rule has a long tradition also does not mean that it is just or that it is consistent with fundamental moral and legal precepts. Enslavement of Africans and the legal subjugation of women to their husbands are obvious examples; they persisted for hundreds of years in Western culture, but few today would argue that these "traditions" were worthy of preservation. Some current members of the Supreme Court nevertheless continue to endorse the jurisprudential line that a liberty is fundamental and protected by the Constitution if it is "deeply rooted in this Nation's history and tradition."[34] Reliance on tradition even appears occasionally in the academic literature as well.[35]

Other members of the Court, though, have disparaged reliance on this criterion as a means of identifying constitutionally protected liberties. Dissenting in *Bowers v. Hardwick*, which held that freedom to engage in homosexual activity is not a constitutionally protected liberty because it is not rooted in the nation's traditions, four justices invoked Oliver Wendell Holmes's famous aphorism "'[I]t is revolting to have no better reason for a rule of law than that so it was laid down in the time of Henry IV. It is still more revolting if the grounds upon which it was laid down have vanished long since, and the rule simply persists from blind imitation of the past.'"[36] Justice White also once observed that "[w]hat the deeply rooted traditions of the country are is arguable; which of them deserve [legal protection] is even more debatable,"[37] while Justice Brennan pointed out that "[e]ven if we could agree . . . on the content and significance of particular traditions, we still would be forced to identify the point at which a tradition becomes . . . too obsolete to be relevant any longer."[38] With similar objections in mind, most legal scholars reject the tradition-based approach to determining fundamental rights. J.M. Balkin, for example, rejects it because "specific historical traditions may often be opposed to our more general commitments to liberty or equality,"[39] and Francis McCarthy explains that "looking backward in time to see whether tradition would support a claim of right can freeze in time very specific rights, but no others, and . . . requires that the entire argument be moved to a different level of abstraction for which the tradition itself provides no direct support."[40]

A more sensible approach would be to engage a rebuttable presumption that a long-standing social practice or legal rule is beneficial and just and potentially deserving of constitutional protection, but to require that when a well-founded challenge to such a traditional practice or rule is presented, courts examine whether it does in fact serve the interests supposed to underlie it and whether it is indeed just and consistent with other legal principles. If a traditional rule or practice fails this test, then it no longer merits legal protection.

THE APPEAL TO CHILDREN'S INTERESTS

Legal scholars and political theorists sometimes justify parents' rights on the ground that they are necessary to protect the interests of children. No one would dispute that because children, at least younger ones, are incapable of protecting or providing for themselves, or of making rational, informed decisions about important aspects of their lives, some adult must be in a position to direct their lives and make important decisions for them. Nor would many people dispute that an optimal upbringing for a child involves an intimate, continuous relationship with a single set of parents that is largely insulated from interference by third parties. Conventional wisdom holds further that parents are in the best position to know what is best for their children and are likely to care more than anyone else about their children's well-being.

Even if one accepts these propositions without qualification, however, it simply does not follow from them that parents should have child-rearing rights. It is particularly illogical to conclude that parents should enjoy plenary rights to effectuate their religion-based preferences concerning their child's life. Significantly, the courts themselves have never taken a child-centered approach to justifying parental free exercise rights. As discussed above, courts have granted parents rights against many forms of state action designed to protect children's interests simply because parents strongly desired such rights and because there is a long tradition of letting parents do what they want with their children absent a threat of grievous physical harm. The courts have not focused on whether, for the child, the costs of such state action would exceed the costs of leaving parents unconstrained. If the courts did focus first and foremost on the interests of children in determining parents' rights, the scope of those rights would undoubtedly be much different from what it presently is.

The first problem with the child-centered approach to defending parents' rights is relevant only in the free exercise context. There is no self-evident connection between parents' religious beliefs and children's temporal interests. Anyone promoting the child-centered justification exclusively would have to demonstrate such a connection in order to justify the rule, established by the Supreme Court in *Yoder*, that parents should have greater rights of control over their children's lives when parental child-rearing preferences arise from religious rather than secular beliefs. They would have to show that the very fact of adhering to a religion—any religion—whose tenets include preferred modes of parenting makes a parent better able or more disposed to further the temporal interests of the child.

The qualification "temporal" applied to "interest" in the preceding passage, and at other points in this book, is critical, of course, and this is an appropriate juncture at which to explain its use. Naturally, religious parents are concerned about more than the secular interests of their children; they are also, often primarily, concerned with children's spiritual interests. However, consistent with the Establishment Clause of the First Amendment, and the principle of state neutrality on religious questions that it embodies, temporal interests are the only interests with which *the state* can properly concern itself in carrying out its responsibility to protect the well-being of children and other incompetent persons. For the state to take account of children's supposed spiritual interests would require *it* to assume the truth of particular religious beliefs—that children *have* spiritual interests in the first place, that those interests are of a certain nature, and that living in a certain way best serves those interests—and therefore to endorse a particular religious view, which the Constitution prohibits it from doing.[41]

Admittedly, this principle of state neutrality is not itself ideologically neutral. It is a distinctively liberal principle. The liberal state is neutral in the sense that it abstains from taking positions on nonsecular issues in its day-to-day operations, though on the higher-order normative question of whether the state *should* be strictly secular in this way, it reflects a partisan, liberal position. Thus, at the level of selecting and justifying a particular type of government, liberalism is directly opposed to those religious views that favor state involvement in promoting religious values and causes. I will not endeavor to defend this nonneutral principle of state neutrality embodied in our federal Constitution but instead simply assume it and explicate its implications for those who endorse it. Suffice it to say that this principle reflects a judgment that, in recognition of the religiously pluralistic nature of our society and the unlikelihood of overcoming disagreements on religious questions, it is best for the state to concern itself only with secular matters while leaving individuals more or less free to determine for themselves what they believe about religion and the role religious considerations should have in their lives—including whether they will sacrifice their temporal interests in some cases to further what they regard as their spiritual interests.

What many political and legal theorists fail to recognize is that the freedom liberalism accords individuals to perform their own balancing of religious and temporal interests extends only to an individual's *self*-determination. Liberal state abstention from religious disagreements does not entail allowing individual citizens to perform that balancing for *other* persons and to determine on that basis the legality of their own actions affecting other persons. For example, it does not mean that I should be able to force my neighbor to attend my church and profess my religion if I decide that doing so would further what I regard as his spiritual interests and that these spiritual interests outweigh his temporal interest in being free from coercion. In our legal system and public morality, religious belief has never been an excuse for violating, or a basis for claiming an exemption from, laws intended to protect the temporal interests of other adult persons. Legislators and judges determine the legality of individuals' actions that affect other persons, based on the material with which they are permitted to work—the temporal interests of the people whom the actions affect.

This same principle should apply when the person affected is the child of the agent. The state should no more allow parents to balance their child's spiritual and temporal interests and decide that they will sacrifice the latter than it should allow me to do this in relation to my neighbor (or my parents, even if they become incompetent). The state should protect the child's temporal interests no matter what the parents believe until the child becomes an adult capable of making his own self-determining choices. This is not to say that the state must completely ignore the parents' beliefs but rather that the state may take the parents' beliefs into account in its decision making, if at all, only insofar as the parents' adherence to those beliefs affects the temporal well-being of the child—for example, if psychological harm might befall a child as a result of his parents' belief that they and the child are damned to an eternity in hell. Any defensible interpretation of the Establishment Clause or of the liberal principle of state neutrality, however, would recognize that it does preclude the state from accepting the parents' belief as true and on that basis weighing the child's alleged spiritual interests against his temporal interests.

We return now to the question whether there is any inherent connection between parents having religious beliefs and children's temporal interests being furthered. Though the motives of persons who promulgate or interpret religious teachings pertaining to child rearing are undoubtedly quite complex, there is no reason to suppose that in most or even many cases their primary consideration in doing so is the temporal well-being of children. Indeed, parents embroiled in conflicts with the state over schooling and medical-care issues typically invoke their own spiritual interests and sometimes also the spiritual interests of their children in support of their parenting choices—against what most members of the larger community, and perhaps they themselves, perceive to be the temporal interests of the children. Given this lack of a connection between parents' religious beliefs and children's temporal interests, a child-centered approach appears particularly unpromising as a defense of the incrementally greater rights of parents under the Free Exercise Clause.

The second problem with invoking children's interests to justify parents' rights applies equally to the courts' construction of such rights under the First or Fourteenth Amendment. It is an odd concept that one individual's interests can and should be protected by giving rights to another individual. Ordinarily we assign rights to the person who needs protection, whose interests are at stake. Why, then, if we are truly most concerned with protecting children's interests, do we not grant children themselves the rights necessary to protect those interests? Why do we instead rely on the conceptually awkward notion of parents' rights? All of the important interests one might attribute to children, including those that parental rights are sometimes said to protect, can be protected by a right residing in the child. For example, the law could attribute to children positive rights to the continuous care, protection, and guidance of a parent or parents and to a suitable education. David Archard expresses this point aptly: "My loving you does not give me rights over you. But if you have a right to certain kinds of treatment and my love for you guarantees that treatment, then it may follow that I am the person to love you. This, however, is your right not mine."[42] In addition, the law could grant children a negative right against any interference—by the state or other third party—in their relationship with their parents or in their schooling that would do them more harm than good. Parental rights are entirely unnecessary to give children these protections.

At bottom, parental rights are necessary only to ensure that parents can treat their children in ways *contrary* to the children's temporal interests. They give parents a legal basis for objecting to state efforts to protect children from harmful actions of the parents, whereas rights of the children themselves presumably would not provide a basis for doing so. For example, in the case of religious schooling, an appropriate set of children's rights could serve as a barrier to any state action that would, on the whole, make the children worse off—for instance, if enforcement of a particular regulation would somehow weaken the bonds between the children and their parents or undermine the efficacy of the parents or teachers without providing a greater, countervailing benefit to the children. What is different under a regime of parental rights is that parents can oppose, sometimes successfully, some forms of state action that would, on the whole, enhance their children's temporal well-being simply by arguing that such action conflicts with their own beliefs and preferences.

As one concrete illustration of this difference, consider the teaching of sexist beliefs in Fundamentalist schools. Assume for the sake of argument that this practice is harmful to the temporal well-being of girls (and perhaps boys also) who attend the schools, and that prohibiting this practice would, on the whole, benefit these students. In that case, Fundamentalist parents could not plausibly object to such a prohibition on the grounds that it violates their daughters' rights. However, under the prevailing judicial interpretation of the Free Exercise Clause, these parents do have a legal basis for objecting to such regulation—namely, that it violates *their* rights. With parental free exercise rights, they have presumptive authority to treat their daughters in this way regardless of the daughters' interests simply because their religion directs them to do so.

One objection to substituting children's rights for parents' rights might be that it locates the operative rights in persons who are not in a position to effectuate them. Most children are not capable of invoking the necessary institutional mechanisms for asserting rights—for example, police protection and investigation, litigation, and the legislative process. However, this objection has no greater force in the case of children than it does in the case of incompetent adults. Persons other than the rightholder can and do act as agents to prosecute the rights of incompetent adults. In a world without parents' rights but with an appropriate set of children's rights, the law could recognize parents as their children's agents (as, in fact, it does now), with the responsibility to assert the children's rights and to invoke the necessary institutional mechanisms when actions by third parties threaten the children's welfare interests. Such actions would include any unwarranted efforts by the state to protect what it perceives, perhaps mistakenly, to be the temporal interests of the child.

Under this legal regime, if a conflict over child-rearing practices were to arise between parents and the state, courts would not balance the child's interests or societal interests against the parents' child-rearing rights, because the parents would have no such rights. Rather, courts would determine as best they could which outcome—that which the parent recommends or that which the state recommends—is more consistent with the rights and temporal interests of the child, taking into account any costs to the child arising from the state's restricting parents' freedom. It would be naive to think that courts can always determine what is best for a child, but it would also be naive to think that parents are always more competent to judge their child's best interests than are state agency personnel who spend their lives studying and thinking about what is best for children, and parents' judgment is particularly suspect when it arises primarily from religious commands, given the disjunction between parents' religious beliefs and children's temporal interests noted above. Courts should acknowledge and draw upon parents' special knowledge of the unique characteristics of their children, and should take into account that parents typically care a great deal about their children, but beyond this there is no reason to assume that the parents' preference regarding their child's schooling or medical care is best for the child. Whether it is in fact so the courts should decide after full and impartial consideration of the evidence both sides present, just as they would in any other dispute about the content and implications of an individual's rights. Where such a determination is beyond the competence of the courts, they should instead decide (or the legislature should decide as a general rule for certain categories of cases) which party is, in general, in the better position to make the kind of decision at issue—in light of the capacities, resources, information, or other variables pertinent to making such a decision—in a manner consistent with the child's temporal interests. They would then apply a presumption in favor of effectuating that party's decision and impose on the other party the burden of presenting sufficient evidence to overcome the presumption.

Undoubtedly, in many aspects of children's lives this approach would support a presumption of parental decision-making authority, but on some issues now left to parental discretion, such as whether children should receive instruction from trained teachers and be protected from sexist instruction, there is good reason to believe it would be better for children in general if the state had presumptive authority to decide (after soliciting input from all interested parties, including parents).

A third problem associated with using parental rights to protect children's interests is that locating the operative rights in parents distracts the attention of everyone—legislators, judges, the public, and parents themselves—away from children's interests and toward parents' desires. Rights in all other contexts are assigned to the persons whose interests the law seeks to protect, so it is natural that when rights are asserted, attention focuses on the interests and wishes of their bearers. As shown in Chapter 2, establishing and giving priority to parents' rights has fostered a tendency in judges to analyze parent-state conflicts over child rearing as if there were no other party involved besides the parents and state officials concerned with societal interests, and scholarly commentary on these cases often reflects this same neglect of children as distinct persons with distinct interests. Rights have the same effect on rights-bearers themselves. Thus, parents' rights incline parents to be self-regarding rather than other-regarding, and to think in terms of how legal rules harm, frustrate, or inconvenience *them* rather than how those rules benefit or harm their children.[43] Characterizing the shield against unwarranted restrictions on child-rearing practices as the right of the child, rather than as a right of the parent, might go a long way toward refocusing governmental, public, and parental attention toward the interests of the children. Were this to occur, we could expect a much more thorough investigation of the effects on children of various child-rearing practices, such as religious schooling, than presently takes place. As noted in Chapter 1, the reluctance of state officials to encroach upon parents' rights has prevented them from adequately studying what goes on inside religious schools and what effects these schools have on the children attending them.

Before we move on to adult-centered rationales for parents' rights, two variations on the "children's interests" rationale warrant examination. The first, an application of the maxim that "ought implies can," contends that because the law imposes on parents substantial duties of care with respect to their children, parents must also have substantial child-rearing rights in order to be able to fulfill their duties. Importantly, this argument would justify only a set of parental rights that extended as far as parents' legal obligations and no further. Thus, it would not support rights to send one's children to a religious school or to refuse necessary medical treatment for a child, since parents are under no legal obligation to do either of these things. And it certainly would not support rights to depart from normal parental legal duties. Moreover, apart from this issue of scope, the reasoning of this argument is simply flawed.

The fact that one person owes duties to another person certainly does not *logically* entail that the first person has any rights—not even rights that might be necessary to fulfill her duties. The logical corollary of a legal duty owed to another person is simply a right residing in that *other* person, not any right residing in the individual under the duty. For example, a doctor owes a duty of care to her patients, but this duty of care does not itself imply that the doctor has any rights against her patients or against third parties. In addition, it is not necessary as a *practical* matter that the state confer on parents any rights in order to ensure that they are able to fulfill their legal obligations to their children. As indicated above, it is sufficient for this purpose to grant parents a legal *privilege* to engage in parenting practices not incompatible with their children's temporal interests and to recognize *the children's* rights against unwarranted interference, by the state or other third parties, in the parents' efforts to fulfill their parenting responsibilities. Analogously, the fact that lawyers do not possess a right to represent their clients in legal proceedings does not prevent them from carrying out their responsibilities to clients or render effective legal representation impossible, because litigants themselves have a right to legal representation that they, through their attorney, can assert against third-party interference in that legal representation (e.g., if counsel were prevented from entering the prison to meet with a client charged with a crime). Furthermore, when the state prevents a parent from performing some action or from making some decision for the benefit of a child, it also to that extent lessens the legal responsibility of the parent, implicitly declaring that the action or decision is no part of the parent's legal duties. Since it is the state that establishes the legal responsibilities of parents, there cannot logically be any conflict between those responsibilities and restrictions that the state imposes on parents. It is thus particularly nonsensical to assert that parents need rights *against the state* in order to carry out their legal responsibilities to their children.

The second variation on the "children's interests" rationale contends that it is better for children in the long run that their parents possess rights to oppose restrictions on their child-rearing practices, even if in some particular instances such restrictions would generate immediate benefits for the child. This is so because if the role of parent were to become substantially more burdensome or less pleasurable as a result of increased state regulation, many parents would become less attached to their children or less devoted to child rearing. They would feel disempowered or resentful of the aggravation that their children have occasioned, and children would suffer as a result. For example, Michael Wald has expressed concern that "if parents lose ultimate authority they will be less willing to assume responsibility for the child."[44]

The main problem with this approach to justifying parents' rights is that it rests upon an exaggerated view of the level of restrictions on parents that would result from eliminating those rights. In actuality, eliminating parents' rights would not in and of itself permit or encourage *any* increase in the level of restrictions. Rather, it would only change the formal procedure for determining what that level should be, substituting a balancing of costs and benefits to the child for the present balancing of parental and societal interests. This alternative procedure would, in practice, be likely to lower significantly the threshold of harm to the child that is sufficient to justify proscription of conduct but not to an enormous degree. The argument for parents' rights itself supposes that children would suffer, on the whole, if state officials interfered to a much greater degree than at present in parents' child-rearing efforts. If that is true, then children should have a right against such interference. The decision-making procedure proposed here requires that the state forbear from interference precisely when doing so would cause more harm to children—taking into account the likely effects on parent-child relationships—than it prevented.

An additional problem with this argument is that it underestimates and implicitly denigrates parental motivation. It presupposes that parents' attachment to their children is fragile and arises primarily from a selfish desire to possess and control another human being, so that once that desire is frustrated little or no motivation to care for children remains. It thus reflects a perspective very different from that of persons who claim parents should have child-rearing rights because their love for their children is so great. Surely there are many parents today who manifest little real love for their children, but it is difficult to see how it benefits their children for those parents to have child-rearing rights. With respect to parents who do genuinely love their children, which I assume to be the vast majority of parents, it is implausible to think that increased regulation of child rearing would weaken their desire to promote their children's well-being. Certainly it would cause many to experience anguish and anger, but it would not cause them to care less about their children. In addition, it should be noted that in a world without parental rights parents would have lesser expectations of control and might therefore experience less frustration when the larger community demanded adherence to majoritarian child-rearing norms. It would also be implausible to claim that parents could not be satisfied in their role without the particular form of social recognition that having rights affords them. Countless people in our society—teachers, judges, and doctors, for example—derive great satisfaction simply from being entrusted with important responsibilities in roles to which they have no right but which they are accorded the privilege of performing. And, finally, it bears mention that anyone who wishes to improve the lives of children and who believes that the family is the best environment for raising children should also be committed to making all parents successful and happy in their role. This includes helping those parents who find it particularly difficult to meet the needs of their children and giving appropriate social recognition to those who carry out this important responsibility. If we as a society did these things adequately, there would be a need for legal action against parents only when they were determined to take actions contrary to the temporal interests of their children.

In sum, child-centered rationales for parents' rights fail to show that these rights are necessary to protect and promote the interests of children. An adequate and more appropriate means of protecting and promoting children's well-being is to attribute certain rights to children themselves, coupled with a parental privilege. This approach is preferable not only because it eliminates a category of rights that is anomalous and that rests on a dubious notion of entitlement, but also because it more directly focuses judicial, societal, and parental attention on the interests of children.

THE APPEAL TO PARENTS' INTERESTS

Raising children is a large component of most parents' happiness. For many adults, raising children is their greatest good, their highest accomplishment, their most profound emotional experience, and a coalescence of their most important beliefs, values, and hopes. The struggle many adults endure just to bear or adopt a child and the sacrifices they make to provide for a child attest to the high priority they give to child rearing within the hierarchy of their desires. Parental rights, some argue, are necessary to protect this aspect of well-being, to enable parents to achieve this noble form of human fulfillment.

This line of reasoning is deficient for at least two reasons. First, neither the intensity of a person's desires nor the nobleness of his motivation determines whether he should possess a right to satisfy those desires. People intensely desire many things to which they have no right—for example marriage to a particular person, great wealth, political office. Predicating parental rights on parental desires fails to explain the anomaly of granting parents rights of control over their children when the courts have abolished or refused to create such other-determining rights in every other area of the law. Given the general, well-established principle that no individual's desire to control the life of another person, no matter how intense and regardless of how benevolent the motive, properly gives rise to a right to do so, an advocate of parents' rights would have to identify some unique feature of parents' interests with respect to children that justifies a departure from the general rule.

One possible distinguishing feature of parents' own interests in connection with child rearing is that they sometimes include an interest in satisfying a desire to re-create oneself in another human being, to shape an entire life as a reflection of one's own. Parents have a uniquely propitious opportunity to do so, given the young child's relatively unformed state. While this desire may reflect negative character traits such as selfishness and narcissism, it may also involve benevolent motives. Regardless of what it reveals about the personality of its possessor, though, this desire does not deserve the protection of a right, for at least two reasons. First, an interest in creating a copy of oneself is not a fundamental interest. A fundamental, or welfare, interest is an objective, universal interest "in conditions that are generalized means to a great variety of possible goals and whose joint realization, in the absence of very special circumstances, is necessary for the achievement of more ultimate aims."[45] In contrast, individually determined desires for higher forms of accomplishment, meaning, and fulfillment are "ulterior interests", interests whose frustration will not impair a person's generalized capacities for pursuing other individualized ends. While fundamental interests presumptively warrant the protection of rights, ulterior interests do not.[46]

The desire to control the life of a child is clearly of the latter, ulterior, kind. Of course, as with any desired end, some individuals' desire for complete control over their children's lives might become so obsessive that frustration of this desire would thoroughly debilitate them. However, we would view such persons as suffering from a failure to realize some universally shared fundamental interest, such as a base level of mental health and/or self-esteem, rather than as having a fundamental interest in exercising this control. Similarly, we do not say, for example, that a person obsessed with forming or maintaining a relationship with another adult person whom he or she loves, or obsessed with circumscribing the experiences, outside relationships, or beliefs of an adult with whom he or she is in an intimate relationship, has a fundamental interest in, and therefore a right to, that relationship or that control. Legal theorists generally agree that persons have no inherent right to others' noninterference or assistance with their pursuit of ulterior aims such as this. The Supreme Court has followed this line in its substantive due process jurisprudence, holding that only fundamental interests are protected under the Fourteenth Amendment Due Process Clause. In the parenting cases it has simply misapplied the notion of fundamentality.

Second, establishing such a right would be inconsistent with a proper respect for the personhood of the individual who is to serve as the medium for the rightholder's re-creation of self. If it were possible to "re-program" or re-create the personality of adults, we would surely find it offensive for the law to treat any adults as involuntary candidates for re-programming in order to satisfy the desires of others to mold another human being in their image. To respect children as equal persons requires finding equally offensive a legal regime that treats them in such an instrumental fashion, as objects for others to manipulate for their own satisfaction.

A further objection to the argument based on parents' interests parallels one of the objections to the child-centered rationale discussed in the previous section. It is simply not true that parents in general must have child-rearing *rights* in order for them to be able to satisfy their desire to be the primary caretaker for a child. As explained above, a child-rearing privilege, coupled with an appropriate set of children's rights, is sufficient to enable parents to maintain an intimate parent-child relationship and to carry out parental responsibilities free from unwarranted interference so long as that is consistent with their children's well-being. At base, the only practical purposes that parental rights serve are to allow some parents to have custody of children when it would be better for the children that they did not and to ensure that parents who have custody can treat their children in ways that are contrary to the children's temporal interests. Thus, to show that it is even *rational* for parents to insist that they have child-rearing rights and not just a parenting privilege, one would have to argue that it is in parents' interest to have custody when they are unable or unwilling to be good parents and to be able to treat their children in ways contrary to their children's temporal well-being. To show further that parental rights are *just*, one would also have to argue that this interest is legitimate and that it outweighs any competing interests or considerations.

Considering just religious child-rearing contexts, it does appear to be rational of parents to demand child-rearing rights if they believe themselves bound by their faith to raise their children in a way that is inconsistent with what the larger society regards as the children's temporal interests, even if they agree with the majority as to the latter. Within their conception of the good, spiritual aims may conflict with and outweigh secular benefits. In addition, many parents, whether religious or not, may derive immediate satisfaction from enjoying unfettered discretion to direct their child's life however they wish. This satisfaction may include positive societal regard flowing from being in such a position of power. However, even if rights to control a child's life in ways inimical to the child's temporal interests do further some interests of parents, these rights may not serve other, long-term parental interests. For example, having such rights may prevent parents from recognizing that their children are separate persons and that their children's well-being is also the legitimate concern of other people. Yet recognizing these things could benefit parents as well as children. It might lead parents to consider that their own views of what is right for their children may not be the same as what the children would choose for themselves if able to do so. This, in turn, might lead parents to adopt certain attitudes—humility, greater respect for their children, openness to dialogue about child rearing with other persons—that would benefit all parties concerned. Much conflict and hostility between parents and children, particularly as children become older and begin to form opinions about their upbringing, as well as between individual parents and other adult members of a community, might be avoided if parents were less possessive of their children and less demanding of their rights as parents. Any determination of whether it is rational for parents to demand parental rights should take these considerations into account. It may well be that parents as well as children would be better off if parents' rights were eliminated.

Moreover, even if it is in the interest of parents to possess rights to direct their children's lives in ways that are harmful to the children, the state should never give that interest precedence over the basic welfare of children (e.g., their physical health, their psychological and emotional development, their education). By elevating such an ulterior interest of parents above fundamental interests of children, the state treats children as less than equal persons, as mere means to the satisfaction of parents' ends, and that is morally repugnant. Indeed, the state should not even recognize this supposed interest of parents as legitimate, as one that must be balanced against the interest of children, any more than it should recognize someone's interest in being able to direct the life of an adult human being in ways the state deems harmful as a legitimate basis for state decision making that must be balanced against the interests of that adult.

Why is it, then, that even people who regard certain religiously motivated child-rearing practices as harmful to children, and who accept that children are persons whose interests the state ought to protect, are reluctant to take a stand against those practices and against parental claims to be free from legal restrictions on their behavior? At least in the case of liberals, I think this reluctance arises out of a misconception that values of state neutrality toward and toleration of diverse ideological views require them to defer to the viewpoint of the parents in determining whether particular child-rearing practices should be permissible.[47] It may be that deference to personal beliefs is appropriate in some cases in deciding what individuals should be permitted to do *to themselves*, or what consenting adults should be free do to each other, based on their own balancing of their own temporal and spiritual interests. Such deference rests upon the principal of respecting personal autonomy that is central to the liberal outlook. However, it is a fundamental confusion to believe that the same principle applies in the case of parenting, because that is not a case in which a person is simply doing something to himself or in which two consenting adults are doing something to each other. It is a case in which a person is doing something to another person who is not capable of giving meaningful consent.

Liberal shyness about endorsing legal prohibition of harmful child-rearing practices thus appears to rest, at base, on a failure to recognize that children are neither the same persons as their parents nor, in general, consenting participants in the religious practices of their parents, and that it is therefore nonsensical to invoke the value of individual autonomy in this context. Child-rearing conduct should be viewed the same as other conduct affecting nonconsenting persons—as subject to legal restriction when it causes what the state regards as harm.

The argument from parents' interests might be put in a slightly different way, though, that would seem plausible to many people. One might
argue that, because parents give so much to children, it *is* fair to give
them rights to direct the lives of their children even in ways that may be
contrary to their children's interests, so long as they do not cause their
children grievous harm. The responsibilities of parenting are a substantial burden, and an entitlement to satisfy one's desires regarding the lives
of one's children or to allow one's religious views to trump the temporal
interests of one's children might be appropriate compensation for carrying that burden. This quid pro quo reasoning may underlie the sense
some people have that parents *are* entitled to determine the course of
their children's lives, that parental authority *should* be seen as a right
and not merely a privilege.

This approach, however, runs up against the problem of having to distinguish rights to control the lives of one's minor children from rights to
control the lives of adult offspring who remain in or have returned to a
parent's care because of some disability—rights that the courts have refused to establish. Indeed, this argument, if generalized, might require
that a whole host of people who shoulder the burden of caring for other
people receive, as a matter of fairness, rights of control over the lives of
those people: persons caring for their elderly parents, teachers nurturing
children's minds, nurses tending to the sick, shelter providers caring for
homeless persons, and many others. The law does not confer such rights
in any of these cases, and few if any persons would sincerely contend
that it should. Even with respect to care providers who receive no mon-
etary compensation for their labors (not even tax credits or deductions),
fairness does not seem to require this result.

It might be objected that there is a basis for distinguishing parents' responsibilities for minor offspring from other kinds of responsibilities—
namely, that they are less voluntary. The law usually demands that persons who accept the role of parents continue in that role in at least some
capacity for as long as they are able and as long as the child needs them
to do so. In contrast, parents caring for adult offspring, adult offspring
caring for their parents, shelter providers caring for the homeless, and
other persons who fulfill caretaking responsibilities can cease doing so
at any time, without legal recrimination. However, this objection, too,
fails to justify giving parents a right to harm their children. In the first
place, in most cases the "some capacity" in which parents must continue to fulfill responsibilities means only providing financial support.
Parents may relinquish custody of their children at any time; the state

does not force parents to act as parents if they do not want to do so. At most, the state compels some parents—those whose ex-partners continue to raise the children—to pay child support. As noted previously, this involuntary obligation simply reflects the reliance interest on the part of the child that parents create when they initially choose to (or negligently) bring a child into the world. And the greater responsibilities of a parent who assumes custody are part of the bargain parents implicitly and voluntarily accept as a condition for being permitted to act as parents.

In the second place, this feature of parental responsibilities actually does not render them unique. There are other situations in which persons who take up duties of care are not permitted thereafter to escape them. For example, a lawyer who undertakes representation of a criminal defendant incurs a responsibility that she cannot thereafter abandon without compelling justification. Because it would be prejudicial to her client for her to cease representing him once proceedings are under way (i.e., because there is a reliance interest), the law requires that she continue to do so even if assisting the defendant conflicts with her personal convictions. Yet the lawyer does not, because of this added burden, thereby acquire any rights in connection with her representation of the defendant. The only rights at issue in the proceedings remain those of her client.

In sum, then, invocation of parents' interests fails to justify the doctrine of parents' rights. This approach ultimately depends either on a suspect understanding of the interests of parents and a morally unacceptable, instrumental view of children or on an aberrant and unsupported notion of fairness.

THE APPEAL TO SOCIETAL INTERESTS

A final category of justifications for parents' rights rests on supposed interests of society as a whole that these rights are said to serve. One such interest might be in the preservation of a particular form of social and political life, such as our liberal democracy. The Supreme Court has in some contexts decided whether asserted liberties are fundamental, and therefore merit heightened protection under the Fourteenth Amendment Due Process Clause, by evaluating whether they are " 'implicit in the concept of ordered liberty' such that 'neither liberty nor justice would exist if [they] were sacrificed'." [48]

It would be implausible to contend, however, that it is implicit in the concept of ordered liberty that parents must have *a right* to control their children's lives. Such a right is no more implicit in the concept of ordered liberty than a right to direct the lives of other adults. This becomes clearer when one realizes that parental rights are not necessary to preserve the institution of the family or the authority of parents to make many decisions on behalf of, and to act as agents for, their children, which many people believe *is* necessary to the maintenance of a free society. Instead, as previously explained, a limited parental privilege coupled with appropriate rights for children would be sufficient for that end, given a child's basic interest in an intimate, continuous relationship with a parent or parents, free from unwarranted intrusions by the state or other third parties and a child's interest in having those who care and know most about him exercise authority over many aspects of his life. In fact, parental rights, particularly as extended under the Free Exercise Clause, violate one premise of ordered liberty, insofar as they enable parents to deny their children basic liberties, as discussed in Chapters 1 and 2.

An additional argument for parents' rights that rests on an appeal to the interests of society as a whole is implicit in the *Yoder* and *Pierce* opinions and explicit in much academic writing. This argument states that conferring on parents the right to depart from majoritarian norms in directing the upbringing of their children allows many different normative communities to survive and thus fosters cultural and religious diversity in our society. In contrast, the argument goes, a uniform, state-imposed education or list of proscribed parenting behaviors would standardize this nation's citizens and forestall cultural progress. It might even indirectly weaken the institutions of democracy if these depend on a substantial measure of heterogeneity.

This argument rests on a shaky empirical foundation and a dubious normative premise. The empirical assumption is that eliminating parental rights and increasing stae regulation of private education would create a culturally and ideologically homogeneous citizenry. However, even if states were to make public school attendance compulsory–a more drastic alternative to the present scheme than I would propose— parents could still model and teach their beliefs to their children at home (and I believe it would be better for children that the state not interfere with belief inculcation in the home unless that inculcation amounts to what the law today recognizes as emotional abuse), and adopting those beliefs would thus remain a very real possibility for the children. Requiring public school attendance would simply result in the children's being exposed to other beliefs and acquiring intellectual skills

that would *enable* them to (but not dictate that they will) choose a belief system and way of life other than their parents'. Furthermore, concerns about the standardizing effect of public schooling are grossly overstated. Surely there is great diversity even among the nine-tenths of
adults in this country who attended public schools during the past half-
century. Moreover, public school teachers today, more than ever before, encourage individuality and teach children to value diversity. Indeed, one is more likely to hear the complaint today that public schools,
with their post-modern focus on multiculturalism, fail to instill any
common norms or common body of knowledge. And if compulsory public school attendance would not extinguish cultural diversity, then certainly merely regulating private schools more stringently to ensure that
they do not harm children and that they meet higher standards of educational quality would not do so either.

In addition, it is not clear that the kind of diversity that parents' rights
preserve, if any, is consistent with the supposed benefits of pluralism.
One benefit of pluralism is that the existence of a marketplace of ideas
and a variety of "experiments in living" spurs progress toward better
ideas and ways of life and allows individuals to discover the particular
way of life best suited to their unique disposition and interests. But giving parents a right to control their children's minds would seem to run
counter to both purposes, insofar as it causes many children to grow up
as unthinking persons chained to a belief system and way of life that
might not be at all suited to them. It does allow for the continuation
of groups, such as the Amish, that might otherwise die out, but most
such groups are neither attractive to nor open to outsiders. Though such
groups may nevertheless provide a model of a different way of life that
the rest of us can learn from, one wonders why they would die out if parents could not prevent their children from learning about other ways of
life, or why we would not learn as much from their extinction as from
their preservation.

Pluralism is also a safeguard against tyranny but is most effectively so
when divergent factions confront one another in the public arena, not
when factions that are petty tyrannies themselves vilify one another and
segregate themselves from the mainstream.[49] Religious difference, in
particular, appears to cause division and distrust more so than respectful engagement. We should not so readily accept promotion of religious
diversity as an aim of social policy, then, without seeing evidence that
it produces benefits outweighing these costs (which is not to suggest
that discouraging diversity should be an aim of social policy). It is not

unreasonable to ask whether diversity of ethnic backgrounds, languages, occupations, political beliefs, and tastes is sufficient to prevent tyrannical majorities from forming and to keep us from feeling that we are all too alike.

More important, however, than this concern about whether parents' rights actually protect pluralism or protect pluralism of the right kind is the concern that this approach to justifying parents' rights rests on a highly objectionable moral premise. It assumes that it is acceptable to sacrifice the welfare interests of certain children, the most vulnerable and politically powerless persons in our society, in order to promote a diffuse public good like pluralism. This is a premise that any adult would surely reject if its principle were applied to him. Suppose that the state granted members of a dwindling religious community a right to force certain adults from outside the community (e.g., homeless persons) to undergo intensive religious indoctrination to ensure the survival of that religious community, or that the state itself intended to force such indoctrination. We would surely be outraged by the notion that our society, or communities within our society, could treat these adults in this way—as nonconsenting means to promote this supposed public good. We would feel the same regardless of whether the adults designated for forced membership had beliefs about religion of their own and regardless of whether they were fully competent. To be consistent in our moral attitudes, we should concede that this notion is equally objectionable when applied to children. The survival of ancient creeds and religious communities may be a good thing, but if it is, it should occur as a result of free choices, not coercion and the sacrifice of children's welfare; if "some traditional ways of life—for instance, that of the Amish—could not survive the requirement that older children be allowed to go to school with children from the larger community and to learn about science and technology . . . then such traditional ways of life have no right to survive, for their survival is at the expense of the liberty of the children who are born into them."[50]

Finally, it is worth noting that a desire for cultural diversity is not what motivates those religious groups who have been most insistent about the rights of parents to control their children's education. Their aim is to standardize children in their own way. The irony of the appeal to pluralism in *Yoder* is that the decision "broaden[s] the range of choices available to adults by decreasing the range of choices available to their children."[51] Indeed, as their efforts to reintroduce Christian teaching and group prayer into public schools suggests, if they could, Fundamentalists would standardize everyone's children in their way. To be sure, "the child is not the mere creature of the state," but the child is also not the mere creature of the parent or of the religious community to which the parent belongs. Rather, the child is his or her own person. A child may lack a fully formed independent character but is nonetheless an individual deserving of the same respect accorded adults.

Conclusion

Relying on the well-established legal and moral principle that rights appropriately protect only a rightholder's own self-determination and personal integrity and that no one is entitled to control the life of another person, and finding no justification for departing from that principle in the case of parent-child relationships, I reach the conclusion that parental child-rearing rights are illegitimate. The law should grant parents only a legal privilege to care for and make decisions on behalf of their children in ways that are consistent with the children's temporal interests. Children themselves should possess whatever rights are necessary to protect their interests, and these would include a right to protection from any state interference that is not, on the whole, to their benefit.

I have emphasized several times that this revised legal framework would not lead to the abolition of the family or radically alter the scope of parental authority, since children's interest in preservation of the family and of some parental authority would justify protecting them. What, then, would change? This is not the place for the kind of careful investigation and analysis of particular fact situations that should underlie decisions on particular policies and laws, but I can suggest, in broad outlines, some of the likely results of the approach I advance. Importantly, though, what matters for my purposes is not whether others agree that these particular results would be good for children, but rather that others agree that this criterion—what is good for children—is the correct criterion for evaluating policies and legal rules pertaining to child rearing.

I believe that my approach would lead courts to make findings of child abuse or neglect upon a showing of less harm than is now required in most jurisdictions, and it would allow earlier intervention to prevent abuse and neglect, either by monitoring and training parents or by removing children. I believe that it would result in earlier and more secure placement of children with adoptive parents when biological parents are absent or unfit to act as parents. I believe my approach would require eliminating religious exemptions to medical neglect and mandatory child immunization laws. And, as discussed in Chapters 5 and 6, I believe it would allow for, and in fact require, extensive regulation of religious schools.

In addition to these legal consequences of adopting the proposed approach, I think eradicating the notion of parental entitlement and substituting the notion of parenting as a privilege would have profound and unqualifiedly beneficial social consequences. The change in attitudes would make parents think about why they should enjoy the opportunity to raise a child and whether they are good parents, and this in turn should lead them to improve their parenting, to seek out information and training, and to engage in dialogue with other parents, as the better parents today do. Relocating the site of entitlement in child rearing from the parent to the child should make parents more respectful of their children as persons, less inclined to treat them as instruments for the parents' own satisfaction, and more accepting of the child's independent interests and beliefs. This would, I believe, greatly strengthen parent-child relationships, for a relationship built upon compliance with authority and conformity to a single model of personality, behavior, and belief is a tenuous one, but a relationship built upon mutual respect and unconditional love is secure.

4 Against a Community Right to Educate

In the background of the Supreme Court's decision in *Wisconsin v. Yoder* was a concern about the consequences of Wisconsin's compulsory school attendance law for the Amish community as a whole. Requiring that children of the Amish receive an education beyond age thirteen might have threatened the survival of Amish communities and have smacked of cultural imperialism. The Court hinted that the Amish community, as a collective entity distinct from individual parents within the community, might itself have a right at stake in the litigation—a collective right to survive and to preserve its religion and religiously grounded way of life, a right that includes the ability to decide whether and what sort of education children born to members of the community would receive. More recent evidence of special solicitude for reclusive minority communities comes from the New York Legislature's creation in 1989 of a separate school district for an Hasidic community (later invalidated by the Supreme Court) so that no children of community members would have to attend a school outside the community.[1] In addition, it is not uncommon to see expressed in political and philosophical discussions of education the view that local school districts have a right to define the nature of education in public schools in accordance with the values of the local community.

The communitarian impulse in philosophy has also generated much interest among political theorists in the notion of culture-protective community rights. Many have argued that insular minority cultural communities, such as the Amish or Native American tribes in the United

States and aboriginal groups in Canada, should enjoy special legal protections, including a collective right to control children's education within their borders to protect their way of life from the encroachments of outsiders and mainstream Western culture. Though these theorists have not explicitly extended their positions to include more mainstream communities, such as Catholics and Fundamentalists, their arguments could in some cases encompass these groups as well.

At first blush, the notion of a community right to educate might seem simply an offshoot of the concept of parental rights that must stand or fall with it. Certainly, if individual parents have a right to determine how their children will be schooled, they can join with other, like-minded parents to educate their children together in the way they collectively choose. The analysis of Chapter 3 would preclude ascription of a community right to educate on that basis. However, the cultural rights idea is more complex than simply a joint exercise of individual rights. As will be seen, it rests on a group interest—cultural preservation—that is not straightforwardly reducible to the individual interests of group members, and it can operate even to constrain the choices of individual parents within a community, in addition to preventing the state from dictating what sort of education children of community members are to receive. In any event, to the extent that arguments for cultural rights depend on a notion of individual rights, they present a quite different approach to the issue of children's education than do the standard arguments for parents' rights because they focus on the collective functioning and transcendent group interests of a subculture within a liberal society rather than on interpersonal relations or the needs of the larger society.

Most arguments for minority cultural rights among political theorists today take one of two forms—an autonomy-based, freedom-of-association rationale or an equality-based rationale. Proponents of both types of arguments include a collective right of control over children's education in the catalogue of rights that they would guarantee to groups satisfying certain conditions—in fact, they give prominence to that particular right. One might expect, therefore, that they have devoted substantial direct attention to children in their theories. In fact, however, they have tended either to disregard children entirely or to conflate children's identity and interests with those of adult members of a community. In this chapter, I explore the implications for community rights theories of recognizing the distinct and equal personhood of children. As an initial matter, it is important to recognize that a community right to educate is, like a parental child-rearing right, a form of other-determining right. It is for all practical purposes a right of adult members of a group to determine collectively how the lives of other persons—children born to community members—will proceed. As with parents' rights, then, community rights to govern children's upbringing are presumptively illegitimate.

Freedom of Association as a Basis for Community Rights

The easier argument to dispense with is the one that grounds community rights in autonomy and free association. This justification posits that where a number of individuals enter into voluntary association, they are entitled to define in concert the terms of their association. As is not the case with individual self-determination, however, initial commitments in the group context, on the freedom-of-association model, remain binding on members so long as they remain within the group, absent a collective decision to amend the rules. One of the initial commitments may be to abide by the particular day-to-day decisions made by a majority of community members to further collective interests even when one disagrees with a decision, including decisions about proper child rearing. The freedom-of-association argument holds that the state should not interfere with a community's collective self-determining decision making and action, just as it should not interfere with an individual's efforts to determine the course of her own life, and that the group may appropriately constrain the freedom of individual members so long as members retain the ultimate freedom to leave the community. This liberty-based argument has wide applicability and would encompass the associative practices of mainstream groups such as Catholics and Fundamentalists in this country as well as those of smaller, more isolated cultural communities. It might also be used to defend so-called family autonomy or devolution of educational authority to local school districts.

I will focus here on one representative statement of this position, that of Chandran Kukathas.[2] Kukathas's principal motivation is to ensure that traditional, nonmajoritarian cultures can continue to exist within the political jurisdiction of a modern state even when the practices of such cultures violate liberal principles, like nondiscrimination and freedom of expression. He contends that a liberal state should view cultural communities as contingent associations among individuals, all of whom possess a right to live on their own terms in concert with others. So long as all members associate willingly and are free to exit if they come to disapprove of the terms of association, the state should refrain from interfering in a minority community's practices, even if some individual members believe these practices to be harmful and request the state's intercession. This argument sanctions extensive communal restrictions on the freedom of both insiders and outsiders. Exclusion of some persons from membership in a community and denial of property or voting rights to new members would be legitimate incidents of the collective exercise of freedom of association. Moreover, internal restrictions on the personal liberties of members, such as freedom of speech or religion, may properly arise from the voluntary agreement of all individual members of a community to live under those restrictions.

In providing examples of specific practices that are protected by the right of free association, Kukathas focuses on the collective decisions of minority groups as to whether and how children born into the group will be educated. The first concrete implication of his thesis is that the "wider society has no right to require particular standards or systems of education within such cultural groups or to force their schools to promote the dominant culture" (117). He illustrates his claim that a liberal state must tolerate illiberal practices within voluntary communities by pointing to the demands of Amish communities in America and gypsy bands in Britain that they be able to keep their children out of school. "Their freedom to associate and live by their own ways," he contends, "would, by my argument, make this permissible" (126). Kukathas clearly recognizes the importance of children's education to the preservation of a culture and therefore to the members of a cultural minority community. Other proponents of community autonomy also uniformly endorse, and even emphasize, community rights to determine the nature of children's education.

Children's education is, however, for obvious reasons, a very odd place to begin in explicating the implications of a position that rests ultimately on voluntary association. Put simply, children do not participate freely in cultural practices, including their education. The freedom-of-association rationale, which entitles individuals to put *themselves* under whatever restrictions they wish in association with others, cannot plausibly encompass situations in which some individuals subject *other* individuals to restrictions and forms of treatment without the latter's informed, voluntary consent, and that is essentially what child rearing involves.

Kukathas is ambivalent about what "free" means in the context of free association, principally because he is not sure what to make of adults who have neither an understanding of cultures other than their own nor the wherewithal to exit the culture in which they were raised. He first suggests that free association entails informed consent to the terms of association, defining cultural communities as associations of individuals "whose freedom to live according to communal practices each *finds acceptable* is of fundamental importance" and who "*recognize as legitimate* the terms of association and the authority that upholds them" (116, emphasis added). The highlighted verbs suggest a substantial epistemic requirement. To wish for, to find acceptable, and to recognize as legitimate the terms of an association presumably entail evaluating those terms against standards of desirability, acceptability, and legitimacy that are external to the terms themselves. Finding a term acceptable seems also to require comparing it with alternatives.

It would strain credulity to suggest that young children assent to the form of education they receive or any other important aspect of their upbringing based upon their evaluation of it against standards of desirability, acceptability, and legitimacy. Their education, particularly in insular, traditional communities, is not a product of their informed, reflective choices. The same is true more generally of their "membership" in a community or in a family: they do not make an informed choice to be members. They are involuntary and unwitting participants in a community's or family's practices. To bar the state from interfering in a community's educational practices therefore cannot be justified as a matter of respect for the informed choices of all the persons whose important interests are at stake.

In fact, this interpretation of free association would actually sanction substantial state-imposed requirements on minority cultural communities—in particular, in the area of education—to ensure that all members of a community are able to evaluate the rules and values of their community in a reflective manner. It could generate a positive right *to be educated* in a certain way and thus weigh in favor of educational mandates that might undermine many traditional cultural communities. Recognizing this, Kukathas ultimately rejects the suggestion that all associations must rest on and foster the exercise of autonomy, conceived of as an individual's ability to choose his own ends and make meaningful choices. Instead, he would require that the state interfere only where a community denies freedom of disassociation to an individual member. "Free" association therefore means simply having a right to leave. Kukathas concedes that the right of exit should be "substantial" and not merely formal, but for him this means merely that (1) a community may not prevent exit by extreme measures such as "forcible induction into or imprisoning of any individual in a cultural community" (125), "cruel, inhuman or degrading treatment," or "physical coercion" (128), and (2) there must exist "a wider society that is open to individuals wishing to leave their groups" (134). These limitations on state interference suggest a respect for liberty *simpliciter* rather than for autonomy; the state should leave individuals free to do what they are inclined to do with their lives, absent harm to others, regardless of whether their inclination is the result of critical reflection or choice among known alternatives.

However, this latter interpretation of free association also fails to support restrictions on the state's authority to regulate the educational practices of a minority community. It would be absurd to suggest that children have a substantial right of exit from their parents' community if they do not approve of the education provided there. In the first place, children do not enjoy even a formal right of exit from the associations into which they are born; the law requires that children who run away from home be returned to their parents, against their will if necessary. Second, even if children possessed a formal right of exit, that right would not be a substantial one. It is common for parents in all cultures to physically restrain their children to maintain control over the children's movements, and they have a legal right to do so. Additionally, the larger society in the United States, and probably in most countries, is not open to the entry of children in the same way it is open to the entry of adults. Children lack the physical, emotional, and intellectual capacities necessary for independent living, and people are generally reluctant to assume the burdens of caring for children who are not their own. As noted above, the usual practice in our society is to return runaway children to their parents whenever possible. Thus, even Kukathas's minimal criteria for a substantial right of exit are not satisfied in the case of children. In addition, children in insular minority communities, at least younger ones, are not likely even to be aware of any alternative culture or to be able to contemplate living in a situation other than their present one; it is simply implausible to say that persons possess a substantial right of exit when they cannot even understand what it would mean to exit.

Community educational rights, in the liberty-based, freedom-of-association model, thus appear to depend on a failure to appreciate the peculiar situation of children or even to recognize them as proper sub-jects of political concern or as persons distinct from their parents. Polit-ical theorists in general need to rethink their understanding of children's status in relation to communities. Kukathas portrays a community as a free association of individuals, and many political and legal theorists similarly speak of the family as a free association of individuals. Other defenders of community autonomy define a community in terms of a shared understanding among community members or a shared sense of commitment to a way of life.[3] One might also define a community in terms of joint participation in decision making about shared resources. By any of these definitions, young children are not members of their par-ents' community at all, even though they live within the community's geographical boundaries, have intimate ties to community members, and in the normal course of events will eventually come to see them-selves as members of the community. Young children do not freely as-sociate with a community, or fully share in a community's common un-derstanding, or participate equally in a community's decision-making processes. Indeed most, if not all, communities view the aim of educa-tion as creating in children an understanding of a culture's traditional values and rules and inducing acceptance of them. Likewise, young children do not freely associate in a family, fully understand or commit themselves to collective family ends, or participate equally in a family's decision-making processes.

Arguably, then, political and legal theorists should evaluate commu-nity practices affecting community members' children formally in the same way they evaluate community practices affecting persons who re-side outside the community and who may or may not choose to become members of it. In other words, they should treat the consequences of particular cultural practices for children as "externalities"—effects on outside parties—even when the purpose of those practices is to integrate the children into the community. A community cannot plausibly justify on the basis of a right to free association any harmful externalities that the community's practices occasion. Viewing community practices af-fecting children in this way has far-reaching implications, not only for the child-rearing independence of insular minority communities but also for the authority of any municipality, state, or nation to determine how children within its political boundaries will grow up and for the sovereignty rights of political entities whose policies threaten the well-being of children within their borders.

Equality among Groups As a Basis for Cultural Rights

The most talked-about and sophisticated defense of community cultural rights today is an equality-based one that Will Kymlicka first popularized with his book *Liberalism, Community, and Culture* and recently restated in *Multicultural Citizenship*.[4] Kymlicka aims to combat two common beliefs among contemporary liberal theorists regarding cultural rights: first, that ensuring universal individual rights is sufficient to address the problems of cultural minorities within a multicultural society, and second, that special group-based rights for certain subcommunities are incompatible with liberalism, which presumes that the state must treat all persons as equals. Kymlicka contends that the peculiar vulnerability of some cultural groups justifies granting them special protections against the actions of outsiders, including the state, in order to protect their fundamental interests. A more nuanced understanding of liberal egalitarianism, he maintains, can actually support their demands for such special protections.

According to Kymlicka, modern egalitarian liberal theory presupposes that individual freedom should operate against a background condition of universal equality in the basic means necessary for the fulfillment of life plans. Inequalities in shares of basic goods are just only if they result from individual free choices, because individuals are morally responsible for their choices but not for unfavorable circumstances over which they have no control. Justice may therefore require special compensation for those in unfavorable, unchosen circumstances.

Within this framework, Kymlicka argues that some minority communities, such as the Amish, Hasidic Jews, and Native American tribes, deserve compensatory legal advantages, including special culture-protective rights, privileges, and powers, because of their unique social situation. The very survival of their distinctive culture is threatened, by outsiders moving in and depleting their resources, by government efforts to assume control over important aspects of their lives, and by the ineluctable influence of mainstream cultural forces such as news and entertainment media. This threat does not exist for members of the majority culture; their cultural structure is secure. Giving vulnerable minority communities the legal tools needed to resist these incursions may enable them to preserve their cultures for a longer time than will be possible if present trends continue.

Kymlicka acknowledges that the survival of minority cultures in and of itself need not be of concern to most liberals, for whom only the lives of individuals have moral significance. However, he draws from the communitarian tradition an empirical argument, termed the "social thesis," that connects cultural preservation to individual well-being. The argument proceeds as follows. Culture is an essential component and precondition for development of any individual's personal identity. It is within a culture that we become aware of the options available to us and acquire the standards and values on the basis of which we choose our individual roles and aspirations in life. Further, a *stable* personal identity requires a stable, enduring cultural context, and a stable identity is essential to any individual's self-respect. Thus, when the culture in which a person was raised is in danger of dissolution, so too is his sense of who he is and thus his self-respect. Finally, self-respect is a fundamental or primary good for individuals, a universal prerequisite for successful execution of particularized life plans. A stable cultural context is therefore a necessary precondition for enjoyment of a basic human good to which all persons are equally entitled.[5]

Combining the social thesis with an appreciation of the special vulnerability of some minority cultures, Kymlicka concludes that members of particular ethnic, religious, and linguistic groups are at an unfair disadvantage relative to the rest of society in securing self-respect because their cultural context is less secure. The disadvantage these people suffer arises from an unchosen circumstance—having been born into and raised within the minority culture—rather than from any choice they have made. Liberalism sanctions the conferral of special benefits to compensate for unfair disadvantages of this sort, and minority rights are an appropriate form of such redress. The particular culture-protective measures for which Kymlicka and others have argued using this line of reasoning are many and varied. Some are special individual rights and some are collectively held rights. Some of the measures are not really rights for the minority groups or their members at all; rather, they are denials of certain rights to outsiders, or powers given to minority groups collectively to define the rights and privileges that insiders and outsiders will hold. For example, some indigenous tribes wish to deny outsiders rights to move onto tribal lands, to own property within the geographical limits of the tribal community, and to vote in tribal elections and referenda. Others seek jurisdiction over certain resources, such as the fish in a local river, with the power to determine what privileges individuals will enjoy to exploit those resources.

The specific measures just mentioned are principally strategies for preserving or enhancing the economic power of a cultural group. They may lessen the likelihood that a culture will disintegrate because outsiders assume control over the community's land and resources or because members of the culture lack the means to support themselves financially within the community and so have to move outside it. The costs these measures entail for outsiders are, in most cases, so small as to be morally and politically irrelevant. For example, the inability of persons outside a particular minority community to move into that community, to purchase property in that community, or to vote in that community's elections is a very slight restriction on their life options, given the broad range of opportunities available to them outside that community. The equality-based argument thus seems unobjectionable with respect to these restrictions. Combined with individual rights against forced assimilation, which political theorists of all stripes would grant, they may go a long way toward ensuring that current members of a cultural community can continue to live together and carry on traditional practices if they wish to do so.

Critical to the long-term survival of a cultural community, however, is the passing on of its belief system and way of life to succeeding generations. Adult members of cultural minorities would not be content to possess protections of their own self-determination without the means necessary to ensure that their children will carry on the traditional way of life and perpetuate the culture. It is not surprising, then, that discussion of the right of minority communities to define the language, methods, and content of children's education within their boundaries has been prominent in political debates and in scholarly writings on the subject of cultural rights, and that Kymlicka and others who argue for culture-protective community rights based on equality have endorsed this particular community right.[6] This right would preclude the larger society from dictating education policy to these communities by, for example, controlling the content and method of instruction, imposing teacher qualification criteria, or requiring that instruction be offered in a particular language. Some proponents of this right—of which Kymlicka does not appear to be one—would go even further and construe it to override, in some circumstances, the choices that individual parents residing within the community might otherwise make about their children's education when those choices pose a threat to cultural survival. For example, if some parents within an insular Hasidic community wanted their children to have a mainstream, purely secular education, that choice might force the community to transfer resources from culture-protective programs to pay for such an education, and the children receiving this education might constitute a culture-weakening influence within the community.

Kymlicka does not include adherents of mainstream religions in this country, such as Catholics and Fundamentalists, among the groups deserving of special culture-protective rights such as a right of control over children's education. These groups do not consciously seek to close themselves off from the rest of society in the same way that the Amish or the Pueblo do; instead they participate willingly in mainstream American culture to a substantial degree (for example, in work and politics) and view themselves first and foremost as citizens of the United States. Moreover, to the extent that they constitute communities, they are robust ones with millions of members, and both continually welcome new adult entrants from outside the community. However, children in the communities that proponents of this argument do have in mind should also be of concern to the state. Some of the child-rearing practices of, for example, Hasidic communities or reclusive religious cults might also be harmful from a secular perspective. Additionally, the equality argument has gained considerable currency in recent years and has the political and theoretical potential for application beyond small, insular groups to any religious or cultural group that does not command a political majority in a given jurisdiction, including Fundamentalists and Catholics. The validity of the equality argument in the context of child rearing is therefore of far-reaching significance.

THE SOCIAL THESIS AND EDUCATION

At least two problems arise with Kymlicka's equality-based argument in relation to a community right to control children's education when the separate personhood and interests of children are taken into account. One has to do with the relationship between the adults' personal identity and children's education and the other with the needs of children themselves.

Adults' Personal Identity and Children's Education

The first problem with Kymlicka's argument is that the social thesis on which it ultimately rests does not show that it is necessary to the stability of any individual's personal identity that her culture survive in perpetuity. The social thesis contends only that a person raised within a particular cultural context may experience a loss of identity if that context disappears during her lifetime or if she is forced to live outside that context, either by overt coercion or by economic necessity. Thus, for example, adult members of an Amish community might be at risk of losing their sense of personal identity if hordes of non-Amish persons suddenly moved into their community, bought much of the land to use for modern factories and shopping malls, and voted to spend the community's assets on secular schools and outdoor rock concerts instead of on traditional Amish projects and ceremonies. Likewise, a person whose primary identity is that of a Pueblo may suffer a loss of that identity if forced to move out of the tribal community to find work.

It is a quite different thing, however, for a person simply to face the prospect that the culture in which he was raised and in which he continues to live may eventually dwindle and come to an end after his own generation has passed away if many members of succeeding generations, including his own children, choose a lifestyle, belief system, and language more in keeping with the majority culture. This may cause the person great sorrow, but the social thesis does not maintain that this experience is itself a threat to personal identity. So long as current adult members of minority communities can continue to live in association with one another without interference by outsiders, they can continue to enjoy a social context for expression and reinforcement of their culturally embedded identity.

In *Multicultural Citizenship*, Kymlicka tones down the discussion of a *threat* to personal identity and individuals' *need* for their culture to survive; he writes instead that certain groups are at a *disadvantage* relative to mainstream society in seeking to satisfy their *desire* that their culture survive indefinitely.[7] This may be because Kymlicka is unable to present the sort of empirical evidence needed to respond to the assertion of some reviewers that cultural extinction occurs not overnight but gradually over many generations, and thus the supposed threat to personal identity may never materialize.[8] But if there is not really a threat to personal identity, then the appeal to primary goods fails and the attempt to fit an argument for cultural rights into a modern egalitarian liberal theory is substantially undermined. I therefore proceed on the assumption that Kymlicka's real concern is extinction of a culture within the lifetimes of current members.

If limited to this concern, the social thesis cannot support a community right to educate children. Children's education bears no inherent relation to the ability of their grandparents and parents to continue their cultural practices to an extent necessary to preserve their sense of self. Continuation of these practices depends primarily on the economic viability of the community, protection of essential community resources such as land, and freedom from forced assimilation. Educating children is itself a cultural practice, but it is only one such practice among many in any given culture. In fact, it is primarily a conduit for transmitting from one generation to the next a language and particular traditions, values, and rituals, all or most of which adults could continue to adhere to themselves even if they were *entirely* unable to pass them on to their children.

It is true that fostering in members of the next generation an exclusive identification with the culture of their parents, and thereby increasing the likelihood that all members of the younger generation will ultimately remain within their parents' cultural community, tends to strengthen the parents' community economically. New generations of workers within communities generally provide financial support for older generations and their associative practices when the latter can no longer work. Thus, a community right to educate is one *possible* practical means of ensuring a stable, supportive cultural context for current adult members of a community throughout their lifetimes. It does not, however, appear to be a *necessary* means. The other culture-protective measures discussed above, such as community powers to control emigration and the use of land and other resources, should be sufficient to enable current adult generations to support their cultural association throughout their lifetimes. If not, the state could provide financial support. In addition, it seems reasonable to expect that even those offspring who chose to enter mainstream culture would provide financial and other support to their elderly parents so that they could maintain their way of life to the end of their days. Such support may be less likely if a group "shuns" persons who leave the community to enter mainstream society, but in that case any hardship created by the lack of support results from the group's own choices.

What children's education does clearly bear on is whether cultural practices will continue beyond the lifetime of current adults, and this, as noted, is not a fundamental aspect of anyone's well-being. In any event, however, the right under consideration here—to control children's schooling so as to prevent exposure to the language, traditions, values, and rituals of mainstream culture—is not necessary in order for adults to teach their language and distinctive cultural practices to children. Even without that right, they could continue to instruct their children in the same ways they always have outside the schoolhouse. They might simply be somewhat less successful in passing on their way of life than they would be if they had control over every aspect of their children's lives. No doubt many offspring in minority cultures would choose to remain in and continue their parents' culture even if they received a liberal education that made it possible for them to enter into mainstream American life without difficulty. Changes would thus come to the community only gradually, over many generations.

In sum, then, a community right to control children's education is not necessary to protect the personal identity of current adult members of a minority community. Thus, even if this aim were a legitimate consideration in deciding what children's upbringing should be like, it would not be sufficiently compelling to overcome the presumption against other-determining rights.

Children's Personal Identity and Children's Education

The second problem for Kymlicka's equality-based argument in relation to a community right to educate is that if the social thesis is true and if there are actually some minority cultures at risk of extinction in the very near future, then equality *for children* may require that those born today into those cultures receive an education that will make the long-term survival of their parents' culture even *less* likely than it is today. These children presumably have the same need to maintain a personal identity within a stable cultural context and thereby to secure the primary good of self-respect. Equal concern for their interests therefore dictates that we as a society do what we can to ensure that they are able to form an identity that is tied to a stable, enduring culture. How are we to do this?

A newborn child does not, of course, yet identify herself as a member of any culture. A newborn's need for self-respect can be met, in the abstract, within any cultural context. She is not under the same disability as a person whose identity is already formed and whose self-respect is therefore, according to the social thesis, tied to the persistence during his lifetime of a particular culture. The child's basic needs therefore do not call for special measures to preserve a culture on the brink of dissolution unless there are controlling reasons to tie her identity exclusively to that culture in the first place, or unless it is simply unavoidable that this will occur. In fact, the newborn child's interests appear to lie in not being put under such a disability if this can be avoided. If her parents' culture is unstable and if it is uncertain whether special measures to prop up that culture would be successful, then a proper respect for the child's fundamental interests seems to require that we prevent her from growing up in such a way that she identifies only, or perhaps even primarily, with that culture. Instead, we should foster at least a partial identification with mainstream culture, provided this can be done without severely impairing the child's relationship with her parents and other members of the cultural community (itself an important precondition for a child's basic well-being).

Whether this is in fact possible and how it might be done are complex questions. Kymlicka's endorsement of freedom for individual parents within a threatened minority cultural community to choose a mainstream, liberal private education for their children suggests that he himself does not believe it necessary for children newly born into these communities to be raised in such a manner that they identify exclusively with the traditional tribal way of life. But the essential point I wish to make here is that if there are any actual situations resembling the one that Kymlicka posits—where a minority culture is on the brink of extinction—the fundamental interests of children in those situations may be in conflict with the desire of their parents to preserve their culture through the children. If they are, then treating children as equal moral persons requires that we give precedence to the former (since fundamental interests trump nonfundamental desires). One approach to doing this might be to provide children born into vulnerable cultures an education that teaches them, in the language of the larger society, about mainstream political and popular culture, that conveys to the children a strong sense that they are valued and equal members of the larger society, and that makes a life within mainstream culture a realistic and healthy option for them. Of course, part of the problem with past efforts to assimilate children born to members of minority cultures has been that many in the majority culture have *not* valued such children as equal members of society but have instead regarded them as inferior. This problem persists and should be taken into account in deciding what particular form the education of these children, and of other children, should take, but there is reason to believe that it is much less severe today as mainstream America has become much more aware in recent decades of its unwarranted prejudices and its insensitivity to difference. The multicultural movement in education has played an important role in this change and can continue to do so.

At the same time, these children also have an important interest in being taught to respect and value the cultural heritage of their parents, and this interest justifies strong condemnation of past efforts in the United States and Canada to coerce children of minority communities into rejecting the culture of their parents, which included forced removal of children from tribal lands to boarding schools and concerted attacks in the classroom on their parents' language, belief system, and way of life.[9] However, the social thesis suggests that these children are better off if their personal identities are never made to depend entirely on the survival of a culture that may soon perish despite efforts to support it, a culture that may be fighting a losing battle for survival throughout their lifetime and may even be largely defunct by the time they reach adulthood. This suggests further that an education that acculturates them to mainstream American life—as public schooling for children of recent immigrants does today—is in their best interests.

It should also be noted that allowing cultural minority communities exclusive control over the education of members' children can pose a threat to the children's self-respect in a more direct way, regardless of whether a community is vulnerable to extinction, if a community's belief system treats some members as inherently inferior. Many religious and ethnic cultures, for example, teach girls that females are inferior to males and train them for lives of subordination to men. Satisfying Kymlicka's requirement that everyone have an equal chance for achieving self-respect might necessitate forcing adherents of these groups to cease their sexist practices, or it might entail providing children of group members an education that fosters a belief that females are the equals of males entitled to the same opportunities and powers, which would be likely to alter both the content and the structure of their culture. More generally, Kymlicka's equality-based argument appears to require that the state prevent any cultural community from teaching or otherwise treating any group of children in ways likely to make life within the cultural community very difficult for them as adults. Such treatment would place these children in the unchosen circumstance of having to decide between a miserable life within the culture and leaving the culture, thereby imperiling their culture-based identity.

The equality-based argument for a community right to define the nature of children's education thus runs up against the problem that children themselves might be better off if the community did not have that right. Justice for children must certainly require that we avoid creating

an inequality in the unchosen circumstances of *their* personal development if we can do so, rather than allowing the inequality to arise and
then trying, with uncertain prospects for success, to compensate for the
results of it later in life. The way to eliminate initial inequality with respect to personal identity and self-respect for children born into cultures
in danger of extinction seems to be to foster in them an identification,
though not an exclusive one, with the mainstream culture. This strategy
would no doubt lessen the likelihood that these children would later
choose to adopt the parents' belief system and way of life. It would thus
also be likely to hasten the demise of the minority cultural community,
possibly ensuring that it would not survive beyond the parents' lifetimes.

   Kymlicka does discuss the possibility of assimilation in both his early
and his more recent work but in a way that fails to account for the separate personhood and special situation of children. He addresses the objection that the social thesis shows only that a person needs *a* cultural
context, not any particular cultural context, and that perhaps the state
should simply facilitate the assimilation of members of minority cultures into the larger society. In his reply, though, he focuses exclusively
on the danger that a person who already has a fully formed identity may
suffer a loss of that identity, and he does not address the developmental
needs of children. In *Liberalism, Community, and Culture*, he writes
that a person cannot simply substitute a new cultural context for the
one in which he was raised: "Someone's upbringing isn't something that
can just be erased; it is, and will remain, a constitutive part of who that
person is."[10] In *Multicultural Citizenship*, he appeals similarly to "the
difficulty of leaving one's culture" and persons' desire "to retain their
cultural membership."[11] Thus, Kymlicka focuses on adults' identity
preservation rather than on children's identity formation. He implicitly
assumes that children will continue to be reared and educated in a way
that fosters in them an identification only with their parents' traditional
world view and way of life, and then will be at risk of losing their identity as a result of mainstream incursions on the traditional community.
When Kymlicka discusses education directly, his concern is with a right
to educate rather than a right *to be educated* in a particular way. He emphasizes in this context the importance for members of a cultural minority to be able to "maintain themselves as a distinct culture, if they
so choose." Absent is any recognition that young children are not in a
position to make such a choice and may not have the same interest as
their parents in maintaining a distinct culture. Kymlicka leaves unex-

plored the possibility that children born into vulnerable minority communities could, and perhaps should, from an early age be acculturated to the larger society in a manner that is responsive to all their developmental interests.

The equality argument thus fails to overcome the presumption against other-determining rights for a second reason—it entails an instrumental treatment of children, a willingness to overlook their needs in order to satisfy the interests of adults, and thus a denial of equality to this group of persons. If protecting adults' interests in cultural survival means sacrificing children's fundamental interests, then this aim is not even a legitimate reason for attributing a community right to educate, let alone a compelling one. Ironically, Kymlicka himself professes to reject the notion of rights to control other persons' lives; in discussing "internal restrictions" on group members, he insists that "nothing in my account of minority rights justifies the claim that a dominant group within a cultural minority has the right to decide how the rest of the community will use or interpret the community's culture or a right to deny adult individuals within the community freedom of choice in religion, political affiliation, or lifestyle." [12] Such a claim would violate the principle of equal respect. The irony is that a claim for a community right to educate is just such a claim: adults demand the right to decide how the rest of the community—children—will use and interpret the community's culture. As such, it treats children in a way Kymlicka deems unacceptable for adults. This is a paradox, I submit, that pervades political theorizing about child rearing.

Conclusion

A community right to educate, like a parental child-rearing right, is conceptually illegitimate. Treating children equally should mean that we deny the legitimacy of any purported rights residing in *any* person or group to direct their lives. Instead, certain persons should simply be accorded a *privilege* of exercising whatever authority and control over a child's upbringing is necessary to promote the welfare interests of the child, pursuant to the positive rights of the child. Even if an assimilationist education of any sort would be inimical to the developmental interests of children born into insular minority communities, a community right to control education would not be the appropriate form of protection against such an education. If there are any legitimate rights pertaining to children's care and education, they must be rights of the children themselves.

To defend efforts by a community decision-making body to control the content and methods of instruction in local schools, therefore, would require showing either that the affected children possess a right to the type of education that the community would choose or that receiving this type of education rather than another is not inconsistent with the children's developmental interests and so may be imposed as a matter of community privilege (but not as a matter of community right). This requirement would be very difficult to satisfy in the case of the educational demands that cultural, linguistic, and religious communities have typically made in recent decades. These generally entail purposefully closing off life options for children that might weaken their identification with the parents' culture, irrespective of whether an expanded range of options would improve the children's prospects for enjoying a happy and fulfilling life. For example, the Amish community in Wisconsin sought an exemption in 1972 from the state's compulsory education law for their high school-aged children because if the children were to attend school outside the Amish community, they would be exposed to views and ways of life different from those of the Amish. The Amish parents did not claim that such exposure would be inimical to the children's developmental interests but rather that it would make it more likely that members of the next generation would choose for themselves a life outside the Amish community, thereby undermining the long-term survival of that community. Within an appropriate conceptual framework for deciding child-rearing issues, such a claim would carry no weight; rather, courts and legislators should ask what is best for the children themselves.

What we adults should be debating when we decide how children will be educated is not whether parents' religious interests outweigh the interests of other adult members of society or what will help adults preserve the culture in which they were raised or which terms of communal association adults desire or find acceptable, but rather, what children need and are entitled to receive.

5 A Right to Equal Treatment

I have assumed in earlier chapters that children are persons and that in a moral sense they are equal persons—that is, that they have equal standing in our society in the sense that their interests should receive equal consideration in decisions about basic principles governing society and in legislative judgments that affect their lives. It is generally agreed today that a basic premise of a just society is that the principles governing people's lives should be the result of a decision-making process that takes into account and gives equal weight to every individual's interests. This assumption rules out standard ways of thinking about parent-state conflicts over child rearing in terms of parental or community rights. In the final two chapters, I build further on this assumption to develop a positive theory of decision making about children's lives.

The first positive implication of children's distinct and equal personhood I wish to explore has to do with the formal way governmental bodies treat different groups of children when they are crafting laws that confer on children benefits or protections from harm. All persons in our society are presumed, as a consequence of their right to equal consideration, to possess a formal right, subject to certain qualifications, to equal treatment by the state in both conferral of benefits and imposition of punishments or other burdens. This right is explicitly set forth in the Equal Protection Clause of the Fourteenth Amendment, which provides: "No State shall . . . deny to any person within its jurisdiction the equal protection of the laws." The courts have interpreted the Due Process Clause of the Fifth Amendment as imposing the same restriction on the federal government. The principal qualification of this general rule is that persons who are different in morally relevant ways may be, and sometimes ought to be, treated differently.

With this basic principle of justice in mind, I examine in this chapter the legitimacy of a dual system of school regulation—that is, one that applies different rules to two and sometimes more categories of schools. In Chapters 1 and 2, I described how legislatures and courts have drawn lines between religious and nonreligious schools, between public and private schools, or between schools that receive state aid and those that do not. This line drawing amounts to discrimination among groups of children in the legal protections they are afforded in connection with their education, and the end result of this discrimination is that some children incur certain harms and suffer a relative educational deprivation. Chapters 3 and 4 showed that this situation is not *compelled* by any entitlements of parents or religious communities. In this chapter, I consider whether the failure to regulate religious schools is even *permissible*, given its apparent inconsistency with our society's fundamental and undisputed commitment to formal equality.

State Action or Private Action?

It might be assumed that any deprivation children suffer as a result of being in a religious school is not the result of state action and therefore does not reflect state discrimination or a failure of the state to treat them as equal persons. Rather, one might believe that since their situation is entirely a result of their parents' religiously grounded choices, it is a purely private matter. Traditionally, the requirement that the state treat all persons as equals has not been understood to demand that the state eradicate discriminatory treatment by private persons. This limitation on the state's responsibility is embodied in the rule that a plaintiff advancing an equal protection claim must show some state action that is discriminatory, rather than simply some deprivation at the hands of private parties.

However, when what is at issue is a statute or a court decision, there can be no question that state action is involved; the real question in such a case is whether the statute or court decision discriminates among groups of individuals unjustifiably. This is true even when the state action itself does not inflict any immediate harm but makes it possible for private parties to inflict some harm. When the state gives two groups of people different levels of legal protection from private harm, or different guarantees of private assistance, there is a potential equal protection problem. Thus, in *Gomez v. Perez*,[1] the Supreme Court decided that a state had violated the Equal Protection Clause by conferring on children generally a judicially enforceable right to support from their natural fathers but denying that right to illegitimate children. That an illegitimate child would fail to receive support only if his or her father chose not to send any money and that the state's involvement was simply a failure to act rather than an affirmative act to prevent illegitimate children from receiving support did not eviscerate the cause of action. Similarly, if a criminal statute prohibiting assault made an exception for assaults against some particular group of persons, such as African-Americans or atheists, and ordered police not to act to prevent assaults against such persons, it would clearly be reviewable under the Equal Protection Clause, even though actions by private parties would be the immediate cause of any resultant physical harm to members of the excluded group.

It should be clear, therefore, that when a legislature enacts a law requiring parents or their proxies to do something for their children's benefit or prohibiting them from doing something the state deems harmful to children but then exempts from the law parents who have certain religious beliefs, thereby removing the protection from children of those parents, the state is acting, and it is doing so in a way that treats different groups of children differently. The fact that parents and their proxies themselves must also act, by claiming the exemption and declining to undertake otherwise mandated behavior or engaging in otherwise proscribed conduct, in order for the children to suffer some deprivation, does not negate the fact that the state has acted in a determinative way. What is at issue in the case of religious exemptions to education laws—the exemptions in Title IX, in some state analogues to Title IX, in many other regulations, and in court decisions—is whether the state's singling out a particular group of children for lesser protection of educational interests because of their parents' religious beliefs violates the constitutional and moral requirement that states treat similarly situated persons similarly.

What about statutes and regulations that apply in the first instance only to public schools? Or legal requirements that extend to all public and private schools receiving government assistance but not to schools that accept no government assistance (which are, for the most part, religious schools)? Here, too, there is quite obviously state action—legislative or administrative promulgation of a legal rule. However, one might think the connection between that state action and any harm to children in schools not covered by the rules is simply too attenuated for any responsibility to be attributed to the state. One might also believe that children in the two categories of schools in each case are not "similarly situated" or that the classifications reflect legitimate state objectives, possibilities I consider below. Here I wish to consider the public/private or state aid/no state aid split primarily in terms of whether the supposed deprivation suffered by children in some of the noncovered schools can reasonably be said to be the result of state action. This question goes to the very heart of the prevailing scheme of government regulation of education in this country and so warrants more than a cursory treatment.

A state might defend a decision to limit the scope of school regulations to public schools or to schools receiving government assistance by arguing that it is simply acting to control its own functions and their effects while leaving the "private" domain unregulated. The notion of a division between public and private domains is a familiar one in our society, which prizes so highly the individual liberty that our system of limited government preserves. In fact, one is more likely to hear the opinion that a state is overreaching its proper bounds of authority when it attempts to regulate private schools than to hear a claim that the state is in some way harming children who attend private schools when it fails to ensure that they receive an adequate education or to protect them from injurious practices.

A state might contend that its school regulations are analogous to restrictions on employment practices that governmental bodies impose on themselves but do not also impose on private employers. Private-sector employees do not complain that this disparate treatment of state and private employment, in terms of the protections afforded employees, violates the Equal Protection Clause. Such a claim would undoubtedly fail, since courts typically treat a legislative decision to abstain from regulating private conduct as immune from constitutional challenge unless it can reasonably be viewed as encouraging the private conduct. They rarely find that a state's decision not to apply all of the rules governing its own internal operations to the private sector encourages any behavior in the private sector. Rather, such a decision is viewed simply as a manifestation of the state's special vigilance over its own affairs. Regulations that apply only to public schools or only to schools receiving state financial assistance might be viewed in the same light.

This notion of separate public and private domains, however, whatever its viability in other contexts, is untenable in the context of children's schooling or of any other aspect of child-rearing.[2] Regulating schooling differs in important ways from regulating the internal practices of government. First, state provision of and support for education is not an internal practice of government but rather the provision of a government benefit to private persons in the community, like any welfare program. Second, education is an essential good that states undertake to guarantee for all children. State education laws as a whole manifest a governmental intent to assume ultimate authority over this fundamental aspect of children's lives. In fact, compulsory education laws typically mandate that all children attend public school and then carve out an exception to this mandate for children whose parents prefer some alternative form of schooling.[3] This fact renders state education law analogous to a law guaranteeing welfare assistance to all persons but allowing some persons to opt out if they prefer to obtain subsistence from a private source. In contrast, regulation of government employment practices inherently relates to a very limited group of persons—government employees—who stand in a special relationship to the government.

Third, with respect to schooling the state affirmatively invests in particular private individuals—parents—plenary legal control over the lives of the intended beneficiaries of the law—children—including the right to decide whether the children will attend a school to which the statutory protections extend or one to which they do not. Children themselves have no legal control, and typically no practical control, over the decision whether they will receive the state-proffered benefit of a public school education or will instead receive some other, possibly inferior, form of schooling. Moreover, the state precludes other private parties from acting to advance the children's welfare; the state grants parents exclusive power and stands ready to prevent its own officials or private parties other than the parents from acting to secure the statutory benefit for the children.[4] Private employers, in contrast, enjoy no comparable state-conferred rights of control over their employees.

With the addition of this crucial third feature, a proper analogy to state education law would be a hypothetical law establishing a universal welfare assistance guarantee, with an individual opt-out provision, that gives some persons (for example, religious leaders) an exclusive legal right to decide for certain other persons (e.g., their followers) whether those other persons will receive the government assistance or will instead receive some private alternative that may be substantially inferior, as well as the right to prevent those other persons from exiting the relationship.

A basic ethical principle in our society, undergirding numerous legal rules, holds that whereas competent individuals may justly suffer as a result of *their own* choices, no one should suffer avoidable harm because of circumstances beyond his or her control, and particularly not as a result of other people's choices.[5] Both this hypothetical welfare law and state education codes that leave some schools unregulated violate this principle. If children in any private school receive a secular education inferior to that in the local public school or incur harms from which public school students are protected, it is a result not of their own choice, but rather of the state's empowering their parents to deny them benefits that public school students receive and that they would otherwise be guaranteed.

The overall effect of laws governing education, then, is to create an absolute bar for a certain class of children to a quality education free from harmful practices that the state proscribes in most schools. Accordingly, this situation is different from that in which states and the federal government, prior to 1976, left private elementary and secondary schools free to engage in racially discriminatory admissions practices, which courts found not to constitute state action. Parents of a child denied admission to such a school readily could, and were motivated to, secure an alternative avenue for obtaining the state-guaranteed benefit at stake, which was simply an education in some school. In contrast, a child who is *in* a school that, for example, imposes on her the belief that she is by virtue of her gender an inferior human being is subjected to this harmful instruction through the state's action in allowing her to be placed in that school rather than guaranteeing her, as it does other children, the benefit of an education that treats her as an equal human being.[6]

A final consideration relating to the question of state action is whether state sex discrimination school laws written to apply only to public schools might be actionable on the basis that they encourage private discriminatory conduct. The Supreme Court has held that it is a violation of the constitution for the government to "'induce, encourage or promote private persons to accomplish what it is constitutionally forbidden to accomplish,'"[7] and it would clearly be unconstitutional for state schools to engage in sexist practices of the kind described in Chapter 1. Though it might seem on the surface that states are simply indifferent to the sexist practices of some religious schools, in fact they do effectively encourage gender discrimination and gender bias in private schools by excluding these schools from the coverage of antisexism laws while at the same time providing them with numerous forms of state aid. The fact that the state does not voice explicit support for discriminatory practices of private schools, and perhaps does not even intend to promote such practices, does not render state support for discrimination unobjectionable.

This conclusion finds support in the context of race discrimination: the Supreme Court has held that merely providing textbooks to private schools that engage in such discrimination constitutes state encouragement of their practices. In *Norwood v. Harrison*, the Court reasoned that *any* significant aid of a kind provided only in connection with schools, whether supplied to the schools directly *or* indirectly through parents, has a "tendency to facilitate, reinforce, and support private discrimination" and that a "state's constitutional obligation requires it to steer clear, not only of operating the old dual system of racially segregated schools, but also of giving significant aid to institutions that practice racial or other insidious discrimination."[8] In the Establishment Clause context, the Court has discussed the additional danger that state aid to religious schools can create the impression—among the public generally and/or in the minds of children in the schools specifically—that the state endorses the beliefs of the benefited religious group. This danger is present in the case of religious schools' sexist training. However, even forms of state aid that pass an Establishment Clause test (for example, because they are provided indirectly, through parents or students, such as textbooks) can constitute encouragement for equal protection purposes.

The federal government and the states provide substantial material assistance to private schools, including religious schools—by conferring tax-exempt status, by allowing tax deductions to parents for private school tuition, by providing textbooks, school lunches, transportation, and other services to private school pupils, and by reimbursing schools for the costs of complying with some regulations. Such aid, by Supreme Court standards, clearly amounts to encouragement of any discriminatory practices of religious schools that the states do not prohibit, and it is therefore state action reviewable under the Equal Protection Clause. Indeed, the supposed purpose of conferring tax-exempt status is to support kinds of activities the government deems beneficial to society and to assist organizations engaged in those activities whose work is consistent with our public policies.[9] In addition, states also confer many less tangible, but nevertheless important, benefits on religious schools—by granting state accreditation to some and by exempting all such schools from certain regulations, such as teacher-certification requirements, that would be costly to comply with. If the states and the federal government wish not to encourage sexist practices in religious schools, they should do nothing to facilitate the operation of those schools. They should withhold tax-exempt status, and all other state-conferred benefits, from schools that engage in such practices, just as they do with respect to racially discriminatory practices.[10]

Reaching the conclusion that nonregulation of religious schools constitutes state action, one might object, leaves the states' entire scheme of school regulation open to constitutional challenge, and so raises the concern that it might require that states impose all the same regulations on all private schools that they impose on public schools, thereby eviscerating the distinction between public and private education in this country. This concern, however, is both overstated and irrelevant. It is overstated because for an equal protection claim to succeed, plaintiffs would also have to show that children in religious schools suffer harm as a result of a state's not extending some regulation universally and that the state lacks an adequate rationale for not imposing regulations. Therefore, states might permissibly give religious schools greater operational and instructional freedom than they give public schools, so long as doing so causes no harm to religious school pupils and serves a sufficient state purpose. There is no reason to believe that a religious school would be unable to maintain a distinctively religious character (even if not exactly the character parents and school administrators want) even if it were subject to all of the statutory regulations (as opposed to constitutional restrictions, such as the Establishment Clause) to which public schools are now subject. Moreover, this concern is irrelevant because if children's right to formal equality requires that states eviscerate all significant distinctions between the regulations governing public schools and those governing nonpublic schools, then *ex hypothesi* they have no sufficient reason for not doing so.

The State's Motivation

Another preliminary objection to treating nonregulation of religious schools as a discrimination problem might be that, unlike racial discrimination, treating groups of children differently based on the religious beliefs of their parents does not reflect any animus on the state's part toward any children. Legislators do not affirmatively desire that some children not receive appropriate schooling. In fact, in many cases they have come to accept the present state of nonregulation of religious schools reluctantly and only after heated battles with religious groups.

Discrimination need not be motivated by a desire to harm the disadvantaged group, however, in order to be morally objectionable or unconstitutional, as Supreme Court decisions striking down affirmative action programs make clear. A government that is simply blind or indifferent to the deprivation it occasions a disadvantaged group, or that has simply given in to the demands of a more powerful group, also fails to respect the equal personhood and equal citizenship of the members of the disadvantaged group. Children in religious schools have a right not simply to be thought kindly of but also to have their interests count equally in state decision making and to receive the same legal protection children in other schools receive absent sufficient justification for disparate treatment.

"Similarly Situated" Children

A final preliminary objection, closely related to the main issue of justification, might be that the groups of children marked out by the existing dual system of school regulation are actually in relevantly distinct situations—or in Fourteenth Amendment parlance, not "similarly situated"—and that the state is simply recognizing and responding to a real difference between the two groups. The two groups do clearly differ in one important respect—the religion-based preferences of their parents with respect to their schooling (I do not consider here the qualifications that many parents who would prefer religious schooling for their children cannot afford it and that some parents who send their children to religious schools do so for nonreligious reasons). Not all differences between the situations of two groups are morally or legally relevant, however, and the determination whether two groups of individuals deserve equal treatment in the state's conferral of legal protections surely cannot turn on whether some third parties want to deny one of the groups such protection. If that were the case, every discriminatory law would pass equal protection review. Rather, a relevant difference must be one that relates to the characteristics of the groups' members and, in particular, to characteristics that render one group less deserving or less in need of the benefits that the law confers.[11]

Certainly it cannot be the case that some children *deserve* lesser educational benefits than others simply because their parents hold certain religious beliefs. In our moral culture, judgments about what a person deserves are based on that person's own choices, voluntary actions, and needs, not on choices made by others. In addition, the religious beliefs of a child's parents do not lessen her inherent need for a good education and for protection from harmful treatment. In fact, children of religious dissenters arguably require *greater* state protection of their educational interests than do other children. With respect to regulations designed to ensure that children receive an adequate secular education, children whose parents choose to send them to a religious school principally for religious reasons (which is usually, but not always, the case), logically stand in greater need of state supervision than children attending a school that their parents chose for them solely because they thought it provided a superior secular education. The former case raises greater concern than the latter that the school chosen does not provide an adequate secular education.

Likewise, parents who for religious reasons favor behavior, such as sexism, that the state deems harmful are likely to subject their child to such treatment at home. Consequently, the child's need for a type of schooling that is free of such behavior is actually *greater* than that of other children. A daughter of Fundamentalist Christian or Orthodox Jewish parents is just as susceptible to suffering diminished self-esteem and the agony of thwarted life prospects as a result of sexist socialization as is the daughter of any other parents. However, because she is likely to receive overt inculcation of sexist views at home from her parents, her need for instruction in the opposing view that men and women are inherently equal—which research has shown to be successful in partly overcoming ingrained gender-stereotyped attitudes[12]—is actually greater than that of other girls. In an analogous situation, children whose parents oppose all medical care on religious grounds stand in even greater need than other children of receiving immunizations, since their parents' likely behavior, in the event that they contract a disease, would make the consequences of not receiving that state-guaranteed benefit more severe.

Thus, children in religious and nonreligious schools are similarly situated with respect to the underlying purposes of school regulations—to ensure a higher-quality education and to protect children from harmful treatment. If the state action in question is encouragement of private discrimination by providing state aid to religious schools that teach sexist views, then the discrimination at issue is based on gender and it is surely true that boys and girls are similarly situated with respect to their need for self-esteem and treatment as equal persons. These conclusions do not, however, determine whether the exemptions are unjust or unconstitutional. They simply emphasize that the state must offer an adequate justification for providing certain legal protections to some children but not to others, when both groups have need for the protections. The discussion above raises concerns about religious freedom, church-state separation, toleration of minority religious practices, and possible adverse effects on children themselves from forcing unwilling parents to conform to majoritarian norms. These concerns suggest that there may be legitimate and important state purposes that justify the religious exemptions.

Justified Discrimination?

Among the myriad statutes federal and state legislatures pass each year are numerous laws that give particular people or groups of people benefits that others do not receive. Some differential treatment is simply unavoidable; government has limited resources and sometimes must pursue its goals in a piecemeal or incremental fashion. But when there is strong reason to suspect that legislators are acting on the basis of prejudice or indifference to the interests of some group, or where very important individual interests are at stake, we more closely examine the decisions they make and demand that those decisions reflect a more scrupulous egalitarianism. The threat to the ideal of equal respect for all persons is greatest when legislative choices reflect a failure to give equal consideration to some persons' interests, and are not simply the result of administrative necessity, or where such choices cause one group to enjoy a lesser share of basic social goods than another.

Judicial review of discriminatory legislation reflects this sensitivity to legislative motivation and to the importance of the interests at stake. Courts tolerate a substantial amount of inequality in the benefits and burdens legislation imposes on different groups of people, and in reviewing most laws under an equal protection analysis apply an undemanding "rational basis test." This test assumes that legislatures have a legitimate reason for making the choices they do, or at least that they are doing their best to manage the complex social and economic problems they face; it requires a person who challenges a law to show that any difference in treatment among groups under the law is not rationally related to any legitimate state purpose. However, when legislation disadvantages a "suspect class"—a group of people likely to be treated with prejudice or indifference by those in power—or has an impact on a fundamental right or important interest of individuals, courts apply a "strict scrutiny" or a "heightened scrutiny" test. This examines discriminatory classifications more closely for their underlying purpose, presumes the legislative choices to be invalid, and imposes on the state the burden of providing greater justification for the choices than simply administrative convenience or incrementalism—a compelling interest under strict scrutiny or an "exceedingly persuasive" [13] state purpose under heightened scrutiny.

Once it is established that religious exemptions to child welfare laws amount to discriminatory state action, the critical question is how circumspect we as a society and the courts in particular should be about the legislative choices these laws reflect. Are legislatures entitled to substantial deference in these difficult areas of conflict between mainstream and minority values? Or is the situation of the children involved, or the nature of their interests that are at stake, such that courts should be especially vigilant to protect them against unfavorable outcomes of the political process?

The Supreme Court's past decisions provide useful guidance as to how stringently laws disadvantaging children of religious objectors should be reviewed. Particularly telling is the Court's past treatment of classifications of children on the basis of characteristics or choices of their parents—for example, parents' marital or citizenship status—with a high degree of suspicion. For example, in *Weber v. Aetna Casualty*,[14] the Court invalidated a state workers' compensation statute that denied benefits to certain illegitimate children, reasoning that "imposing disabilities on the illegitimate child is contrary to the basic concept of our system that legal burdens should bear some relationship to individual responsibility or wrongdoing. Obviously, no child is responsible for his birth." In *Plyler v. Doe*,[15] the Court applied heightened scrutiny to a law allowing school districts to deny a public education to undocumented alien children, whom the Court described as "children not accountable for their disabling status." Although these cases involved a societal hostility toward the parents that was unjustly extended to the children, and religious exemptions do not, an equal danger exists in the latter case that legislators will disregard the interests of, and impose disabilities on, children as they react to parental choices. It is as unjust to visit suffering on children based on their parents' "pieties" as it is to visit suffering on them based on their parents' "sins." In both cases, children are wholly unaccountable for their disabling status.

Not only do children denied protection by religious exemptions lack control over their defining characteristic, but they also lack control over how the political process reacts to that characteristic. From its first identification of the need for heightened judicial protection of some groups, the Court has treated a group's ability to affect the political process as an important determinant of whether its members constitute a suspect or "quasi-suspect" class,[16] and for good reason. That ability is precisely what ensures that members of a group receive the equal consideration in state decision making to which their personhood entitles them. As Justice Thurgood Marshall once stated, a group's political powerlessness points to "a social and cultural isolation that gives the majority little reason to respect or be concerned with that group's interests and needs."[17]

Children of religious objectors arguably have less political power than any other group in this country, less than even illegitimate or alien children, and that makes the judiciary's role in ensuring that they receive equal consideration crucial. Not only are these children unable to influence the political process themselves, but the persons who ordinarily would represent their temporal interests in the public sphere—their parents—do not do so in this context. In fact, the parents advocate *against* those interests. Moreover, unlike other groups of legally or practically disabled persons, including other groups of children, children of religious objectors today have no substantial third-party constituency advocating for them. In the past, individual legislators, state education and social services officials, teachers' associations, and medical organizations did look out for these children to some degree, but they have largely given up, wearied by heated confrontations with and relentless lobbying by groups of religious parents.[18] Feminist scholars and women's advocates have been surprisingly silent about the sexist practices of conservative religious schools, as if unaware that the girls in these schools are incurring harm that is unquestionably worse than that incurred by girls in the average public school or by women in many of the employment situations that they rightly and vehemently condemn.

For these reasons, we should treat classifications on the basis of parents' religious beliefs with great suspicion. In addition, the interests at stake for children in relation to education regulations, child medical care laws, and many other areas of law governing their lives are undeniably of the utmost importance, even if our adult-centered federal constitution does not explicitly recognize them as such. What the Supreme Court said of education in *Brown v Board of Education*,[19] is even more true now: "Today, education is perhaps the most important function of state and local governments. . . . Today it is a principal instrument in awakening the child to cultural values, in preparing him for later professional training, and in helping him to adjust normally to his environment. In these days, it is doubtful that any child may reasonably be expected to succeed in life if he is denied the opportunity of an education." It is simply perverse, even if not logically inconsistent, that the Supreme Court in *Yoder* read into the Constitution an implicit fundamental right of some parents *to deny* their children an education beyond the eighth grade while declining in *San Antonio Independent School District v. Rodriguez*[20] and subsequent cases to find that children have a fundamental right *to receive* an education.[21] In contrast, a number of state courts have declared that, under their respective state constitutions, education is a fundamental right.[22]

Fortunately, and wisely, the Court in *Plyler v. Doe* did recognize education as an important interest triggering heightened review. In doing so, it identified an essential connection between education and the central purpose of the Equal Protection Clause. A law denying an education to a discrete class of children, the Court wrote, creates "a lifetime hardship" for each child and an underclass of persons unable to participate in and contribute to society: "The inestimable toll of that deprivation on the social, economic, intellectual, and psychological well-being of the individual, and the obstacle it poses to individual achievement, make it most difficult to reconcile the cost or the principle of a status-based denial of basic education with the framework of equality embodied in the Equal Protection Clause."[23]

Of course, to say that education is extremely important does not mean that every aspect of schooling is of great moment for a child's life. But many of the particular regulations from which religious schools are exempted—such as those relating to teacher qualifications, selection of basic curricular materials, and sex discrimination—go to the core of a child's educational experience. Indeed, it is difficult to imagine any state officials arguing that, for example, the sexist practices in which many religious schools engage do not impair a critical developmental interest of the girls subjected to those practices. The "inestimable toll" of sexist instruction on the "social, economic, intellectual, and psychological well-being" of girls, like the toll that racial segregation of schools has taken on African-American children, is undeniable given the crucial role that self-esteem plays in child development and education. Legislatures that have passed regulations prohibiting sexism in schools have clearly recognized this fact and so would not be in a position to credibly contend that protection against sexist treatment is actually not very important.

We as a society, and courts in particular, should therefore not be complacent about or deferential toward the legislative choices reflected in religious exemptions to education regulations. Rather, we should be highly skeptical about their appropriateness and demand of our government that it demonstrate at least an "exceedingly persuasive," if not compelling, justification for denying to children of religious objectors the protections it grants to other children. This is a novel proposition, and many people would be resistant to thinking about religious exemptions in equal protection terms at all, but that reaction is itself evidence of the obstacle these children face to being treated as equal persons, because it reflects an inclination not to think about these children as persons in their own right, distinct from their parents, and as having interests potentially at odds with their parents' wishes. Legislators who vote for religious exemptions no doubt share this inclination to ignore the independent interests of these children, and that is precisely what it means to violate a person's right to formal equality, the right to equal consideration in the formulation of laws affecting one's life.

Applying Heightened Scrutiny to Religious Exemptions

Probably most people assume that there are several legitimate purposes served by having religious exemptions in child welfare laws, and that the real question is how important those reasons are, relative to the deprivations to children caused by the exemptions. However, some of the purposes one might imagine to support these exemptions turn out not even to be legitimate. One basic prerequisite of legitimacy is that, consistent with the notion of equal citizenship, an asserted state purpose must be an impartial one—that is, it cannot be simply a "naked preference" for one group over another.[24] Indeed, the foremost aim of the Equal Protection Clause is to eliminate legislative decisions made on the basis of such preferences, rather than on the basis of equal consideration of the interests of all.[25] This does not mean that no law may further interests of only one particular group of citizens, or even that the state may never act in such a way that some people are benefited while some are burdened. Rather, it means that in those cases the state must have decided which group's interests to satisfy after giving equal consideration to the interests of both. There is nothing illicit in deciding that one group's interests outweigh those of another or that two groups' interests are equal and that limited state resources require satisfying only one. Ordinarily the state is assumed to have properly balanced interests in establishing policies and laws. However, as noted above, when a disadvantaged group's interests are important and/or there is reason to think the state is acting on the basis of hostility or indifference to that group, the state may rightly be called upon to demonstrate an impartial basis for the distribution of benefits and burdens it chose—in other words, a rationale that reflects a balancing of interests in which every individual's interests count equally.

Usually the "naked preference" at issue in an equal protection case is between persons within a legislatively designated class and persons not within that class. For example, a law excluding people of minority races from public office would reflect a naked preference for white people over all other people. However, the right of formal equality is equally offended when the preference is between a particular group of persons receiving a special legislative benefit (e.g., certain parents) and persons who incur a corresponding burden as a result of the others' having that benefit (e.g., their children). Conversely, denying a benefit to one group of individuals (e.g., certain children) that other, similarly situated persons receive in order to satisfy the wishes of a third group (e.g., their parents) may also run afoul of the equal consideration principle, by giving preference to the third group's interests over those of the first. Thus, for example, an exemption from rape laws for husbands who rape their wives cannot permissibly be based on a legislative preference for the interests of husbands over the interests of wives. Likewise, any legitimate justification for parental religious exemptions cannot be based upon a preference for parents' interests over those of their children.

Parents' Preferences and Constitutional Rights

The actual reason that legislators and courts exempt some parents from child welfare laws is clear: they wish to satisfy the religious preferences of those parents, or they simply capitulate to parental demands.[26] In doing so, as shown in Chapter 2, neither legislatures nor courts have given much consideration to the interests of children that religious exemptions sacrifice; in reaching their decisions, they have instead typically weighed only parental interests and the interests of the larger society in having self-sufficient citizens. Neither legislatures in their declarations of purposes and findings nor courts in their opinions make any pretense that their decision furthers, or is even consistent with, the interests of the individual children involved. Nor do they claim that they gave appropriate consideration to the children's interests and simply found them outweighed by the parents' interests. Existing religious exemptions therefore reflect a naked preference for parents' interests over children's interests, which is illegitimate.

It is no defense to say that legislatures are respecting parents' constitutional rights and that complying with the Constitution is a legitimate state purpose. In the first place, many existing statutory exemptions go beyond what courts have held to be constitutionally required. In fact, religious schools are statutorily exempted from some requirements, such as teacher certification, that courts have explicitly held the states may constitutionally impose on such schools. Second, to the extent courts have held that parents are constitutionally entitled to an exemption from any child welfare laws, this simply shifts the locus of responsibility for discrimination from the legislative branch of government to the judicial branch, which must also conform to the equality principle. Consistent with the basic premise of liberalism that equality is the most fundamental principle of a just political order,[27] the Supreme Court has treated the Equal Protection Clause as a higher-order constraint on judicial interpretation of substantive constitutional rights. For example, in finding that a lower court's enforcement of a racially restrictive covenant in a private real estate contract violated the equal protection rights of African-Americans, even though protection of property rights is a fundamental principle in our constitutional scheme, the Supreme Court stated that "[t]he Constitution confers upon no individual the right to demand action by the State which results in the denial of equal protection of the laws to other individuals."[28] As the review of judicial decisions in Chapter 2 makes clear, judicial creation of child-rearing rights that are more expansive for religious objectors than for other parents has rested solely on the interests of parents, with no serious consideration given to the interests of children. In fact, as noted in Chapter 2, the Supreme Court in *Yoder* summarily dismissed considerations of the children's interests, indicating that parents' religious rights control even when inconsistent with their children's interests so long as what parents do to their children does not impose substantial costs on the larger society.

An equal protection perspective on child rearing thus leads to the startling conclusion that the *Yoder* decision, that icon of liberalism and free exercise jurisprudence, in addition to having the infirmities identified in Chapter 3, was actually itself unconstitutional. It is for children of religious objectors what *Plessy v. Ferguson*[29] was for African-Americans—the Supreme Court's imprimatur upon discriminatory laws that foster subordination and social isolation, made to seem reasonable by a perfunctory dismissal of the interests of the disfavored class. The ultimate question regarding religious exemptions to child welfare laws is whether the state, in the form of a legislature *or* a court—even the Supreme Court—had a legitimate and "exceedingly persuasive" justification for creating the inequalities among groups of children that those exemptions entail, and that justification must be something other than simply sympathy with or a desire to placate religious parents.

Now what if the state, in considering whether to create a religious exemption to a particular child welfare law, did give equal consideration to the temporal interests of children, and found that their parents' interest in religious freedom was weightier? Would it be appropriate to grant an exemption based on that balancing? Here the plot thickens, for it turns out that there are some kinds of interests that the state may not even take into account in crafting laws that discriminate among groups of people. One of those interests is a desire, whatever its basis, to deny another person certain goods, such as legal protection from harm, to which they would otherwise be entitled. For example, it would be inappropriate for the state to take into account the desire of some white people, even if religiously motivated, to deny certain legal protections—for example, protections against assault—to African-Americans in deciding whether to extend those protections universally. Similarly, if some minority religion encouraged husbands to beat their wives if they engaged in unorthodox behavior, a religious exemption to domestic abuse laws based on a balancing of the religious interests of men in this community against the health and safety interests of women in the community would be inappropriate. The husbands' interest in denying their wives the legal protection other women enjoy should not even factor into the state's deliberations, and protection of these women should not depend on a finding that their interests outweigh those of their husbands.

Under this same principle, it is inappropriate to deny equal protection of the laws to a group of children by balancing their interests against the preferences of their parents or of any other persons (e.g., other adults who believe they have a religious duty to save the children, or liberals wishing to preserve diversity in our society) that they not enjoy that protection. Thus even though it is certainly the case that children's interests in receiving an education and proper medical care outweigh any desires of their parents (or other persons) to deny them those goods, it is not necessary to demonstrate that in order to conclude that satisfying such desires is not an adequate justification for the religious exemptions, for the state may not properly even consider those desires.

The actual state purpose behind religious exemptions to child welfare and education laws, therefore, is not even a legitimate purpose, regardless of whether it is understood as respecting parents' supposed constitutional rights or as simply gratifying parents' wishes. Courts applying heightened equal protection review ordinarily do not look beyond the actual purposes of a discriminatory classification to find justification, perhaps believing that where there is reason to be suspicious of legislative motives or where the stakes are high for disfavored individuals, the courts should not allow the government to construct post hoc rationalizations for their actions. In these situations, legislatures should be forced to make decisions on an appropriate basis in the first place. Given the long-demonstrated tendency of policy makers to ignore the plight of children in general[30] and of children of religious objectors in particular, courts perhaps should refuse to allow them to fabricate justifications after the fact when it is clear that the thinking that governed their actions when they passed the laws did not involve a proper respect for the equal personhood of the children affected and equal consideration of their interests. Striking down parental religious exemptions on this basis would have the salutary effect of bringing to the forefront of public attention the situation of groups of children that have previously been ignored. This would generate open public discussion of the needs and interests of these children and of children generally and their claims to the protections of the larger society.

Nevertheless, I will consider other possible justifications the state might offer for parental religious exemptions. It is worth exploring whether there might be less salutary consequences of eliminating such exemptions. Any possible adverse consequences of extending child protective laws universally—particularly, any adverse results for the excluded children themselves—might provide sufficient reason for not doing so, even if the state's failure to do so in the past was merely the result of legislative indifference. In speculating about alternative justifications for religious exemptions to child welfare laws, though, we must keep in mind that the exemptions are tied not to parental choices in general but to those based on religious belief. Indeed, if parents were exempt from a legal responsibility whenever they chose for any reason not to fulfill it, the laws would be vacuous. Any hypothesized purpose for these exemptions must therefore relate in some way to religious belief.

PROTECTING FAMILY RELATIONSHIPS

The potential justification that comes most readily to mind is the promotion of close family relationships. This aim is indisputably a legitimate state purpose, in light of the importance of these relationships to the temporal well-being of all members of a family and to the functioning of our society, and it might bear some relation to religious exemptions to child welfare and education laws. Specifically, parents' ability to act on the basis of their religious beliefs in raising their children might promote peaceful stability and close relationships within the family. Parents thwarted in their child-rearing preferences might become very upset and react in a way that disturbs the tranquillity of the home and the bond between parent and child. Avoiding this outcome might appear to be a legitimate state purpose because it protects interests of the children and interests that the children share with the parents, rather than interests of parents that are at odds with those of the children. The state, too, has an interest consistent with these, since overcoming parental resistance to extending legal protections to their children might entail substantial enforcement costs. In fact, although not a stated purpose for existing exemptions, enforcement problems clearly played an important causal role in the creation of many of them, particularly in the education context.[31]

However, while the general aims of promoting close family relationships and conserving state resources are legitimate ones, the more specific aim of avoiding adverse parental reactions to ensuring children equal protection of the laws is highly problematic. The Supreme Court has held on numerous occasions that in determining whether to implement and enforce the constitutional rights of some class of persons, states may not consider the possibility that other private parties will have negative reactions to or resist such state action, even where those reactions may have adverse consequences for the persons whose equal protection rights are being upheld. For example, in *City of Cleburne v.*

Cleburne Living Center, the Court considered the potential for neighborhood resentment toward the mentally retarded inhabitants of a proposed group home, and the effect that resentment might have on them, but concluded that "mere negative attitudes, or fear, unsubstantiated by factors which are properly cognizable in a zoning proceeding, are not permissible bases for treating a home for the mentally retarded differently from apartment houses, multiple dwellings, and the like."[32] The Court likewise dismissed concerns about private resistance to school desegregation in the 1950s[33] and to desegregation of other areas of social life such as public parks and restaurants in the 1960s,[34] when the harm from resistance would have fallen primarily on the individuals whose equal protection rights were at stake and secondarily on the government agencies that would have to enforce the laws.

These precedents appear to rest on assumptions that also apply in the case of child-rearing religious exemptions: that securing for individuals, even especially vulnerable ones, their constitutional rights is more important than protecting them from social friction; that states have alternative means available for protecting individuals from the adverse reactions of private parties to state enforcement of their rights; and that states would create perverse incentives if they backed down in the face of resistance to enforcement of some individuals' constitutional rights.[35] Allowing states to exclude some children from the protection of education and medical care laws because the children's parents might be very upset about and resist application of the laws to them certainly raises a concern about creating perverse incentives—encouraging parents to become increasingly resistant to any legal obligations of which they disapprove and further endangering children's welfare. Conversely, making clear to parents that the state will not shirk its responsibility to protect children's temporal interests, regardless of parental opposition, should over time weaken parents' sense of entitlement and inclination to do battle with the state. If the state also employs alternative means to minimize parents' sense of defeat and to demonstrate its respect for their role despite present disagreements, the outcome for children and families in the long run should be far preferable to the current state of affairs.

There is an additional concern regarding family relations, though, that is more vexing. Some parents might become alienated from their children, viewing their children as different or separate from them or as morally tainted or impure if the state ordered education or medical care of the children that was antithetical to the parents' religious worldview and self-conception. For example, Christian Science parents whose children received immunizations might have a different attitude toward their children as a consequence. Similarly, Fundamentalist parents might feel estranged from a daughter who is taught and comes to believe that she is morally equal to any male and who develops an ambition to attend college and have a career outside the home. Estrangement from their children might cause parents to become less nurturing, which could substantially harm the children.

In these types of situations the feared parental reaction and a state aim to avoid it do not appear objectionable. To distinguish this aim from that addressed in *Cleburne* and the desegregation cases, we might contend that opposition to enforcement of the legal rights of others is, in a sense, beyond the constitutional pale; a willingness to abide by the law and to respect others as equal citizens is a basic condition for membership in our democratic community, and states simply should not brook such opposition. In contrast, emotional attachment to another person, including one's child, does not have this political dimension. It is not something the state can presume to exist or demand as a prerequisite of citizenship. Thus it may be appropriate for the state to take cognizance of and attempt to avoid discouraging such attachment.

If this reasoning is sound, a state purpose of avoiding parental alienation from children might be a legitimate one for some parental religious exemptions, and if so, it becomes necessary to examine whether it is a sufficiently important purpose and is sufficiently related to the legislative classification. The state should have to show, at a minimum, that the alienation of parents from their children that would result from the teaching of facts or viewpoints inconsistent with the parents' beliefs and the encouragement of critical thinking would be so great as to outweigh the benefits to the children—their liberty, opportunities, and psychological well-being—from receiving that kind of education.

As I have argued, children incur great and lasting harm from failing to receive competent instruction, from the repression of independent thought, and from being trained for lives of subordination. This harm includes diminished self-esteem, lesser chances for success in careers, frustration of ambitions, and lesser self-fulfillment. On the other side of the equation, preserving parental attachment is not only important but is in fact compelling; however, if one considers the actual effects of children's receiving a more liberal education, they do not seem to pose a substantial threat to this goal. Any diminution in parental attachment to children (as opposed to parental outrage) would surely be only modest; religious objectors would not abandon their children if the children were to learn in school that most people think women are morally and politically the equal of men and that humans evolved from apes, and if they developed the capacity to think critically about political views and scientific and historical conclusions. Unsurprisingly, court decisions regarding challenges to school regulations mention no claims by parents that they would no longer accept, love, or nurture their children if the children were to receive instruction that the parents opposed on religious grounds. Many religious minorities, such as the Jehovah's Witnesses, have in fact manifested a doctrinal adaptability to the legal environment in which they live, deeming even adult members of the sect absolved of moral responsibility for receiving medical treatment prohibited by their faith when under a court order to do so.[36]

In addition, one might also speculate that a modest psychological detachment of parent from child in these cases would actually be a good thing. The children involved might actually be better off if their parents came to see them to a greater extent as distinct persons rather than as appendages, reproductions, or property of the parents. Inducing parents to see their children as persons in their own right might clear the way for formation of a different, more mutually rewarding bond and make parents feel less inclined or less entitled to sacrifice the children's temporal developmental interests for the sake of religious principles. All these considerations suggest that concern regarding the parent-child bond is illusory, or at least too insubstantial to justify any parental religious exemptions.

CHILDREN'S RELIGIOUS INTERESTS

Another post hoc rationalization a state might offer for parental religious exemptions is that they protect children's religious interests. But what could those interests be? One might understand them to include a need to grow up within a religious belief system, following the rules and joining in the practices of a religious community. However, the state may not assume that children have religious needs of this sort, and courts have consistently held as such in custody cases where the issue has arisen;[37] to do so the state would have to assume the truth of particular religious beliefs, which, as already noted, the Establishment Clause prohibits it from doing.

One might instead understand children's religious interests not as a need for a religious upbringing, but rather as an interest in religious liberty. The Supreme Court no longer views such an interest by itself as a legally sufficient basis for demanding an exemption from a neutral, generally applicable law—even a law designed to protect the religious individual's own interests. However, the Court has suggested that it is a constitutionally permissible basis on which a legislature may gratuitously grant an exemption (despite the equal protection and religious establishment concerns raised by treating religiously motivated claims to freedom as more important than other claims to freedom).[38] Moreover, a purpose of securing the religious liberty of religious objectors' children would not present the same problems that a purpose of securing parents' religious liberty presents, since it would not entail denying children legal protections in order to satisfy the preferences of some *other* persons.

Nevertheless, there are several problems with this hypothetical justification. First, religious exemptions to child welfare and education laws are in almost all cases tied to the religious beliefs of parents, not of children, so an argument that they are intended to protect children's religious liberty would simply be implausible. Second, these exemptions, particularly in the area of education, appear to result principally in the denial to many children of the freedom to think about and discuss religion; indeed, that is the reason why many parents demand the exemptions. Third, this justification is untenable even with respect to children who have no inclination to question the religious beliefs they have been taught and who would voice support for their religious education, since there are obvious problems with attributing to children an interest in religious liberty that would justify allowing them to make major life decisions—such as a decision to attend a school that will cognitively handicap them or a school that inculcates sexist views—inimical to their overall well-being and especially to their liberty and opportunities throughout the rest of their lives. Most children lack the cognitive abilities, knowledge, psychological and emotional independence, and self-control necessary for making such momentous life-determining choices, and this is especially true of those growing up in an authoritarian, restrictive environment. Moreover, placing on children the burden of making such decisions could itself be quite traumatic for them and would no doubt induce many parents to take coercive measures to ensure that their children made the "right" choice. Thus the consistent practice of courts not to base decisions in custody, medical care, school regulation, and other situations on the "religious liberty" of younger children makes a great deal of sense.[39]

Finally, one might understand a child's religious interests to include an interest in avoiding confusion or disorientation as a result of witnessing a clash of values and authority between her parents and the larger society, or as a result of being forced to receive medical care or instruction that is in conflict with the religious beliefs her parents have taught her. Certainly, potential for emotional harm to children is a permissible state consideration. However, there is no empirical evidence that exposure to competing belief systems is harmful to children, and courts have consistently rejected that argument in disputes between divorced parents over parenting practices and in parental challenges to elements of instruction in public schools.[40] In fact, courts have, after reviewing the opinions of child psychologists on the subject, concluded that such exposure is a potentially valuable learning experience for children. Confronting the more liberal values of the larger society may also be a salutary antidote to repressive and subordinating treatment the child receives at home.

At the same time, it is indisputable that forcing a child to do something that he believes will displease God can be traumatic. It is difficult to imagine, though, how most education regulations—for example, those requiring certified teachers or those prohibiting sexist teaching (as opposed to mandating antisexism teaching)—could ever have this result if imposed on religious schools, unless parents went to extraordinary lengths to make these changes appear frightening to the children (at which point the discussion of parental resistance above would become relevant). These regulations do not require children to do anything; they only constrain the behavior of teachers and school administrators.

On the other hand, some regulations, such as requiring instruction in, or use of textbooks that promote, views inconsistent with parents' religious beliefs, might have this consequence. Schoolchildren are likely to be aware of parental beliefs that certain ideas are sinful and thus may experience anxiety about hearing those ideas taught or reading books containing them. As discussed in Chapter 1, one troubling aspect of some forms of religious upbringing is precisely that they set children up to experience excessive anxiety by warning of divine vengeance for violation of moral codes that may be difficult to satisfy. Avoiding trauma in children thus might serve as a legitimate reason for exemptions from some regulations (though a concern about creating a perverse incentive for parents arises), and we should consider how persuasive that reason is.

A purpose of protecting children from anxiety, like that of protecting parental attachment, loses its force when one looks at the specific danger school regulation would pose. One might reasonably expect that parents and religious school teachers genuinely concerned for children's welfare would act to alleviate the children's concerns, reassuring them that they are not responsible for things that the state compels. Presumably parents of religious school pupils have a positive attitude toward the schools their children attend, and the children have a well-established relationship with their teachers that creates a sense of stability and security. Moreover, some children in conservative religious schools might actually experience relief from anxiety if the state ordered their schools to provide a better education, perhaps because they have hopes for their lives that require strong academic preparation. With respect to antisexism regulations, anxiety is probably inevitable for female children of persons with strongly sexist religious views regardless of what the state does. By extending these regulations to religious schools, the state may create new anxiety but may also alleviate a great deal of existing anxiety, while also ameliorating the many other harmful effects of sexism.

Finally, even if some religious exemptions do result in a net reduction in anxiety for children in some cases, we must balance that benefit against the costs for children of not receiving the same kind of instruction and training that children in public schools are supposed to receive. Imagine that tomorrow you were going to be a child again and that your parents would send you to a religious school. Ask yourself what you would rationally prefer—to receive an education that fosters higher-order thinking skills, promotes self-esteem, and provides the knowledge that most other children in society are acquiring (even if you would experience some anxiety because of your parents' opposition to this education), or instead to receive schooling that thwarts cognitive development, undermines self-esteem, provides distorted and false information, and, if you are female, constrains you to a life of subordination. Would you not conclude that the harms attendant upon the latter form of schooling far outweigh any anxiety the former might occasion?

In any event, exempting all religious schools from regulation would be a grossly overbroad means of avoiding trauma to children. This concern would probably not even arise with respect to the majority of religious schools. For example, Catholic schools and Lutheran schools, which together comprise well over half of religious school enrollment in this country, are much closer to the mainstream in their outlook than the Fundamentalist schools that have fought vehemently against state regulation in recent years. In particular, the American Catholic church now professes an aim to overcome its history of sexism. A national conference of Catholic school educators a few years ago in fact produced a "directional statement" to the effect that "Catholic education works toward the elimination of sexism . . . in its own structures and curricula, in the Church and in society."[41] Many Catholic parents might even welcome some state inducement to move that process along.

Conclusion

The actual purpose of parental religious exemptions, it turns out, is not even legitimate, nor are many of the hypothetical justifications we can imagine a state might claim: avoiding parental resistance to enforcement of child welfare and education laws, satisfying children's "need for religion" or respecting children's religious liberty, and sparing a child from exposure to beliefs inconsistent with those of his parents. In addition, the only two alternative justifications we can hypothesize that might be legitimate—promoting parental attachment to children and sparing children from anxiety—are too insubstantial to justify the failure of the state to regulate religious schools; in fact, the concerns they raise are largely illusory. It is difficult to imagine a state even arguing that it must accept the educational deprivation and subordinating treatment of millions of children as the necessary cost of avoiding parental alienation from, or psychological trauma to, those children. In particular, it would be shocking for any court to uphold a legislative tolerance for sexist teaching in some schools on the basis that this promotes healthy parent-child relationships or reduces children's anxiety.

We should conclude, therefore, that excluding religious schools from any school regulations intended to guarantee a high-quality education or to protect children from harmful practices violates the most basic right of children in these schools—the right to formal equality. Children's entitlement to equal consideration in government decision making yields a presumption that the state must treat all children equally. Any substantive legal protections for children in relation to their education should apply to all children, including those whose parents have religious objections to those protections, absent a convincing demonstration that some group of children would in fact be better off if their parents and schools enjoyed an exemption from the laws.

6 Justice for Children

The task of this final chapter is to identify some of the particular substantive protections that children in general—both those in religious and other private schools and those in public schools—should receive in connection with their schooling. It seeks to determine, in particular, whether children in general should possess rights against any of the pedagogical practices described in Chapter 1, which available evidence suggests take place in Fundamentalist and Catholic schools. This analysis, too, is very much one about the implications of children's equal personhood and presumptive right to equal treatment. Here I will draw comparisons between the liberties enjoyed by adults and those enjoyed by children, in addition to comparing further the situations of different groups of children—this time to determine what affirmative obligation the state has to counteract unequal social circumstances (rather than to avoid discriminatory legislation) in order to ensure equal educational opportunity for all children.

A New Framework for Determining Substantive Policy

One possible analytical approach to defining children's substantive educational rights would be to focus exclusively on children and to make their interests completely determinative of state policy affecting their lives—in other words, to decide what is best for children without considering effects on any adults. However, though it might be an appropriate policy outcome to establish rules designed to protect and promote the interests only of children in religious schools, a *theory* of state policy regarding education or any other basic social institution should begin with an equal concern for *all* persons potentially affected by that policy. Although the preceding analysis showed that the interest of parents and other adult members of a community in inculcating their religious beliefs in children is not a fundamental interest, does not merit the protection of rights, and cannot justify sacrificing the welfare of children, it did not show that such an interest is in all its possible forms illegitimate or that it should not be a factor at all in the formulation of public policy. To the extent that parents and communities can satisfy this interest without undermining the well-being of children, it may be appropriate to permit them to do so.

A proper theoretical framework for deciding on a scheme of state regulation of religious schools will therefore arise from and reflect an equal regard for children, parents, and other members of our society. Fortunately, a highly developed model of such a framework is readily at hand—that put forward by John Rawls in *A Theory of Justice*.[1] Rawls suggested reasoning about political principles and social policies from a perspective of hypothetical ignorance about features of oneself and one's situation in life that are morally arbitrary—that is, not earned or a reflection of personal merit but rather the result of chance genetic and environmental circumstances. In other words, in deciding what the basic constitutional principles, particular laws, and distribution of important goods in our society should be, we should abstract from our individual situation and try to imagine that we could actually be any kind of person in any kind of circumstances in our society. This effectively compels us to give equal weight to the interests of all persons; operating behind this "veil of ignorance," we must sympathetically identify with persons of all different types and imagine what their lives would be like under various political and legal regimes. The outcome of such a process of reasoning should be the selection of political principles that reflect a fair balancing of any competing interests and are therefore the ones under which we should be willing to live no matter what personal characteristics we turn out to possess once the veil is "lifted." We should recognize these as just precisely because they are the outcome of this fair and objective process of decision making.

This description of the model makes plain that it is critical to define the personal characteristics and social circumstances that are morally arbitrary. Some of these features are more widely recognized as such than others. There is, for example, a broad, though not universal, consensus in our society that the state should not deny benefits or impose burdens based upon the race of individuals. On the other hand, there is much debate among political theorists about whether talents and abilities are morally arbitrary features of persons. However, we need not determine here all the features that belong on the list. For the purposes of the discussion below, we need principally to assume only the moral arbitrariness of a person's age, gender, and parentage. Surely these are all things over which persons do not have control and for which they therefore are not morally responsible.[2] That is not to say that these characteristics are never relevant to state decision making but rather that they cannot properly be a basis for the state's giving less consideration or weight to a person's interests.

For purposes of determining children's substantive educational rights, therefore, one must assume when reasoning from this artificial perspective—which Rawls terms "the Original Position," in which, in a sense, one does not know who one is—that once the veil of ignorance is lifted, it might turn out that one is a child. One must therefore imagine what it would be like to live as a child and grow toward adulthood under various possible political regimes. One must also assume that if one is a child, one is likely to become an adult and so should be concerned with one's well-being over the course of an average lifetime. Moreover, since persons behind the veil of ignorance do not know their parentage, they must take into account that it might turn out, when the veil is lifted, that they are children whose parents are Catholics, Fundamentalist Christians, Jews, Muslims, adherents of some other major religion, members of a smaller religious sect or cult, atheists, agnostics, Satanists, Ku Klux Klan members, or persons of any other ideological stripe. In addition, one should assume in the Original Position that one might be or become a parent, or some other adult related in some way to a particular child, or an adult with no attachments to or concern for children.

We must therefore arrive at conclusions regarding children's education after considering the situation of all such persons and must, if possible, devise overarching principles, constitutional provisions, and legislative enactments that represent a fair accommodation of all persons' interests and so could be accepted as just by all moral persons in society. The information constraints I have woven into the veil of ignorance represent the fact that parents of *any* ideological disposition might wish to send their children to a school that indoctrinates them with the same ideology, and these constraints reflect the normative premise that as a matter of fairness and neutrality the same basic principles should apply to all parents and all children and to all potential forms of schooling.

It is important to recognize, though, that reasoning in the Original Position does not take place in a moral vacuum; we retain awareness of certain basic moral principles—"fixed points" in our normative culture—and test the conclusions we reach for their consistency with these fixed points. When a conflict arises between conclusions reached behind the veil of ignorance and these widely held norms, we must modify or reject one or the other, according to which seems less rationally supportable or less compelling. This process of "reflective equilibrium" should yield a coherent scheme of moral beliefs, constitutional principles, and particular legal rules.

At the same time, however, an additional and critical constraint on decision making in the Original Position is that decisions cannot be premised on assumptions about the truth or falsity of religious beliefs. Thus, no particular religious sect's theology can constitute one or more of those fixed points. This is because the Original Position is a model of state decision making, and one of the higher-order fixed points in our liberal democratic culture is that the state should not decide theological issues but should act only on the basis of more-or-less uncontested "secular" moral and nonmoral values and beliefs about the likely temporal consequences of various political regimes. Some might reasonably dispute whether there is any real or clear distinction between moral norms and religious precepts, or whether secular morality is a coherent concept, but we do recognize this distinction in our political culture in a way that is satisfactory to most people. In any event, I will not rely much on "moral" values in the following discussion; my concern here is simply to show the need to suspend one's religious beliefs about the spiritual interests of children when reasoning from the Original Position.

I have already identified, in Chapter 3, one fixed point—the principle that no one is entitled to control the life of another person and that rights protect only self-determination and individual integrity. Beyond this, in defining children's educational rights, I endeavor to rely in this chapter only on substantive secular values that I believe are broadly accepted. Thus, I eschew reliance on a comprehensive moral liberalism that presupposes moral autonomy—the capacity to reflect critically upon and choose from among a range of conceptions of the good—to be intrinsically valuable and necessarily an aspect of basic well-being for all persons, since this is a highly contested position and one I do not hold. I do consider, though, whether moral autonomy has *instrumental* value for some or all persons in our society at this time because it advances other, largely undisputed aspects of well-being. The conception of justice employed here is, nevertheless, a distinctively liberal one insofar as it assumes that individual (self-determining) liberty is a fundamental human good, which I take to be a relatively uncontroversial position in our society. It also assumes that the state may, if fairness dictates, take steps to counteract inequalities in the circumstances of children's birth, which is somewhat more controversial but endorsed by most Americans, I believe, when they are able to put self-interest aside. My aim is not to defend these limited assumptions but to show their implications for state regulation of religious schooling for those who happen to share them.

The implications I draw would generate quite robust requirements for children's education and so provide an independent basis for state-imposed restrictions on the educational practices of religious schools that are much more extensive than those now existing, and also more extensive than most liberals today would endorse. In particular, they are much greater than Rawls himself proposes in his latest discussion of the subject, in *Political Liberalism*.[3] Rawls and other liberal theorists have in recent years become increasingly troubled by the extent to which a liberal theory of justice conflicts with the belief systems of some people in our society, particularly religious conservatives. They worry that their substantive conclusions are therefore at odds with the liberal principle that political institutions should be tolerant and neutral in their treatment of competing reasonable conceptions of the good.[4] But as Chapters 3 and 4 showed, this concern is entirely misplaced, and the value of toleration is simply irrelevant, in the context of children's education. The failure of political theorists to recognize this may be attributable to their failure to see children as separate persons with distinct interests rather than as appendages or belongings of their parents or instruments of social reproduction. This leads them to confuse matters of self-determination with the essentially other-determining matter of child rearing. If treatment of children raises toleration concerns at all, it must be with respect to *children's* conceptions of the good, and I suggest reasons in Chapter 5 and in this chapter why children's religious beliefs should not preclude the state from assuming an important role in their intellectual formation. Whether and to what extent the state may assume such a role depends on how one fleshes out a general theory that gives equal regard to children.

Applying the Principles of Justice to Children in Religious Schools

Rawls contends that persons operating from within the Original Position, deciding without knowledge of their individual characteristics or situation, would endorse two fundamental principles to govern the basic institutions of society. My aim here is to show the implications of these principles for children's education. The first is the equal liberty principle, which requires, subject to important qualifications discussed below, that all members of society enjoy an equal share of basic personal liberties. The notion of equal fundamental freedoms is not particularly controversial, and for the most part our constitutional rights jurisprudence is consistent with it. However, parties behind the veil of ignorance would not limit legal protection of their liberties to rights against the state, as the Constitution does, but would also wish to guard against incursions on their freedom by private parties, as statutes and common-law rules do in every jurisdiction of this country today. Moreover, the list of specific basic liberties Rawls endorses is somewhat more extensive than those presently recognized. The second principle has two components, one requiring a "fair equality of opportunity" for all persons and the other effectively mandating a roughly equal distribution of wealth. The second component of the second principle is highly contested but is not directly relevant to the issues I will address. Only the first component of the second principle, requiring some form of equal opportunity, is important in the analysis below.

Bringing children more directly into the theory should not alter the general formulation of these basic principles. The special implications of giving equal consideration to children arise primarily in applying the principles to define specific rights.

EQUAL LIBERTY

The first principle requires that all competent individuals enjoy an equal share of basic liberties. Restrictions on a competent adult's liberty are therefore justified only to ensure that the liberty of others is protected. The conclusion that behind the veil of ignorance we would wish, first and foremost, to protect individual liberty follows directly from the starting assumption that individual liberty is a value of the highest order in our society. The additional requirement of *equal* liberty reflects the impartiality engendered by ignorance of our personal characteristics and situation in the Original Position. Putting ourselves in the place of all kinds of (competent) persons in all types of social circumstances, we would recognize and weigh heavily the value to each of having basic freedoms. At the same time we would give little weight to any preferences some persons might have to deny certain freedoms to others (or no weight, if we believe that such preferences are illicit and should not even factor into our deliberations), since such preferences do not constitute important aspects of a person's well-being.

What about incompetent or less competent persons? In light of the fact that we could find ourselves to be such a person, once the veil is lifted, we would seek to ensure for all such persons the greatest amount of liberty possible, but with several qualifications. As with competent adults, we would authorize restrictions on children's liberty in order to ensure the equal liberty of others—that is, to prevent children from harming others, interfering with the self-determining activities of others, or impeding the efficient functioning of institutions or organizations to which they belong (e.g., a school or a family). In addition, though, we would also permit restrictions on children's liberty in order to promote their own overall well-being, for we would reasonably assume that, absent some greater restrictions on their freedom, children would likely cause themselves serious and lasting harm (I leave aside the question whether greater or lesser paternalistic restrictions on adults than presently exist would be appropriate). However, we would sanction paternalistic constraints on our freedom, should we turn out to be a child, *only* to the extent *necessary* to promote our temporal well-being on the whole and in the long run.[5] If we assume that liberty is important to individuals at every stage of their lives (and anyone with children can attest that it is), the interests of children promoted by denying them liberty on paternalistic grounds in a particular instance should be substantial.

Rawls suggests that the only interest that could justify paternalistic denial of liberty to incompetent persons is an interest in more liberty—in other words, an interest in having the greatest possible overall quantity of liberty over the course of a lifetime. I would not rule out in principle the possibility that other, non-liberty-related temporal interests of children could sometimes justify denying them certain liberties, but I do not believe there are any such interests affected by state regulation of their schooling that justify allowing schools to deny them liberty on paternalistic grounds. In particular, as I argued in Chapters 3 and 5, children's interest in a close relationship with their parents, and in their parents' feeling motivated and competent as parents, would not be threatened to any significant degree, if at all, by state imposition of substantial requirements for the content and methods of instruction in religious schools. In any event, the presumption lies in favor of freedom, and the burden rests on those who would deny it to demonstrate the necessity of doing so.

The Basic Liberties Defined

The particular liberties that parties in the Original Position would guarantee are primarily the same as those enshrined in the United States Constitution: freedom of the person (i.e., physical freedom), freedom of association, freedom of thought and expression, freedom of religion, and basic political rights (e.g., to vote and hold office). Freedom of the person entails the freedom to move about, cross borders, and engage in physical activities, such as athletics or sex with other consenting persons, as well as the right not to allow public officials or private persons to harm, restrain, or otherwise violate the integrity of one's physical being. Freedom of thought and expression is the mental analogue of freedom of the person; it includes the freedom to mentally explore the intellectual landscape and to interact verbally with others and a right against others' injuring, restraining, or otherwise violating one's mind and expressive capacities. Religious liberty is really a special instance of both freedom of the person and freedom of thought and expression, insofar as it involves the freedom to act, think, and speak in the special context of religious practice, belief, and expression. Individuals possess a liberty of conscience "when they are free to pursue their moral, philosophical, or religious interests without legal restrictions requiring them to engage or not in any particular form of religious or other practice, and when other men have a legal duty not to interfere."[6]

Political liberty in the Rawlsian scheme does go beyond the rights now provided for by our Constitution and in that respect is a somewhat novel concept. In Rawls's view, an individual's political liberty should not only include the formal right to participate on an equal basis in the electoral process and in the pursuit of political office and to assemble with other persons to discuss political matters. It should also include a positive right to government assistance in securing the preconditions for meaningful exercise of these privileges. This means that a just society would ensure all citizens an education that provides the necessary information and fosters the necessary capacities for political deliberation and for advancing their interests and political views in the political process. Richard Arneson and Ian Shapiro suggest what the content of such an education would be:

> To be able to participate competently in democratic decision-making, voters should have an adequate knowledge of contemporary science in its bearing on public policy issues, an understanding of modern world history and particularly the history of democratic institutions and the culture of their own society, and critical thinking skills that include the ability to represent the situations of others in imagination, to intuit their experience, and sympathetically to analyze and assess their attitudes, principles, and policy arguments. Citizens should have the capacities to keep themselves briefed on current events that are relevant to governmental decisions to be made. In a diverse democracy composed of disparate creeds, faiths, races, worldviews, and concerns, arriving at fair and reasonable decisions about public policy is a task of delicate and complex judgment.[7]

Conservative religious groups would probably not deny the importance—at least for males—of being prepared to engage in political debate; they would be more likely to insist that parents have the right to impress their own political views on their children and to give them only the ability to defend those particular views. In the Original Position, however, the possibility that one might be a child and that one's parents could be of any ideological persuasion would lead one to guarantee for all children an education that promotes a more generalized capacity and a broad understanding of competing political views, since the (self-determining) importance of receiving such an education as a child would be greater than the (other-determining) value of being able to deny such an education to one's own child if one turned out to be a parent when the veil lifted.

These, then, are the particular liberties that persons in the Original Position will want most to ensure for themselves no matter what type of person they may turn out to be. Some actual persons in our society may not deem certain liberties to have preeminent value, perhaps because of religious beliefs that discourage self-expression or political participation or that demand the sacrifice of freedom to a moral authority. But in the Original Position we would nevertheless guarantee equal liberty for all, since all persons have an interest in possessing the basic liberties should they wish at any time to exercise them, and no one suffers as a result of having this option.[8] In any event, the concern here will be with children's liberties. Since children do not enter the world with ideologically based objections to or desires to forgo liberties, it would be rational to assume in the Original Position that if one turns out to be a child, it would be best to have the fullest share of liberty compatible with one's limited but developing abilities as he grows older, as well as an education that develops the capacity for meaningfully exercising these liberties.

Before applying the equal liberty principle to the case of religious schooling, a few words about parental "liberty" are in order. I argued in Chapter 3 that no person's liberty can properly be said to include a right to determine how another person's life should proceed. This argument was based on assumptions concerning the inherent nature and purpose of rights and principled limitations on the notion of moral entitlement. In Chapter 5 I showed how special rights for parents to depart from generally applicable child-rearing norms on the basis of religious liberty were illegitimate because they conflicted with the higher-order principle of equal treatment. The Original Position construct now offers a third means of demonstrating the inappropriateness of parental rights.

Parties in the Original Position are concerned first and foremost to secure protection for the most basic interests of every member of society, since they could turn out to be any one of those members. Because some measure of self-determination is a basic interest in itself and also instrumental in satisfying other basic interests, it would be rational for parties in the Original Position to insist on legal protections for their self-determining acts and decisions as citizens. On the other hand, the ability to control the lives of other people, though strongly desired by many persons in our society, is simply not a basic or fundamental interest in the sense of requiring satisfaction before a person can pursue higher aims in life. When parties in the Original Position consider, moreover, that they might turn out to be one of those persons whom others are likely to want to control—for example, an elderly person, a developmentally disabled person, a member of a minority race, a woman, or a child—and that the persons who seek control over them could hold any one of the diverse conceptions of the good available or could simply be very selfish and mean-spirited individuals, they would rationally conclude that no person should have the right to determine the life of another person and that the freedom to do so should not be guaranteed.

At the same time, one's exercise of even self-determining rights can and often does affect other people, particularly when one is in intimate association with others. Parents and teachers should certainly possess self-determining rights, including rights to freedom of speech and religion, and their exercise of these rights will necessarily influence children. The equal liberty principle provides that competent individuals should enjoy the greatest measure of freedom compatible with others' having an equal freedom, and this suggests that parents' and teachers' self-determining behaviors should be protected so long as they do not result in less liberty for children. This suggests, though, that parents and teachers may be required to give up some measure of their personal liberty as a condition for enjoying the privilege of participating in children's upbringing, For example, they might justifiably be proscribed from expressing sexist views in the presence of children in a way that damages children's self-esteem (i.e., such expression could be deemed to fall within legal definitions of psychological and emotional abuse in child welfare laws now in place), since, as discussed further below, self-esteem is a prerequisite to the meaningful exercise of one's liberties.

Infringements of Children's Liberties in Religious Schools

The implications of the equal liberty principle for children's education depend on the interpretation we give in this context to the basic liberties identified above, taking into account whether any special characteristics of children would lead a person in the Original Position to sanction a lesser or different type of liberty for them, in relation to their education, than adults ordinarily enjoy.

Freedom of the Person

Freedom of the person would proscribe any physical attack on or physical restraint of a student or coercing a student to engage or not engage in any conduct, except as necessary to protect other persons from harm, to allow for the orderly operation of the school, or to promote a greater total liberty for the child over the course of her lifetime. Imposing on students some measure of discipline in conduct is justifiable because the same would be required of adults in an educational setting and because learning self-discipline is necessary to enable students to participate effectively in society as adult citizens with a full measure of individual liberties. However, enforcement of otherwise reasonable codes of conduct by physically striking a child is not justifiable because it is not a necessary means to the desired end of self-discipline; thus, any paddling of students in Fundamentalist schools is a violation of children's right to freedom of the person.

Moreover, imposing a code of conduct that goes beyond what is necessary to prevent students from harming others or disrupting the learning process or to teach self-discipline is not justified. Thus, Catholic and Fundamentalist schools that condemn all playfulness in the school, even outside of class time, Fundamentalist schools that prohibit forms of physical self-expression such as dancing or attending non-Christian music concerts, and A.C.E. schools that confine children to workstations all day thereby violate their students' right to physical freedom unless they can demonstrate that doing so enhances the students' overall liberty. There should be a presumption against their doing these things, which schools could overcome only by providing reliable evidence that the children are in fact better off, in terms of their *temporal* interests, by being so restricted.

The equal liberty principle would also approve of preventing children from engaging in sexual activity that would harm others or that would have worse consequences for them than the denial of sexual freedom—for example, contracting AIDS, becoming pregnant, or suffering serious and lasting psychological harm. Both Catholic and Fundamentalist schools, however, appear to impose on children, with warnings of divine retribution, the belief that *all* pre-marital sexual relations, even between consenting adults, homosexual relations in any context, and even modest forms of affection between boys and girls are sinful. Such haranguing would ordinarily not be deemed to violate an adult's personal liberty, since adults are legally and practically free to avoid and/or disregard it. However, the children in these schools are not able to avoid it and are in general more susceptible than adults to external control of their wills, particularly by adults who occupy positions of authority in their lives. As a result, these moral exhortations by educators effectively prevent many children from freely expressing themselves physically, exploring their sexuality, or even giving affection to others. The equal liberty principle would therefore require a school to demonstrate that condemning *all* sexual activity—including activity short of intercourse and intercourse with appropriate precautions, as well as merely dating—and doing so by threat of divine retribution rather than by respectful discussion of the practical consequences, is necessary to prevent students from making liberty-defeating choices. Unless the school can do this, it is violating the students' right to freedom of the person.

Finally, forcing children to participate in a school's religious activities, such as worship services, if they would prefer not to violates their freedom of the person, since it cannot be liberty-defeating, from a secular perspective, to decline to engage in religious rituals or services. Of course, policing a prohibition against forced worship, and perhaps some of the other suggested prohibitions as well, might be too difficult and too intrusive to benefit the children on the whole, but we can still say that they have a right not to be coerced into being practitioners of any religion.

Liberty of Thought and Expression

Liberty of thought and expression includes the right to consider and discuss any ideas and to express one's opinions to others on religious or any other matters. It also generally includes a right not to be compelled to listen to the speech of others. The equal liberty principle sanctions restrictions on this freedom for adults only so far as is necessary to protect the liberties of other persons (for example, proscription of speech that because of its content diminishes the psychological capacity of others to speak) or to make the shared right of expression meaningful (for example, time, place, and manner restrictions that make it possible for expression by many speakers to take place in an orderly fashion). In the case of children, it would also permit compelling students to attend school and to receive instruction necessary to prepare them for adult life with the full range of individual liberties. It might also sanction some limits on the range of appropriate subjects of discussion and for younger children perhaps even insistence on unquestioning acceptance of some core, nonsectarian social values (e.g., hitting and ridiculing are wrong), in order to train them in the mental self-discipline and mores they will need to participate freely and effectively in our society.[9]

However, squelching all independent thought in matters of faith, personal morality, social policy, or any of the other subjects of study in a school cannot possibly be conducive to students' enjoying a greater overall measure of liberties during their lifetimes, let alone the least restrictive means for securing such enjoyment. Thus, schools that deny students the freedom to question or express a view contrary to what they are being taught, as both Fundamentalist and Catholic schools appear to do, violate the students' liberty of thought and expression. In addition, compulsory religious instruction and religious expression cannot be justified as necessary to promote children's liberty or any other aspect of their temporal well-being, which suggests that religion classes and liturgy in religious schools should be voluntary for students.

Moreover, given children's particular susceptibility to control by adult authority, it seems correct to say that they are denied intellectual liberty not only when schools explicitly prohibit or condemn questioning or disagreement or explicitly command participation in religious instruction or activities, but also when teachers create an environment of fear in the classroom that prevents students from thinking freely and exercising independent judgment. Likewise, degrading treatment that diminishes students' sense of the worth of their own thoughts and opinions effectively denies them intellectual freedom. Thus, if Catholic and Fundamentalist schools, as the evidence suggests, devalue students' interests and opinions in ways likely to diminish the students' sense of self-worth as thinking persons, they violate students' liberty of thought and expression. And when teachers or textbooks convey to female students the belief that they are inferior to males and should be subservient and nonassertive, they violate the intellectual rights of those students. Adults have the right not to be held captive and subjected to degrading treatment, and it is difficult to imagine that denying this same right to children could be justified in secular terms as conducive to their overall well-being.

Political Liberty

As noted above, the basic formulation of political liberty includes certain education rights. In the Original Position, we would want to guarantee for ourselves, no matter who we turn out to be, not only the rights to vote, join political associations, and hold office (at least during that portion of our lifetimes when we are competent to exercise those rights), but also an education that prepares us to exercise these rights intelligently and effectively. This is quite plausible, particularly since adding this component to a school's curriculum should involve little added cost. Thus, in addition to the negative right not to be thwarted in the development of their capacity for reasoned debate on issues of public concern, students should perhaps possess certain positive political rights: a right to be encouraged and trained to deliberate about opposing political views, a right to have and participate in a student government, and a right to form associations with other students and hold meetings on school property outside of instructional periods, with only as much adult supervision as the students request or as is necessary to protect their well-being.

Students' negative political right is violated by religious schooling that mandates rote learning and rigid thinking and that inculcates hostility toward and condemnation and distrust of persons of other faiths or other political outlooks simply because they think differently. Students who receive this sort of schooling may become capable as adults of voting, running for office, and organizing with like-minded persons to push their political agenda onto a party platform or through the legislative process, but they are unlikely to be able to engage in constructive, reasoned, and respectful dialogue with unlike-minded persons in order to resolve differences, reach compromises, or simply achieve mutual understanding in a civil manner. In addition, just as in the case of free expression, schooling that inculcates sexist views clearly has the tendency to undermine the capacity of females to participate fully in public discourse and electoral politics, as well as the capacity of males to engage in respectful dialogue with women on political or any other matters.[10]

Many religious schools do have student governments, but these are more likely to be forums for planning the next bake sale or discussing some other task teachers assign rather than forums for open discussion of issues important to the students. Nor is there any evidence that these schools even welcome, let alone encourage, free discussion of current political issues or uncensored student political organizations. Consequently, they fail to satisfy their students' positive political rights. In addition, Fundamentalist schools that exclude females from positions of leadership or otherwise discourage full participation in student government add injury to insult, undermining in a very concrete way female students' will and ability to participate in the democratic political process.

In sum, Fundamentalist and Catholic schools appear to infringe, in one way or another and to varying degrees, all of the basic liberties that we would guarantee for children if deciding from within the Original Position. Undoubtedly many public schools also violate one or more of their students' liberties, and they should be taken to task for it. Catholic and Fundamentalist parents and school officials might dispute the charge against their schools in at least two ways. First, they might claim that any loss of liberty is more than compensated for by a gain in spiritual well-being for the children. As previously discussed, however, this claim rests on a premise that the state cannot endorse, inasmuch as it embodies particular religious beliefs. Second, they might claim that their children are quite happy with their schooling and that state-mandated changes to curriculum and teaching methods would violate their children's right to the free exercise of religion. The next section addresses that claim.

Religious Schooling As Children's Free Exercise of Religion

I have argued that religious schools constitute an impediment to students' enjoyment of freedom of religion insofar as they stifle any inclinations students have to question the religious beliefs of their parents' community or to discuss or act on beliefs relating to religion that are different from those of the schools' sponsors. Some children in religious schools, though, might never develop such inclinations. Moreover, in any religious school there are undoubtedly some students who would express a sincere preference to remain in that school if presented with the option of changing to another, and probably also some who would echo any religiously based objections their parents have to state regulation or supervision of the school. With respect to these children, significant state control over the methods and content of education in religious schools might itself infringe upon their religious liberty, and the state would be in the position of having to justify *its* restriction of one of the children's basic liberties.

One response to this situation might be to deny that children are capable of exercising religious liberty. This would mean that no action by the state (or by the schools) could infringe upon religious liberty simply by virtue of thwarting the existing preferences of these children relating to religious training. The standard view of developmental psychologists is that children below the stage of formal-operational reasoning, which children normally reach between the ages of twelve and fourteen, are not capable of freely and reflectively choosing a conception of the good and are instead likely to echo their parents' views on religious matters simply on the basis of parental authority.[11] Moreover, children who grow up in a conservative, authoritarian religious environment are likely to reach the stage at which they are capable of independent choice regarding values and religious belief at a later age than other children; research has demonstrated that such an upbringing retards cognitive development.[12]

However, it is not normally part of our conception of religious liberty that one must have arrived at one's beliefs about religion through reflective, informed, and uncoerced rational choice among a range of alternative beliefs, or even simply with awareness that there are alternatives and that one is free to choose. This is, rather, what we ordinarily mean by "autonomy." "Liberty" means simply the freedom to effectuate existing preferences, without legal restriction or interference by others, even if these preferences are not self-originating or viewed by their holder as the product of free choice.[13] It is therefore difficult to deny that children are capable of exercising religious liberty at a very early age, perhaps even before they enter the first grade, or to deny that legal restrictions on the practices of religious schools would infringe the religious liberty of any children who prefer that their school be able to continue its current practices.

What makes us uncomfortable about saying that state regulation designed to protect children's liberty could itself violate the right to religious freedom of some children is, first, that such children most likely do not fully appreciate what is at stake for them and in fact may be entirely uninformed or incapable of understanding what the conflict between the state and their parents is about, and second, that we think the children's choices are irrational. The first concern arguably is not a sufficient reason to override children's preferences; we do not think it appropriate for the state to override adults' religious preferences solely because they are based on ignorance or incompetence, and it is not clear why we should treat children differently in that respect. However, if children's expressed preferences relating to religious practice are clearly irrational, in the sense that effectuating them would result in their suffering greater harm than denying them would cause, then the equal liberty principle would sanction overriding those preferences.

A state could convincingly argue that by requiring some children to receive an education less hostile to their other liberties than the form of education for which they express a preference, it is acting to ensure the children greater total liberty in their lifetimes. The legal changes suggested so far are ones that would eradicate liberty-defeating practices of religious schools—in particular, those that deny children freedom of thought and expression, which is a greater incursion upon a person's liberty than denial of the ability to act upon one's beliefs, as courts routinely point out in free exercise cases. Even students who are not presently inclined to question the religious beliefs they have been taught and who would express opposition to state regulation would have a greater total liberty if given the freedom to change their minds about religion and to think about and discuss alternative views in other areas of their studies as well. Further, forgoing a quality secular education can seriously affect a student's opportunities for careers and other means of fulfillment. It seems clear, therefore, that a child's expressed preference for a kind of schooling that includes the practices described in Chapter 1 would be irrational, and overriding that decision on paternalistic grounds would be appropriate and even morally requisite.

The state might also justify increased regulation as necessary to promote students' interest in religious liberty as adults. Persons who develop an inclination to question inherited religious beliefs later in life but because of admonitions received in childhood suffer severe anxiety at the thought of abandoning those beliefs might plausibly be said to enjoy a lesser measure of religious liberty. External constraints initially introduced in childhood continue to be effective later in life and become internalized constraints on thought and expression. Chapter 1 cited evidence that this is an extremely common experience among adults who were raised in the Fundamentalist or Catholic traditions. Most of the children in Fundamentalist and Catholic schools today can be expected one day to confront the reality of religious pluralism in our society, and as a result of this or some other experience may be induced to ask themselves why they believe what they do and perhaps to consider the merits of competing conceptions of the good. If their schooling has constructed formidable psychological and social barriers—that is, extreme guilt and fear of recrimination—to questioning their religious beliefs, these individuals will effectively be deprived of religious liberty at that later stage of life.

Finally, the state could also justify on nonpaternalistic grounds overriding any student opposition to increased regulation, by pointing out that effectuating the present preferences of those students would entail the continued denial of basic liberties to any fellow students who *are* now inclined to question received views and to act in proscribed, but not necessarily disruptive or irrational, ways. Thus, overriding those preferences (while not denying the students the freedom to hold and express them) may be necessary to ensure equal liberty for all students.

In sum, considerations of justice, as reflected in the first principle chosen in the Original Position, point in favor of regulations designed to eradicate the repressive features of religious schools and to ensure that all schools positively assist their students in acquiring the capacities necessary for full political participation. The regulation necessary to effectuate children's liberties would itself substantially transform many Catholic schools and perhaps all Fundamentalist schools. However, the conclusions thus far do not include a requirement that schools positively assist their students in acquiring the capacities and knowledge necessary for moral autonomy—that is, for making a free and informed selection of a conception of the good from among a range of alternatives. The first principle seems to preclude assaults and unjustified restrictions on the bodies and minds of children in religious schools, as well as discussion of other faiths intended to generate in students fear and hostility toward people who adhere to them, but nothing said thus far indicates that the first principle accords children a positive right to a fully liberal (in a Kantian sense) education.

Religious schools might therefore be able to satisfy the equal liberty principle while teaching their students only about their own respective creeds so long as they did not stifle student-initiated inquiry about other faiths and religious matters and so long as they nurtured in their students the critical and deliberative capacities and the interpersonal skills and attitudes necessary for meaningful exercise of political liberty as adults. They might therefore be able to remain, in a limited way, distinctively proselytizing institutions. Of course, requiring religious schools to nurture certain capacities, skills, and attitudes in relation to political deliberation might lead students to become morally autonomous because of the connections between reasoning about public policy and reasoning about morality and religion. It may be possible, though, for teachers to generate critical thinking about politics, economics, organizational management, and other subjects while also successfully instilling in students the belief that religious matters are of a different order and not properly subject to critical inquiry. In addition, meaningful exercise of a capacity for moral autonomy may require possession of information—for example, in the areas of theology, comparative religions, history, and sociology—that children might not receive in the course of learning to think critically about political issues. In any event, the equal liberty principle itself does not appear to require that schools directly promote moral autonomy.

Equal Opportunity

The second principle of justice is a substantive conception of equal opportunity, requiring that all social positions be equally open to all persons possessing the native talents and abilities suited to the positions. We have reached a consensus in this society that all persons should enjoy a formally equal opportunity to employment and educational programs—that is, that persons equally qualified for a job or school program should receive equal consideration and, if possible, equal treatment; persons should not be given lesser opportunities because of characteristics, such as race or gender, that have no relation to the necessary qualifications.

There is clearly less of a political commitment to a substantive equality of educational opportunity in this country than there is to formally equal employment and educational opportunity, even if one looks only at public schools. Gross disparities remain in the quality of public schools and in the level of resources at their disposal from one state to the next and from one district to the next within states. Few would contend, however, that this is a just situation for the children in the poorer public schools. Opposition to equalizing the quality of public education arises principally from the self-interest of those who would have to pay for it. Most people, it seems, simply do not care that other people's children have an unjust lot in life or at least do not care enough to accept significant sacrifice to redress the situation. In the case of religious schooling, the tendency to neglect the plight of other people's children is compounded by a lack of awareness of what these schools are doing and by a sense that parents alone are responsible for any deprivation their children suffer in a nonpublic school, since they chose to place the children there.

It is in precisely this kind of situation that the Original Position construct is most useful. It compels us to put aside self-interest (or to use it creatively to achieve greater insight) and to overcome our inclination to neglect the plight of those far removed from our own situation. By imagining that we are to occupy various other positions in society, thinking seriously about what we would want for ourselves in each of those positions, and giving the interests of persons in each position weight equal to that given the interests of persons in other positions, we should be able to determine what justice requires for those who are presently disadvantaged in our society.

The outcomes of this thought process are more straightforward regarding use of increased regulation to ensure equal educational opportunity for children in religious schools than they are in the context of public school financing, which has been the subject of most academic debate and litigation over the substantive equality of educational opportunity.[14] Changing the regulatory environment in which religious schools operate would not require a great transfer of wealth from one group to another and in fact would principally require from the rest of us simply a commitment to impose and enforce those regulations necessary to ensure children attending religious schools a roughly equal education. Doing so would likely result in closure of some religious schools, which would in turn increase public school enrollment, but the consequent burden on society of increased public school funding would likely be outweighed by the greater prosperity of a better-educated citizenry.

The real trade-offs are between the life prospects of children in religious schools and the interests of parents and others in their religious communities in directing children's lives in accordance with their religious beliefs and in creating a new generation of believers. If we take a moment to reflect, imagining that tomorrow we will be reborn and that our parents will be members of a religious community that strives to repress the minds of children so that they are incapable of rejecting the community's beliefs or pursuing a life outside the community as adults, we would surely want to have guaranteed for us an education that counteracts this effort, that makes it possible for us to choose and live successfully within other ways of life and systems of belief. Such a guarantee would be of objectively fundamental importance to our lives. The only reason for not wanting such an education would be a belief that the religious tenets of the community were true, but in the Original Position we do not assume any particular religious beliefs to be true. Not knowing whether any possible religious claims are true, parties behind the veil of ignorance rationally would ensure for themselves the opportunities for success in this world that they know they are likely to want, rather than gamble these opportunities away for the radically indeterminate possibility that the particular persons who will be their parents hold true religious beliefs and would choose for them an education that steers them toward other-worldly benefits.

Now we should also imagine that when the veil of ignorance is lifted it will turn out that we are parents who belong to a religious community and who wish to control the mental lives of our children so that they come to believe what we believe. We would want this not only for the satisfaction it would bring us but also because of our love for our children and our desire that they attain salvation. This would be of very great subjective importance to us, but as the discussion of fundamental versus nonfundamental interests in previous chapters found, it cannot plausibly be said to be of objectively fundamental importance to our lives in the sense of being necessary for us to pursue higher aims in life. Our conclusion, after imagining ourselves in both positions, should therefore be that justice requires that the educational needs of children be met and that the state guarantee that they are met. The only plausible *explanations* for why the state does not do so now—a desire to respect the religious preferences of parents and a lack of political will to enforce regulations over the objections of parents—cannot serve as *justifications* because they are inconsistent with what a proper balancing of the respective interests of children and adults would require.

It remains, then, to identify which of the practices described in Chapter 1 effectively deny equal opportunity to children in religious schools. Some of these practices I have already found to be proscribed by the equal liberty principle, which is to say that violations of children's liberties can also result in lesser life prospects for them. For example, persons possessing native talents that suit them for highly complex tasks would suffer a lesser opportunity for self-realization if their schooling severely restricted their freedom of thought and expression. As shown above, the equal liberty principle should not only preclude religious schools from denying freedom in this way but arguably should also require that these schools actively foster deliberative rationality in students in the context of political principles. Fair equality of opportunity would also appear to require that religious schools affirmatively nurture in their students a more generalized capacity for complex and independent thought to the same degree as do other schools, since this capacity is required for an increasing percentage of jobs in today's world. Thus, schools that promote only rote learning and fail to encourage independent thought in many subject areas violate the fair-equality-of-opportunity principle and work an injustice to their students, who will be less able than other persons with the same native abilities to pursue rewarding careers.

Successful pursuit of careers requires not only intellectual skills but also interpersonal skills, knowledge, and self-confidence. Among the interpersonal skills necessary for positions in the mainstream work world is the ability to treat other persons with understanding and respect no matter what their religious beliefs or affiliation, and to take seriously the opinions and views of others. Schools that foster contempt for persons of other faiths and instruct students not to associate with them, and schools that instill a dogmatic disposition, create an obstacle to harmonious interaction with persons outside their faith community. Extreme inflexibility in one's views and an inability to respect the views of others are likely to lead to repeated conflicts. Indeed, even a lack of exposure to alternative ways of life and ideologies handicaps students; this suggests that students may have a right to interscholastic programs that foster understanding of other cultural groups and harmony with persons outside their religious community—a kind of ideological desegregation program.

Schools that instill a dogmatic and intolerant disposition also thereby create an obstacle to students' enjoyment of an equal opportunity for an advanced education. An aversion to associating with persons outside one's faith community severely limits the pool of higher educational institutions that one can attend, certainly eliminating all the best universities in this country. Even for those who are able to attend a college with a heterogeneous student population, despite an aversion to associating with persons holding views different from their own, their experience and performance in courses are likely to be substantially poorer than that of students who are more open to interaction with and more respectful of others and who are capable of free and open discussion of competing viewpoints.

Schools that deny their students access to a substantial body of information, such as standard views on scientific, sociological, and historical matters, or that distort those views seriously handicap their students. They are likely to perform less well than other students on college entrance exams, in college courses, in doing independent research, in interviewing for jobs and establishing connections with professionals, and ultimately in carrying out any jobs they do obtain that require knowledge of such information. It is significant that most state colleges and universities do not accept diplomas from A.C.E. schools as equivalent to high school diplomas.[15] Fair equality of opportunity thus also provides justification for the state's assuming control over the content of what students in religious schools learn in nonreligious subjects.

Self-esteem is also obviously important to success. To have an equal chance at a range of jobs at the highest level for which one is suited, a person requires both a general sense of self-worth and competence and a sense that exercising one's talents through challenging jobs is valuable. Rawls suggests that self-respect is "the most important primary good," one that persons in the Original Position would strive to protect "at almost any cost."[16] Without it, a person may not be able to see anything as worth doing or muster the will to strive for anything in life.

Schools that routinely denigrate children as sinful persons and humiliate them to induce compliance foster a negative general self-image. This causes some students to carry with them throughout their lives a belief that they do not deserve success and so thwarts their ambition and undermines their performance. Schools that teach that assertiveness and creativity reflect sinful pride may effectively prevent students from ever being assertive or creative, because doing so makes them feel worse rather than better about themselves. In addition, inculcating sexist attitudes is clearly antithetical to female students' self-esteem and results in underachievement. These particular teachings about what is good and bad and about the inherent moral worth of persons, which are integral to the religious mission of certain types of schools, thus violate the second principle of justice. Considerations of justice for children, based on judgments about their temporal interests, therefore support state control over the content even of religious instruction in religious schools.

Other potential conflicts between religious education and equal opportunity are also readily identifiable. A person whose greatest native talent is in the artistic realm would need to develop a facility for bodily and/or oral expression in order to have an equal chance at succeeding in the arts. For women in general to enjoy an equal opportunity for careers, many have argued, they must have effective control over their reproductive lives, including knowledge about abortion rights and services and about the use of contraceptives.[17] Carrying severe anxiety and anger in one's person can also interfere with the development of useful relationships and distract one from work. Fair equality of opportunity thus requires not only that schools refrain from repressing children's physical and verbal expression and denigrating their bodies and minds, but also that they actively encourage free self-expression and a positive attitude toward one's body and mind, and that they provide sex education to their students.

Does equal educational opportunity also require that all schools nurture moral autonomy? I have argued that it requires them to foster the capacity for critical, independent thinking generally, which is likely to affect a person's thinking about every aspect of life, and requires them to make students somewhat familiar with the beliefs of other groups in society. Let us assume, however, that schools could foster a generalized intellectual autonomy in students, but that by not encouraging the students to apply that capacity in the moral realm, they would succeed in securing unreflective acceptance of the moral doctrines they teach. Would this violate the equal opportunity principle?

The goal of this principle is simply an equal shot at the best sorts of jobs, measured in terms of the level of income, authority, and self-actualizing possibilities they entail, for which one's native talents are a good fit.[18] Persons behind the veil of ignorance would not feel compelled to ensure that they are prepared to perform *every* job at their proper level but rather merely some job or some subset of jobs at that level. Someone with a very high native intelligence, for example, should be prepared to occupy a range of roles in society that call for and reward high intelligence but need not be prepared to occupy all such roles. This would be impracticable even if it were theoretically possible. And there are undoubtedly occupations at every level of income, authority, and complexity for which moral autonomy is not required.

However, there may be a contingent connection between moral autonomy and self-respect in our society today, and self-respect, as noted previously, is important to one's life prospects and possibly also to one's exercise of liberties. It entails a sense of the value of oneself and one's aims in life, which requires, in part, "finding our person and deeds appreciated and confirmed by others." [19] It is therefore dependent to a substantial degree upon one's social environment; whether we value our own aims turns in large part on what others whose opinion matters to us appreciate, value, and respect. Parties in the Original Position would take into account that "their confidence in the value of their own system of ends cannot withstand the indifference much less the contempt of others." [20] Of course, it is not necessary that the entire society positively value a person's plan of life. A person might receive sufficient support for her plan of life so long as the smaller communities to which she belongs affirm the worth of her activities. However, it is also important to a person's self-esteem that her plan of life not be scorned by the bulk of the larger society to which she belongs. [21]

I wish merely to suggest that, in mainstream American culture today, moral autonomy may be a necessary precondition for social respect. The great majority of those who populate this culture tend to regard negatively adults who appear not to possess this attribute. This is evident in the readiness of many to disparage those who espouse ideologies or engage in practices for which they can give no reason other than an appeal to authority internal to their belief system. We may confront them, ridicule them, or simply look askance at them for their blind adherence to the dictates of authority or imitation of others. This negative regard may be strongest among highly educated liberals (who, so it is said, control the mainstream media), but less educated persons and political conservatives, if they do not themselves belong to a religious community that disavows self-determination in the realm of morality, are also likely to condemn unreflective dogmatism when they perceive it.

This attitude must pose a self-respect problem for any individual who participates in mainstream American life—for example, by working in a plant or office with persons of diverse backgrounds and beliefs, by getting involved in politics at a level that brings together diverse constituencies, or by receiving information through the mainstream media—but who is not, or is not perceived to be, morally autonomous. The aftermath of the Scopes Trial in the 1920s, with widespread ridicule of the Fundamentalist Christians who opposed the teaching of evolution, led Fundamentalists to withdraw almost entirely from the political realm. Their reappearance on the political landscape in the 1980s generated fear and hostility on the part of mainstream Americans, liberal and conservative. The backlash against them triggered complaints by Fundamentalists and even some mainstream scholars that they were being denied their place in our democracy, silenced in the public sphere. Some see this as a matter of fairness to persons with religious outlooks, but I see it as a problem for the education of their children. Knowing that these children will incur the scorn of mainstream America if they grow up to be like their parents, why do we not act to prevent that, for their sake, rather than expect mainstream Americans to develop a respect for people who argue dogmatically for reactionary policies based upon religious premises we do not share?

We should also consider, when thinking about how to ensure self-respect for all persons in the Original Position, the self-respect of parents. In a perfectly just society, parents would not wish to deny their children anything important to their well-being and so would not oppose or feel threatened by the school regulations proposed here. In the nonideal world of today, however, mandating a transformation of their children's education in ways directly contrary to the parents' religious beliefs would certainly make the parents feel disrespected, which in turn could undermine their self-respect. This is a serious concern but one clearly outweighed by the needs of the present and succeeding generations of children. We should not perpetuate a problem in order to avoid short-term costs, particularly if the latter can be ameliorated by other means. Allowing parents to deny their children a liberal education may allow them to preserve their sense of dominion, but it prevents our society from advancing to a point where *all* persons would have an equal chance for self-respect, and it preserves an ideology that is incompatible with justice toward children.

Fair equality of opportunity, if legally enforced, would thus effect a substantial transformation of many religious schools, beyond what is required by the equal liberty principle. It would require schools to foster a much broader intellectual autonomy, to refrain from instilling intolerant or dogmatic attitudes, and to impart considerable knowledge, including mainstream views in secular subjects and basic information about other faiths and cultures. The equal opportunity analysis may also have implications for affirmative action programs today; any graduates of religious schools as they are presently constituted who do develop ambitions for careers that require higher-order thinking skills and extensive knowledge may be at a great disadvantage in pursuing those careers when compared with persons who have equivalent native talents and abilities and received a high-quality liberal education. The "cognitive handicap" with which these graduates struggle may very well be a greater obstacle to success than that which most current beneficiaries of affirmative action programs have had to overcome. Arguably, then, employers and universities should give preferential treatment to graduates of conservative religious schools who seek to rise above their social situation and to overcome the disabilities their schooling inflicted on them.

Conclusion

Constructing a positive theory of state policy toward religious education is inevitably an extremely complex undertaking. The Rawlsian decision-making model of the Original Position has proven a very useful framework for accomplishing this task, yielding a number of definite conclusions and clarifying the values at stake. Since it is a theory that many modern liberals find compelling, applying it to the case of religious schooling offers the prospect of generating a broad consensus on appropriate public policy in this area.

The basic conclusion of Chapter 6 is that a number of features of Fundamentalist and Catholic schools (as described in Chapter 1) violate basic principles of justice. Excessive restrictions on children's physical and intellectual freedom violate the equal liberty principle, as does a failure to foster in students a capacity for rational deliberation on political issues. Failure to nurture in students the skills and knowledge needed to enjoy an equal chance at occupations for which their native abilities suit them violates the fair-equality-of-opportunity requirement. And practices that directly impair students' self-respect, including inculcation of sexist beliefs and denigration of children and their individual interests and perspectives, violate both the equal liberty principle and the fair-equality-of-opportunity requirement, since persons require self-respect in order to exercise their liberties and to succeed in a fulfilling career. It is not clear whether the schools' failure to foster moral autonomy violates either of these principles. If moral autonomy is a necessary precondition of self-respect for participants in mainstream American culture, then states should require all schools to promote it.

Rawls scholars may wish to contrast the conclusions I have reached by developing and applying Rawls's model of justice in the specific context of religious education with the position Rawls himself has recently taken regarding the requirements for children's education in conservative religious communities. As noted in the introduction, Rawls has been pushed, by liberal clamorings about the seeming intolerance of nonliberal beliefs and ways of life in his theory, to a minimalist view of what society can expect of parents in these communities. He now would impose only the following two requirements for the education of children within religious sects: (1) that it provide children with "knowledge of their constitutional and civic rights," including their right to exit the sect when they become adults if they so choose, and (2) that it "prepare them to be fully cooperating members of society and enable them to be self-supporting," by encouraging in them "the political virtues so that they want to honor the fair terms of social cooperation in their relations with the rest of society."[22]

Schools might satisfy the first requirement by informing children of their legal rights while also informing them that they will burn in hell and be ostracized from their community should they ever elect to exercise their legal right to leave the faith and while repressing the children's minds and bodies in all the ways described in Chapter 1. The second requirement is somewhat more demanding. It would require that all schools teach their students the rationality for them of obeying the social rules that emanate from a scheme of pure procedural justice. Rawls appears to intend that schools teach children to understand and appreciate the liberal political conception of justice, to recognize the equal claim of all citizens to the liberties and other social goods that the sect members demand for themselves, and thereby to perceive the benefits and fairness of the scheme of social cooperation in place in the just society. To accomplish this would probably require nurturing in children a respect for others as equal citizens and a capacity for rational deliberation about various possible political systems. The requirement that sects prepare the children in their midst to be self-supporting would generate an additional restriction on religious instruction, precluding the channeling of girls into adult lives of dependency on men.

Even with this more demanding second requirement, however, Rawls does not appear to rule out forms of education that (1) repress physical and verbal expression and stifle intellectual inquiry in nonpolitical subject areas, (2) discourage students from ever invoking rights against persons who hold authority within their religious community, (3) teach children that persons outside their church community, though equal as citizens, are inferior as moral persons and are condemned to eternal damnation, (4) teach children that females, though equal before the law and capable of being self-supporting, are inferior to males in God's eyes, and (5) teach children that all desires of the flesh and desires to enjoy the culture of the larger society are sinful and lead to damnation. In other words, this requirement preserves some measure of political liberty and liberty of thought and expression but goes no further to protect children's basic liberties, opportunities, or psychological well-being.

Rawls does note that in practice it might be quite difficult for schools to make a distinction between the political and the nonpolitical, and thus modes of thought learned in one realm might carry over to the other. This seems a slender reed on which to hang the intellectual autonomy of children, however, and it is troubling that Rawls actually sees this potential for slippage as cause for regret.[23] It is also troubling that the apparent reason that Rawls scaled back his formal demands regarding education within religious sects in recent years is that his primary concern is for adults who "wish to lead their common life apart from" the modern world and its "unwanted influences."[24] He appears only secondarily concerned for children's "role as future citizens," and he manifests no concern for the well-being or equal claim to justice of the children in these sects.

As explained in Chapters 3 and 4, this concern about tolerating illiberal conceptions of the good cannot properly translate into sanctioning illiberal treatment of children, who themselves are not choosing to opt out of the modern world or liberal democratic society. Toleration should mean respect for atypical modes of *self*-determination, not for anyone's desire to determine the lives of other people. Moreover, the notion that until a person emerges as an adult into the world of electoral politics and public discourse on political matters, she is outside the political realm is simply fallacious; thus the assumption that a theory of justice need be concerned about children only as "future citizens" is unwarranted. In one way or another, the law determines the contours of a child's life, either by authorizing agents of the state to assume responsibility for certain aspects of that life or by explicitly or implicitly granting parents control over it. A complete political conception of justice must therefore account for every aspect of a child's upbringing. This chapter has aimed to take a first step toward that end.

Conclusion

This book began with a concern that millions of children in this country are presently attending schools whose pedagogical practices harm them in serious ways. The harm could be characterized in the most general terms as a severe repression of their minds and bodies. One purpose of the book was to demonstrate the inappropriateness of the current, adult-centered legal and standard academic approaches to determining what legal protections children should have against harmful child-rearing practices. Judges, legislators, and theorists under the thrall of the notion that parents have a fundamental right to raise their biological offspring and to do so as they see fit, or that in a liberal society toleration requires deference to the religious or cultural preferences of parents or communities regarding children's lives, are failing to treat children as equal persons. An appropriate analytical framework would accord rights in connection with child rearing only to children themselves, who alone have fundamental interests at stake. It would determine the proper scope of parental freedom or community discretion, on the one hand, and of state control, on the other, in connection with children's upbringing by weighing the costs and benefits to children of various legal rules and practical outcomes. This approach would not make children "creatures of the state," as many liberals and conservatives have long assumed is the only alternative to strong parental rights. Rather, it would effectuate the belief that children are no one's creatures.

I explored the implications of this alternative framework only in the context of religious schooling, but it also has implications for legal treatment of other religious or cultural child-rearing practices. For example,

I believe it would require eliminating all religious exemptions to laws mandating medical care for children. Religious groups that believe it sinful to seek medical treatment would nevertheless be required to secure medical care for their children for any significant illness or injury and would be required to have their children immunized against more serious contagious diseases. Moreover, the implications of the approach I urge extend beyond disputes involving minority child-rearing norms to reach every aspect of the law governing child rearing. The determination whether and when to charge parents with abuse or neglect, to remove a child from parents' custody, and to terminate foster care and place a child for adoption would be based on the best interests of the child rather than on rights of the parents. The best-interest standard would also be extended in custody cases to govern not only disputes between biological parents but also disputes between a biological parent and a psychological parent.

The second purpose of the book was to construct a positive theory of what children are entitled to in connection with their education. The first part of that theory built upon a principle of formal equality and determined that the state should not discriminate among children based upon the ideological beliefs of their parents in extending legal protections and other benefits. Religious objectors' children have a fundamental right to equality before the law, and the current failure of states and the federal government to apply to religious schools the same regulations they apply to other schools is a clear violation of this right. The second part of the theory employed an egalitarian liberal framework to determine what substantive rights children should have in connection with their schooling, and concluded that religious (or other schools) violate children's rights when they deny children basic liberties or a fair equality of opportunity for pursuit of fulfilling careers.

These conclusions suggest that states not only must extend current regulations governing public schools—including teacher certification requirements, curricular and teaching guidelines, antisexism measures, and prohibitions of corporal punishment—to cover religious schools as well. They must also fashion new regulations to deal with harmful practices that exist (or at least are now constitutionally permitted to exist) only in religious schools, such as compelling religious expression and practice, teaching secular subjects from a religious perspective, denigrating persons of other faiths, and making children's sense of security and self-worth depend on being "saved" or meeting unreasonable, divinely ordained standards of conduct.

The objection will be made that such extensive regulation of religious

schools would so radically alter their nature as to make them un-
recognizable as Fundamentalist or Catholic (or Jewish or Muslim) institutions. The changes would certainly be radical for Fundamentalist
schools and substantial for most Catholic schools. That Fundamentalist
and Catholic schooling as presently constituted would no longer exist
should not, however, be cause for mourning, at least not for anyone who
respects the personhood of children. It should rather be cause for cele-
bration, because any form of schooling that systematically violates the
rights of children should not exist. That said, an ideal set of school regulations would not preclude the existence of distinctively religious
schools altogether. It would allow for religious instruction (subject to
certain restrictions on content), prayer, and religious ceremonies in private schools, so long as children were genuinely free not to participate.
There are undoubtedly some liberal religious schools in existence today,
including some Catholic schools, that would have to adjust very little to
comply with such regulations.

A related objection is that enforcing such extensive regulation of the
content and methods of instruction in religious schools would inti-
mately involve state actors in the operation of those schools. Such involvement would conflict with the principle of church-state separation,
thereby implicating the Establishment Clause of the First Amendment,
and would generate fierce resistance from parents and church leaders.
As for church-state separation, government entanglement in religious
institutions should not be viewed as raising Establishment Clause concerns when the entanglement clearly inhibits an institution's religious
cause rather than advancing it, and does so to advance secular aims
rather than to promote the cause of another religion. In such cases, the
entanglement should be viewed solely as a potential violation of the
Free Exercise Clause, and I have demonstrated that there are no free exercise rights at stake in connection with religious schooling. As for resistance, it is undoubtedly true that to protect the interests of children
and avoid having to put parents in jail, states must take a very gradual
approach to effecting change. I have offered a vision of what educational
rights children should have, as a goal toward which states should strive,
and will close by suggesting what steps a state might now undertake toward reaching that goal.

As a first step, states should require that all schools obtain state approval in order to operate. Requirements for approval should include, at
a minimum, that teachers in the schools have state certification, that
schools use only approved instructional materials for secular subjects,

and that they submit to periodic unannounced visits by state education officials. States could then use their power to control teacher training and curricular materials to influence what and how teachers in all schools instruct their pupils. They could require, as states now typically do, that persons seeking teacher certification have received training that discourages practices the state deems harmful to children and that shows them how to promote children's self-expressive and rational capacities. States could also make adherence to a code of professional conduct a condition for teachers' retaining their certification. Focusing their efforts on teachers would enable the states to have the greatest influence on religious schools while requiring the least overt intrusion into the schools.

Nevertheless, past experience makes clear that such a change in the laws governing religious schools would generate fierce resistance. The hope is that persons who are committed to, and fully understand the implications of, the fundamental principles of a liberal society will come to understand the appropriateness and moral necessity of making this change and muster the political will to overcome such resistance. At the same time, of course, we should make every reasonable effort to minimize such resistance and to avoid adverse effects from the change on the self-respect of parents and children. For example, in addition to an incremental and "least intrusive means" approach to transforming religious schools, providing parents with tuition subsidies—through tax credits or vouchers—might go a long way toward gaining their acceptance of and cooperation with the changes. In my view, this should not present an Establishment Clause problem; so long as religious schools further the state's aim of providing a high quality secular education to children and have no practices inconsistent with the temporal well-being of their students, the state should be free to let public funds be used to pay for children to attend these schools, just as it allows public funds to be used to pay for medical treatment at hospitals operated by religious orders. Needless, to say, the state should attempt to engage parents and religious community leaders in dialogue concerning proposed changes and should do anything it can to communicate to them, and to the larger society, that the actions it is taking are not motivated by hostility toward any group of adults but rather by respect and concern for the children in their care.

As was the case with school desegregation, though, it may be that change can only come about, if at all, through litigation and enforcement of court orders; legislatures may continue to prove too sensitive to the threats of religious groups and too insensitive to the just claims of children. If there will ever be a day when children in religious schools enjoy the same legal protections that children in public schools enjoy, and enjoy equal educational opportunity, it will no doubt be in the far distant future. That no one has ever before asserted their educational rights in a legal forum is cause for regret and even shame, but also cause for hope that when someone does so, the legal foundation on which the institution of religious schooling in its present form now rests will begin to crumble.

Notes

Chapter 1. Catholic and Fundamentalist Schooling Today

1. For citations to the state education statutes discussed in this section, and to the secondary materials on which the description of religious school regulation below relies, see James G. Dwyer, "The Children We Abandon: Religious Exemptions to Child Welfare and Education Laws As Denials of Equal Protection to Children of Religious Objectors," *North Carolina Law Review* 74 (1996): 1321–1478.

2. Cal. Educ. Code § 44790 (West 1993).

3. Cal. Educ. Code § 60200(h) (West Supp. 1996).

4. Cal. Educ. Code § 51201.5 (West 1993).

5. 20 U.S.C. § 1681 (West 1997). The implementing regulations, however, exclude sexist textbooks and curricular materials from their coverage. 34 C.F.R. § 106.42 (1995).

6. See 20 U.S.C. § 7231 et seq. (West 1997). But see Barbara Anne Murphy, "Education: An Illusion for Women," *Southern California Review of Law and Women's Studies* 3 (1993): 19–108 (arguing that both Title IX and the Women's Educational Equity Act are inadequate means of addressing sexism in education).

7. Wash. Rev. Code Ann. § 28A.640.020(1) (West Supp. 1996). Other states with such provisions include Alaska, California, Florida, Nebraska, and Rhode Island. Alaska Stat. § 14.18.030, 14.18.060 (West 1996); Cal. Educ. Code §§ 40, 45, 220, 230, 51500, 51501, 60040, 60044 (West 1989); Fla. Stat. § 228.2001(1)(e) (West 1997); Neb. Rev. Stat. § 79-3003 (1994); R.I. Gen. Laws § 16-38-1.1 (1988).

8. Ill. Comp. Stat. Ann. ch. 105, para. 5/27–20.5 (West 1993). See also Cal. Educ. Code § 51204.5 (West 1989); Fla. Stat. § 228.2001(4) (West 1997), requiring public schools to develop and implement strategies for increasing

participation of female students in programs and courses in which they traditionally have been underrepresented.

9. Some of the many sources for these empirical conclusions are Joanne H. Meehl, *The Recovering Catholic: Personal Journeys of Women Who Left the Church* (Amherst, N.Y., 1995, pp. 69–98); Peggy Orenstein, *School Girls: Young Women, Self-Esteem, and the Confidence Gap* (New York, 1994); Janice Streitmatter, *Toward Gender Equity in the Classroom: Everyday Teachers' Beliefs and Practices* (Albany, N.Y., 1994), pp. 57, 61, 66; Lyn Yates, *The Education of Girls: Policy, Research and the Question of Gender* (Hawthorn, Victoria, 1993), pp. 35–41 ; Murphy, "Education: An Illusion for Women," in *How Schools Shortchange Girls*, ed. American Association of University Women Educational Foundation (Washington, D.C., 1992); Sharyl Bender Peterson and Mary Alyce Lach, "Gender Stereotypes in Children's Books: Their Prevalence and Influence on Cognitive and Affective Development," *Gender and Education* 2 (1990): 185, 194; Anne O'Brien Carelli, ed., *Sex Equity in Education: Readings and Strategies* (Springfield, Ill., (1988), pp. 25, 26; Dale Spender and Elizabeth Sarah, eds., *Learning to Lose: Sexism and Education* (London, 1988); and Michael Marland, ed., *Sex Differentiation and Schooling* (London, 1983).

10. See Edward B. Fiske, "America's Test Mania," *New York Times*, 10 April 1988, sec. 12 (Education Supp.), pp. 16, 19, col. 2; Robert J. Sternberg, "Misunderstanding Meaning, Users Overrely on Scores," *Education Week*, 23 September 1987, 28, 22 .

11. Cal. Educ. Code § 221 (West 1994); Ky. Rev. Stat. Ann. § 344.555(1)(b) (West 1997).

12. See Data Research Inc., *Private School Law in America*, 7th ed., (Rosemount, Minn., 1996), p. 36; Note, "The Latest Home Education Challenge: The Relationship Between Home Schools and Public Schools," *North Carolina Law Review* 74 (1996): 1913–16.

13. See Data Research Inc., *Private School Law*, pp. 300–20, 345; John D. Colombo, "Why Is Harvard Tax-Exempt? (And Other Mysteries of Tax Exemption for Private Educational Institutions)," *Arizona Law Review* 35 (1993): 845–47, 855–56.

14. Sources for the description of Fundamentalist schools presented here include Edward T. Babinsky, *Leaving the Fold: Testimonies of Former Fundamentalists* (Amherst, N.Y. 1995); Alfred Darnell and Darren E. Sherkat, "The Impact of Protestant Fundamentalism on Educational Attainment," *American Sociological Review* 62 (1997): 306–15; Peter P. Deboer, *The Wisdom of Practice: Studies of Teaching in Christian Elementary and Middle Schools* (Lanham, Md., 1989); Ed Doerr and Albert J. Menendez, "Should Tax Dollars Subsidize Bigotry?" *Phi Delta Kappan* (October 1992): 165–67; Mary Beth Gehrman, "Reading, Writing, and Religion," *Free Inquiry* (fall 1987): 12–18; Albert J. Menendez, *Visions of Reality: What Fundamentalist Schools Teach* (New York, 1993); Paul F. Parsons, *Inside America's Chris-*

tian Schools (Macon, Ga., 1987); Alan Peshkin, "Fundamentalist Christian Schools: Should They Be Regulated?" *Educational Policy* 3 (1989): 45–56; Alan Peshkin, *God's Choice: The Total World of a Fundamentalist Christian School* (Chicago, 1986); Susan D. Rose, *Keeping Them Out of the Hands of Satan: Evangelical Schooling in America* (London, 1988); Melinda Ballar Wagner, *God's Schools: Choice and Compromise in American Society* (New Brunswick, N.H., 1990); and Marlene Winell, *Leaving the Fold: A Guide for Former Fundamentalists and Others Leaving Their Religion* (Oakland, Cal., 1993).

15. Sources for the description of Catholic schools presented here include Nancy Lesko, *Symbolizing Society: Stories, Rites, and Structure in a Catholic High School* (Philadelphia, 1988); Peter McLaren, *Schooling As a Ritual Performance: Towards a Political Economy of Educational Symbols and Gestures* (London, 1986); Patrick H. McNamara, *Conscience First, Tradition Second: A Study of Young American Catholics* (Albany, N.Y., 1992); Meehl, *The Recovering Catholic*; and Gary Schwartz, *Beyond Conformity or Rebellion: Youth and Authority in America* (Chicago, 1987).

16. United States Department of Education, National Center for Education Statistics, *Digest of Education Statistics: 1996* (Washington, D.C. 1996), pp. 12, 72; Mary Mahar, ed., *NCEA/Ganley's Catholic Schools in America* (Montrose, Colo., 1996), p. 13.

17. Kline Capps and Carl H. Esbeck, "The Use of Government Funding and Taxing Power to Regulate Religious Schools," *Journal of Law & Education* 14 (1985): 554 n. 5.

18. A distant third in enrollment are Lutheran schools, followed by Jewish schools, and, in uncertain order, Seventh Day Adventist, Episcopal, Calvinist, Quaker, Mennonite, Assembly of God, and Greek Orthodox schools. James and Levin, *Comparing Public and Private Schools*, p. 33.

19. *The Concise Columbia Encyclopedia*, s.v. "Fundamentalism."

20. Harold Bloom, *The American Religion: The Emergence of the Post-Christian Nation* (New York, 1992), p. 222.

21. Ibid., pp. 221–32. See also Robert N. Bellah et al., *Habits of the Heart: Individualism and Commitment in American Life* (New York, 1985), pp. 231–32, 244.

22. See, e.g., Dalton Farrell Ham, "Reasons Why Parents Enroll Their Children in Fundamentalist Christian Schools and Why Churches Sponsor Them" (Ed.D. dissertation, University of Missouri, 1982), pp. 43, 64–66. This appears to be the case in other countries as well. See, e.g., Cathy Speck and David Prideaux, "Fundamentalist Education and Creation Science," *Australian Journal of Education* 37 (1993): 279.

23. Speck and Prideaux, "Fundamentalist Education," pp. 283–84.

24. Parsons, *Inside America's Christian Schools*, p. 72.

25. Speck and Prideaux, "Fundamentalist Education," p. 284.

26. Ibid., pp. 285–86, 288–90, 292–93; Menendez, *Visions of Reality*.

27. See Gehrman, "Reading, Writing, and Religion," p. 14.

28. Speck and Prideaux, "Fundamentalist Education," p. 284.

29. Figures in this paragraph derive from Mahar, *NCEA/Ganley's Catholic Schools in America*, pp. 16–21.

30. See Ham, *Why Parents Enroll Their Children*, p. 78 (quoting Paul Kienal).

31. Peshkin, "Fundamentalist Christian Schools," p. 48.

32. See Gehrman, "Reading, Writing, and Religion," p. 18.

33. Rose, *Keeping Them Out of the Hands of Satan*, p. 162.

34. Wagner, *God's Schools*, p. 50.

35. Schwartz, *Beyond Conformity*, p. 151.

36. McLaren, *Schooling As a Ritual Performance*, p. 207.

37. Ibid., p. 178.

38. Ibid., p. 228.

39. Ibid., p. 163.

40. Ibid., p. 217.

41. Meehl, *The Recovering Catholic*, p. 60. See also ibid., chap. 1 and pp. 54, 59, 67, and 88.

42. Gehrman, "Reading, Writing, and Religion," p. 16.

43. McLaren, *Schooling As a Ritual Performance*, pp. 151, 152.

44. Ibid., p. 144.

45. Meehl, *The Recovering Catholic*, pp. 28–29.

46. Ibid., p. 59.

47. Peshkin, *God's Choice*, p. 238.

48. Ibid., p. 127.

49. Ibid., pp. 101, 175.

50. Rose, *Keeping Them Out of the Hands of Satan*, p. 179. See also Speck and Prideaux, "Fundamentalist Education," pp. 288–93; Peshkin, "Fundamentalist Christian Schools," pp. 49, 50.

51. Wagner, *God's Schools*, p. 23.

52. Rose, *Keeping Them Out of the Hands of Satan*, pp. 132, 139–40, 176.

53. Ibid., p. 179. See also Winell, *Leaving the Fold*, p. 80. ("Thinking in ways that are contrary to orthodox doctrine is dangerously sinful. Therefore, believers are taught techniques to prevent too much independent thinking.").

54. Peshkin, *God's Choice*, pp. 55, 141.

55. Menendez, *Visions of Reality*, pp. 3, 144.

56. Peshkin, *God's Choice*, pp. 55, 141, 190 (citation omitted).

57. Menendez, *Visions of Reality*, p. 3. See also Wagner, *God's Schools*, pp. 157, 159.

58. Ibid. (1986), p. 59.

59. Rose, *Keeping Them Out of the Hands of Satan*, p. 107; Peshkin, "Fundamentalist Christian Schools," p. 48.

60. Parsons, *Inside America's Christian Schools*, p. 135. See also Deboer, *The Wisdom of Practice*, p. 138.

61. Deboer, *The Wisdom of Practice*, p. 138.

62. Peshkin, *God's Choice*, pp. 219–20.

63. Ibid., p. 175.

64. Gary B. Melton, "Decision Making by Children: Psychological Risks and Benefits," *Children's Competence to Consent*, ed. Gary B. Melton, Gerald P. Koocher, and Michael J. Saks (New York, 1983), p. 27.

65. Rose, *Keeping Them Out of the Hands of Satan*, p. 179.

66. Ibid., pp. 144, 175, 179, 200–204.

67. Darnell and Sherkat, "The Impact of Protestant Fundamentalism," pp. 310, 313; Speck and Prideaux, "Fundamentalist Education," pp. 291–93.

68. McLaren, *Schooling As a Ritual Performance*, p. 182.

69. Ibid., pp. 183, 212.

70. Schwartz, *Beyond Conformity*, pp. 165–67.

71. Ibid., pp. 151, 153.

72. See, e.g., William Sander and Anthony C. Krautmann, "Catholic Schools, Dropout Rates and Educational Attainment," *Economic Inquiry* 33 (1995): 219.

73. Peshkin, "Fundamentalist Christian Schools," p. 50.

74. See Gehrman, "Reading, Writing, and Religion," p. 18.

75. See June Louin Tapp and Gary B. Melton, "Preparing Children for Decision Making: Implications of Legal Socialization Research," in *Children's Competence*, p. 228.

76. See Gehrman, "Reading, Writing, and Religion," p. 17.

77. See Menendez, *Visions of Reality*, p. 25.

78. See Wagner, *God's Schools*, p. 159.

79. Peshkin, *God's Choice*, p. 136.

80. Parsons, *Inside America's Christian Schools*, p. 135.

81. Menendez, *Visions of Reality*, p. 148.

82. Peshkin, *God's Choice*, p. 108.

83. Ibid., p. 121.

84. Menendez, *Visions of Reality*, p. 4.

85. Ibid., p. 187; Peshkin, "Fundamentalist Christian Schools," p. 53.

86. Ibid., p. 290.

87. Menendez, *Visions of Reality*, p. 3.

88. Peshkin (1986), p. 296.

89. McNamara, *Conscience First*, p. 109.

90. See Schwartz, *Beyond Conformity*, p. 163.

91. Wagner, *God's Schools*, pp. 84, 85; Winell, *Leaving the Fold*, pp. 20, 73–75.

92. Peshkin, *God's Choice*, pp. 223, 234, 237, 245.

93. Meehl, *The Recovering Catholic*, p. 77.

94. McLaren, *Schooling As a Ritual Performance*, pp. 168, 179.

95. Meehl, *The Recovering Catholic*, p. 50.

96. Ibid., p. 47.

97. Peshkin, *God's Choice*, p. 137.

98. Meehl, *The Recovering Catholic*, p. 71.

99. Judith Blake, "Catholicism and Fertility: On Attitudes of Young Americans," *Population and Development Review* 10 (1984): 337.

100. Meehl, *The Recovering Catholic* , p. 34.

101. Parsons, *Inside America's Christian Schools*, p. 34; Rose, *Keeping Them Out of the Hands of Satan*, p. 186.

102. Peshkin, *God's Choice*, pp. 125–26.

103. Ibid., pp. 152, 219, 246, 286.

104. Ibid., p. 120.

105. Ibid., p. 231.

106. Winell, *Leaving the Fold*, pp. 18, 21, 200–201.

107. Meehl, *The Recovering Catholic*, p. 43.

108. Ibid., p. 44.

109. Schwartz, *Beyond Conformity*, pp. 157, 191. See also McNamara, *Conscience First*, pp. 119–20.

110. Schwartz, *Beyond Conformity*, p. 175.

111. Bernard Lubin, Lisa Terre, and Eros DeSouza, "Comparison of Public and Parochial School Patterns of Student Affect," *Adolescence* 27 (1992): 413.

112. Meehl, *The Recovering Catholic*, p. 54.

113. Ibid., pp. 28–29, and ch. 9; Schwartz, *Beyond Conformity*, p. 191.

Chapter 2. The Constitutional Backdrop

1. See Denise M. Bainton, "State Regulation of Private Religious Schools and the State's Interest in Education," *Arizona Law Review* 25 (1983): 192; Parsons, *Inside America's Christian Schools*, pp. 146–50.

2. Wesley Newcomb Hohfeld, "Fundamental Legal Conceptions As Applied in Judicial Reasoning," *Yale Law Journal* 23 (1913): 30–36.

3. Hohfeld's taxonomy of legal relations included several other terms as well, and some facets of parents' legal position could be characterized using these terms instead of or in addition to "right" and "privilege." For example, parents' decision-making authority with respect to their children's education could be characterized as a "power" to determine the duties (of noninterference or of assistance) that the state owes to the parents or their children. Parents' ability under the Constitution to resist state-imposed limitations on their control over children's lives could be characterized as an immunity against state legislative alterations of the parents' existing statutory or common-law rights. Courts and the general public, however, typically use the term "rights" to denote all the protections—including any powers or immunities—that parents enjoy against limitation of their behavior and authority in connection with child rearing (and this usage does not conflate concepts that need to be kept distinct in the analysis that fol-

lows), so I do the same. The critical distinction is between those things captured by the term "right" and what I wish to denote by the term "privilege." The latter includes not only a "mere" freedom to act, but also what Hohfeld termed "liability" (or the absence of an immunity) to having one's legal relations with the state altered—for example, by having one's freedom to act or one's power to decide curtailed. I believe "privilege" serves as a useful shorthand, one consistent with popular understanding of the term, for the situation of having no basis for objecting on one's own behalf to the state's restricting one's actions or authority.

4. 262 U.S. 390 (1923).

5. 268 U.S. 510 (1925).

6. 273 U.S. 284 (1927).

7. 321 U.S. 158 (1944).

8. 406 U.S. 205 (1972).

9. E.g., Mozert v. Hawkins County Board of Educ., 827 F. 2d 1058, 1067 (6th Cir. 1987), *cert. denied*, 484 U.S. 1066 (1988); Blackwelder v. Safnauer, 689 F. Supp. 106, 135 (N.D. N.Y. 1988), *appeal dismissed*, 866 F. 2d 548 (2d Cir. 1989).

10. E.g., New Life Baptist Church Academy v. Town of E. Longmeadow, 666 F. Supp. 293 (D. Mass. 1987); Moody v. Cronin, 484 F. Supp. 270 (C.D. Ill. 1979); Kentucky State Bd. for Elementary Secondary Educ. v. Rudasill, 589 S.W.2d 877 (Ky. 1979), *cert. denied*, 446 U.S. 938 (1980); State v. LaBarge, 357 A.2d 121 (Vt. 1976); State v. Whisner, 351 N.E.2d 750 (Ohio 1976); In re Green, 292 A.2d 387 (Pa. 1972).

11. See James G. Dwyer, "The Children We Abandon: Religious Exemptions to Child Welfare and Education Laws As Denials of Equal Protection to Children of Religious Objectors," *North Carolina Law Review* 74 (1996): 1345–46.

12. Ibid., p. 1350.

13. 368 N.W.2d 74 (Iowa 1985).

14. 885 F.2d 940 (1st Cir. 1989).

15. 368 N.W.2d 74, 82 n.2 (Iowa 1985) (describing decision of trial court).

16. 351 N.E.2d 750 (Ohio 1976).

17. People v. Bennett, 501 N.W.2d 106, 117; People v. DeJonge, 501 N.W.2d 127, 129 (Mich. 1993).

18. For citations to judicial decisions and statutes regarding medical care for children, see Dwyer, "The Children We Abandon," pp. 1353–63.

19. 267 N.E.2d 219 (Mass. 1971).

20. See, e.g., C.M. v. Catholic Children's Aid Society of Metropolitan Toronto, 2 S.C.R. 165, 200–201 (1994) (in deciding whether state must return child to custody of parents, "the best interests of the child must always prevail").

21. 603 F.2d 1271 (7th Cir. 1979).

22. 494 U.S. 872 (1990).

Chapter 3. Why Parents' Rights Are Wrong

1. See Barbara Bennett Woodhouse, "Hatching the Egg: A Child-Centered Perspective on Parents' Rights," *Cardozo Law Review* 14 (1993): 1747–1865, for a discussion of how a child-centered perspective would be likely to change the outcome of many custody disputes.

2. Allen Buchanan and Dan W. Brock, *Deciding for Others: The Ethics of Surrogate Decision Making* (Cambridge, Eng., 1989), p. 237.

3. See Alan R. White, *Rights* (Oxford, 1984), pp. 152–53.

4. See Ronald Dworkin, "What is Equality? Part 3: The Place of Liberty," *Iowa Law Review* 73 (1987): 7 ("we are now united in accepting the abstract egalitarian principle: government must act to make the lives of those it governs better lives, and it must show equal concern for the life of each").

5. Tying personhood to autonomy is still unsatisfactory, however, because it fails to account for the situation of nonautonomous adults and of children who will never become autonomous—either because they are terminally ill or because they are severely mentally disabled—neither of whom we regard as nonpersons or semipersons.

6. School District v. Schempp, 374 U.S. 203, 222 (emphasis added).

7. Downes v. Bidwell, 182 U.S. 244, 282 (1901).

8. Meyer v. Nebraska, 262 U.S. 390, 399 (1923).

9. 667 P.2d 395 (Kan. Ct. App. 1983).

10. West Virginia State Bd. of Educ. v. Barnette, 319 U.S. 624, 631 (1943) (emphasis added).

11. Wooley v. Maynard, 430 U.S. 705, 714 (1977) (emphasis added).

12. First Nat'l Bank of Boston v. Bellotti, 435 U.S. 765, 816 (1978) (White, J., dissenting).

13. Doe v. Bolton, 410 U.S. 179, 213 (1973) (Douglas, J., concurring) (emphasis added).

14. Cruzan v. Director, Mo. Dep't of Health, 497 U.S. 261, 269 (1990).

15. Ibid., p. 287 (O'Connor, J., concurring) (emphasis added). See also ibid., p. 305 (Brennan, J., dissenting) ("'Anglo-American law starts with the premise of thorough-going self-determination'").

16. Rust v. Sullivan, 500 U.S. 173, 216 (1991) (Blackmun, J., dissenting, joined by Stevens and Marshall, JJ.).

17. Planned Parenthood v. Casey, 505 U.S. 833, 851 (1992) (plurality opinion of O'Connor, Kennedy, and Souter, JJ.) (emphasis added).

18. Thornburgh v. American College of Obstetrics and Gynecology, 476 U.S. 747, 777 n.5 (1986) (Stevens, J., concurring) (quoting Charles Fried, "Correspondence," 6 *Philosophy and Public Affairs* 6 (1977): 288–89).

19. Doe v. Bolton, 410 U.S. 179, 211 (1973) (Douglas, J., concurring).

20. Bailey v. Alabama, 219 U.S. 219, 241 (1911).

21. Hodges v. United States, 203 U.S. 1, 17 (1906).

22. Akhil R. Amar and Daniel Widawsky, "Child Abuse As Slavery: A

Thirteenth Amendment Response to Deshaney," *Harvard Law Review* 105 (1992): 1364.

23. 41 *American Jurisprudence 2d*, "Husband and Wife" §§ 9–10 (1995).

24. Ibid., § 2; People v. Liberta, 474 N.E.2d 567, 572–73 (N.Y. 1984).

25. E.g., People v. Liberta, 474 N.E.2d 567, 573 (N.Y. 1984).

26. E.g., Planned Parenthood v. Danforth, 428 U.S. 52, 70 n.11 (1976); Eisenstadt v. Baird, 405 U.S. 438, 453 (1972).

27. The Supreme Court recognized that children are persons under our Constitution in, among other cases, Tinker v. Des Moines Indep. Community Sch. Dist, 393 U.S. 503, 511 (1969) (upholding children's First Amendment rights in public school context), and In re Gault, 387 U.S. 1, 13 (1967) (holding that children have due process rights in connection with their confinement to an institution for juvenile delinquents).

28. 497 U.S. 261 (1990).

29. In re Quinlan, 355 A. 2d 647, 661–62 (N.J.), *cert. denied sub. nom.* Garger v. New Jersey, 429 U.S. 922 (1976).

30. 509 U.S. 312 (1993).

31. 410 U.S. 113, 156–57.

32. See, e.g., Donald H. Regan, "Rewriting Roe v. Wade," *Michigan Law Review* 77 (1973): 1569, 1622, 1630–31; Judith Jarvis Thomson, "A Defense of Abortion," *Philosophy and Public Affairs* 1 (1971): 47.

33. E.g., Allison v. City of Birmingham, 580 So.2d 1377,1381–82 (Ala. Crim. App. 1991).; State v. O'Brien, 784 S.W.2d 187 (Mo. App. 1989); Crabb v. State, 754 S.W.2d 742 (Tex. App. 1988), *cert denied*, 493 U.S. 815 (1989).

34. See, e.g., *Cruzan*, 497 U.S. at 294, 295 (1990) (Scalia, J., concurring) (noting that there is no tradition and therefore no liberty to commit suicide); Michael H. v. Gerald D., 491 U.S. 110, 123 (1989) (plurality opinion of Scalia, J., joined by Rehnquist, C.J., and in part by O'Connor and Kennedy, JJ.).

35. E.g., Stephen L. Carter, *The Culture of Disbelief: How American Law and Politics Trivialize Religious Devotion* (New York, 1993), p. 184.

36. 478 U.S. 186, 199 (1986) (Blackmun, J. dissenting, joined by Brennan, Marshall, and Stevens, JJ.) (quoting Holmes, "The Path of the Law," *Harvard Law Review* 10 (1897): 457, 469).

37. Moore v. City of E. Cleveland, 431 U.S. 494, 549 (1977) (White, J., dissenting).

38. Michael H. v. Gerald D., 491 U.S. 110, 138 (1989) (Brennan, J., dissenting).

39. J. M. Balkin, "Tradition, Betrayal, and the Politics of Deconstruction," *Cardozo Law Review* 11 (1990): 1618.

40. Francis G. McCarthy, "The Confused Constitutional Status and Meaning of Parental Rights," *Georgia Law Review* 22 (1988): 984.

41. See County of Allegheny v. ACLU, 492 U.S. 573, 593 (1989) (holding that religious displays on government property are impermissible: "[T]he Establishment Clause, at the very least, prohibits government from appearing

to take a position on questions of religious belief"); Texas Monthly, Inc. v. Bullock, 489 U.S. 1, 8 (1989) (plurality opinion) (striking down a tax exemption benefiting only religious publications because "the Constitution prohibits, at the very least, legislation that constitutes an endorsement of one or another set of religious beliefs or of religion generally").

42. David Archard, *Children: Rights and Childhood* (New York, 1993), p. 103.

43. See Katharine T. Bartlett, "Re-Expressing Parenthood," *Yale Law Journal* 98 (1988): 293–340; Carl E. Schneider, "Rights Discourse and Neonatal Euthanasia," *California Law Review* 76 (1988): 162–63. ("Thinking in terms of rights encourages us to ask what we may do to free ourselves, not to bind ourselves. It encourages us to think about what constrains us from doing what we want, not what obligates us to do what we ought.")

44. Michael S. Wald, "Children's Rights: A Framework for Analysis," *University of California at Davis Law Review* 12 (1979): 277.

45. See Joel Feinberg, *The Moral Limits of the Criminal Law*, vol.1, *Harm to Others* (Oxford, 1984), p. 37.

46. Ibid.

47. See, e.g., Amy Gutmann, "Children, Paternalism, and Education: A Liberal Argument," *Philosophy and Public Affairs* 9 (1980): 352–53.

48. Thornburgh v. American College of Obstetrics and Gynecology, 476 U.S. 747, 790 (1986) (White, J., dissenting). In *Palko v. Connecticut*, 302 U.S. 319, 325 (1937), for example, the Court held that the right to trial by jury and to immunity from prosecution except as the result of an indictment are "not of the very essence of a scheme of ordered liberty," and therefore are not among the liberties that the Fourteenth Amendment protects against state encroachment.

49. See Christopher L. Eisgruber, "The Constitutional Value of Assimilation," *Columbia Law Review* 96 (1996): 102–3.

50. See Kenneth Henley, "The Authority to Educate," in *Having Children: Philosophical and Legal Reflections on Parenthood*, Onora O'Neill and William Ruddick ed. (New York, 1979), p. 262.

51. Schneider, "Rights Discourse," p. 160.

Chapter 4. Against a Community Right to Educate

1. See Board of Education of Kiryas Joel Village School District v. Grumet, 114 S. Ct. 2481 (1994).

2. See Chandran Kukathas, "Are There Any Cultural Rights?" *Political Theory* 20 (1992): 105. Subsequent references to this article appear in the text. See also Chandran Kukathas, "Cultural Rights Again," *Political Theory* 20 (1992): 674. Other formulations of a liberty-based approach to opposing state interference in the practices of minority communities include Abner S. Greene, "Kiryas Joel and Two Mistakes About Equality," *Columbia*

Law Review 96 (1996): 1–86; Jan Narveson, "Collective Rights?" *Canadian Journal of Law and Jurisprudence* 4 (1991): 329; Robert Nozick, *Anarchy, State, and Utopia* (New York, 1974), chap. 10; and Beth J. Singer, *Operative Rights* (Albany, 1993), pp. 174 ff.

3. E.g., Michael McDonald, "Should Communities Have Rights? Reflections on Liberal Individualism," *Canadian Journal of Law and Jurisprudence* 4 (1991): 218–19; James W. Nickel, "Equal Opportunity in a Pluralist Society," *Social Philosophy and Policy* 5 (1987): 105; Vernon Van Dyke, "The Cultural Rights of Peoples," *Universal Human Rights* 2 (1982), p. 32.

4. Will Kymlicka, *Liberalsim, Community, and Culture* (Oxford, 1989); Will Kymlicka, *Multicultural Citizenship: A Liberal Theory of Minority Rights* (Oxford, 1995).

5. Kymlicka, *Liberalism, Community, and Culture*, pp. 164–67.

6. See Kymlicka, *Multicultural Citizenship*, pp. 105, 111–13; Kymlicka, *Liberalism, Community, and Culture*, pp. 147, 149–50, 184, 194–95; McDonald, "Should Communities Have Rights?" p. 236; Joseph Raz, *The Morality of Freedom* (Oxford, 1986), p. 423; Vernon Van Dyke, "Collective Entities and Moral Rights: Problems in Liberal-Democratic Thought," *Journal of Politics* 44 (1982): 27, 31, 37.

7. Kymlicka, *Multicultural Citizenship*, pp. 85–86, 109.

8. E.g., John Tomasi, "Kymlicka, Liberalism, and Respect for Cultural Minorities," *Ethics* 105 (1995): 580.

9. See Patrice Riley, ed., *Growing Up Native American: An Anthology* (New York, 1993), p. 116.

10. Kymlicka, *Liberalism, Community, and Culture*, p. 175.

11. Kymlicka, *Multicultural Citizenship*, pp. 85–87.

12. Kymlicka, *Liberalism, Community, and Culture*, pp. 196–97.

Chapter 5. A Right to Equal Treatment

1. 409 U.S. 535, 538 (1973).

2. See Susan Moller Okin, *Justice, Gender, and the Family* (New York, 1989); Frances E. Olsen, "The Myth of State Intervention in the Family," *University of Michigan Journal of Law Reform* 18 (1985): 835–64.

3. See, e.g., Ill. Comp. Stat. Ann. ch. 105, para. 5/26–1 (West 1995): "Whoever has custody or control of any child between the ages of 7 and 16 years shall cause such child to attend some public school in the district wherein the child resides the entire time it is in session during the regular school term. . . . Provided, that the following children shall not be required to attend the public schools: 1. Any child attending a private or a parochial school where children are taught the branches of education taught to children of corresponding age and grade in the public schools. . . .

4. See David A. Strauss, "Due Process, Government Inaction and Private Wrongs," 1989 *Supreme Court Review*, 53, 64–66 ("the family unit is to a

significant extent the product of state action" because of the vast and exclusive control it gives parents over children's lives); Lawrence H. Tribe, "The Curvature of Constitutional Space: What Lawyers Can Learn from Modern Physics," *Harvard Law Review* 103 (1990): 12.

5. See Kymlicka, *Liberalism, Community, and Culture*, pp. 186, 190; Plyler v. Doe, 457 U.S. 202, 220 (1982) (noting " 'the basic concept of our system that legal burdens should bear some relationship to individual responsibility or wrongdoing,'") quoting Weber v. Aetna Casualty & Surety Co., 406 U.s. 164, 175 (1972).

6. The seeming inconsistency between current civil rights laws prohibiting racially discriminatory admissions policies in private elementary and secondary schools and exemptions to prohibitions against sexist teaching and other practices can be explained, I think, by the fact that both protect parental choice. Neither set of laws appears to confer any benefit on children; in fact, both result in children's being thrust into an environment where they are regarded as inferior.

7. Norwood v. Harrison, 413 U.S. 455, 465 (1973).

8. Ibid., pp. 466–67.

9. See John D. Colombo, "Why Is Harvard Tax-Exempt?" (And Other Mysteries of Tax Exemption for Private Educational Institutions)," *Arizona Law Review* 35 (1993): 846, 851–55.

10. See Grove City College v. Bell, 465 U.S. 555 (1984) ("Congress is free to attach reasonable and unambiguous conditions to federal financial assistance that educational institutions are not obligated to accept").

11. See New Jersey Welfare Rights Org. v. Cahill, 411 U.S. 619, 621 (1973) (invalidating exclusion of families containing illegitimate children from state welfare program and arguing that "the benefits extended under the challenged program are as indispensable to the health and well-being of illegitimate children as to those who are legitimate"); Railway Express Agency v. New York, 336 U.S. 106, 112 (1949) (Jackson, J., concurring) ("Government must exercise [its] powers so as not to discriminate between [its] inhabitants except upon some reasonable differentiation fairly related to the object of regulation").

12. See Sharyl Bender Peterson and Mary Alyce Lach, "Gender Stereotypes in Children's Books: Their Prevalence and Influence on Cognitive and Affective Development," *Gender and Education* 2 (1990): 194–95.

13. See Clark v. Jeter, 486 U.S. 456, 461 (1988); City of Cleburne v. Cleburne Living Ctr., 473 U.S. 432, 440–41 (1985); Mississippi Univ. for Women v. Hogan, 458 U.S. 718, 724 (1982).

14. 406 U.S. 164, 175 (1972).

15. 457 U.S. 202, 223 (1982).

16. United States v. Carolene Products Co., 304 U.S. 144, 152–53 n.4 (1938).

17. City of Cleburne v. Cleburne Living Ctr., 473, 472 (1985) (Marshall, J., concurring).

18. See Neal E. Devins, "Fundamentalist Christian Educators v. State: An Inevitable Compromise," *George Washington Law Review* 60 (1992): 825–34; Jennifer L. Rosato, "Putting Square Pegs in a Round Hole: Procedural Due Process and the Effect of Faith Healing Exemptions on the Prosecution of Faith Healing Parents," *U.S.F. Law Review* 29 (1994): 59, 61.

19. 347 U.S. 483, 493 (1954).

20. 411 U.S. 1, 35 (1979).

21. See Susan H. Bitensky, "Theoretical Foundations for a Right to Education under the U.S. Constitution: A Beginning to the End of the National Education Crisis," *Northwestern University Law Review* 86 (1992): 550 (arguing that an implicit fundamental right to education can be predicated upon several explicit provisions of the federal Constitution).

22. E.g., *School Dist. of Wilkensburg Educ. Ass'n*, 667 A.2d 5, 9 (Pa. 1995) ("[P]ublic education in Pennsylvania is a fundamental right"); *Skeen v. State*, 505 N.W.2d 299, 313 (Minn. 1993): *Claremont Sch. Dist. v. Governor*, 635 A.2d 1375, 1378 (N.H. 1993) ("The language commands, in no uncertain terms, that the State provide an education to all its citizens and that it support all public schools."); Serrano v. Priest, 487 P.2d 1241, 1263 (Cal. 1971); Salazar v. Honig, 246 Cal. Rptr. 837, 842 (Cal. Ct. App. 1988).

23. 457 U.S. at 223.

24. See City of Cleburne v. Cleburne Living Ctr., 473 U.S. 432, 439, 446–47 (1985); Weinberger v. Salfi, 422 U.S. 749 (1975); United States Dept. of Agriculture v. Moreno, 413 U.S. 528, 534 (1973).

25. See Cass R. Sunstein, "Naked Preferences and the Constitution," *Columbia Law Review* 84 (1984): 1693–94.

26. See James G. Dwyer, "The Children We Abandon: Religious Exemptions to Child Welfare and Education Laws As Denials of Equal Protection to Children of Religious Objectors," *North Carolina Law Review* 74 (1996): 1425–26; Devins, "Fundamentalist Christian Educators v. State," pp. 826, 831.

27. See Ronald Dworkin, "What is Equality? Part 3: The Place of Liberty." *Iowa Law Review*, 73 (1987): 7 ("Any genuine contest between liberty and equality is a contest liberty must lose").

28. Shelley v. Kraemer, 334 U.S. 1, 14–18 (1948).

29. 163 U.S. 537 (1896).

30. For an illuminating account of societal and governmental neglect of children's interests in recent years, see Lucia Hodgson, *Raised in Captivity: Why Does America Fail Its Children?* (St. Paul 1997).

31. See Devins, "Fundamentalist Christian Educators v. State."

32. 473 U.S. at 448.

33. Cooper v. Aaron, 358 U.S. 1 (1958); Brown v. Board of Education, 349 U.S. 294, 300 (1954).

34. Watson v. Memphis, 373 U.S. 526, 535 (1963); Wright v. Georgia, 373 U.S. 284, 293 (1963).

35. See, e.g., Steffan v. Aspin, 8 F.3d 57, 68 (D.C. Cir. 1993). ("Even if the

government does not itself act out of prejudice, it cannot discriminate in an effort to avoid the effects of others' prejudice. Such discrimination plays directly into the hands of the bigots; it ratifies and encourages their prejudice.")

36. See, e.g., In re President and Directors of Georgetown College, 331 F.2d 1000, 1007 (D.C. Cir.), *cert. denied*, 377 U.S. 978 (1964); In re E.G., 515 N.E.2d 286, 288–89 (Ill. App. Ct. 1987).

37. See Zucco v. Garrett, 501 N.E.2d 875 (Ill. App. Ct. 1986); Zummo v. Zummo, 574 A.2d 1130 (Pa. Super. Ct. 1990).

38. Employment Div. v. Smith, 494 U.S. 872 (1990).

39. See, e.g., Zummo v. Zummo, 574 A.2d 1130, 1149 (Pa. Super. Ct. 1990); In re Sampson, 317 N.Y.S.2d 641, 655–58 (N.Y. Fam. Ct. 1970).

40. See, e.g., Zummo, 574 A.2d at 1155–56; Mozert v. Hawkins County Bd. of Educ., 827 F. 2d 1058, 1067 (6th Cir. 1987), *cert. denied*, 484 U.S. 1066 (1988).

41. Mary A. Grant, *Catholic School Education in the United States: Developments and Current Concerns* (1992), pp. 238–39.

Chapter 6. Justice for Children

1. John Rawls, *A Theory of Justice* (Cambridge, Mass., 1971). For a different and very effective approach to elucidating what justice demands in terms of treatment of children born to members of conservative religious groups, see Nicholas Humphrey, "What Shall We Tell the Children?" *Social Research* (forthcoming fall 1998).

2. Readers familiar with Rawls's work will recognize that placing age and parentage among the characteristics about which persons in the original position are ignorant marks a significant extension of Rawls's theory. It brings children, whose situation Rawls has largely ignored, directly into the account of a just society. Rawls's Kantian focus on *moral* personhood (i.e., on certain cognitive capacities), as the basis for an individual's claim to equal consideration in the fashioning of a society's political principles and laws, which may explain the relative neglect of children, is unnecessary to his theory and unwarranted. Rawls offers no reason why beings should be subjects of our moral concern only insofar as they possess or have the potential to develop certain moral capacities. He does raise the pragmatic consideration that the stability of a just society depends in part on people's accepting the basic principles as just, which they can do only if they possess moral powers. However, he does not argue, nor could he plausibly, that *every* member of society must have moral powers and perceive the justice of the chosen scheme of cooperation in order to achieve stability. It should be sufficient that the vast majority do so. And beyond this pragmatic consideration, there is no argument in the theory for according justice to beings on the basis of their having moral powers or the potential to develop them. A more plausible view is that any sentient being whose life our decisions

significantly affect should be a subject of our moral concern. In this view, even terminally ill infants and profoundly mentally handicapped children should have an equal claim to just treatment.

3. John Rawls, *Political Liberalism* (New York, 1993).

4. See John Rawls, "The Priority of Right and Ideas of the Good," *Philosophy and Public Affairs* 17 (1988): 266 n.25.

5. Rawls, *A Theory of Justice*, p. 214.

6. Ibid., pp. 202–3.

7. Richard J. Arneson and Ian Shapiro, "Democratic Autonomy and Religious Freedom: A Critique of *Wisconsin v. Yoder*," in Ian Shapiro and Russell Hardin, eds., *Nomos XXXVIII: Political Order* (New York, 1996); Rawls, *A Theory of Justice*.

8. Rawls, *A Theory of Justice*, pp. 142–43.

9. See Susan H. Bitensky, "A Contemporary Proposal for Reconciling the Free Speech Clause with Curricular Values Inculcation in the Public Schools," *Notre Dame Law Review* 70 (1995): 769–843 (arguing in favor of public schools' inculcating moral norms that "transcend the status of debatable values and have effectively become 'ideational prerequisites' to collective human existence").

10. See Susan Muller Okin, *Justice, Gender, and the Family* (New York, 1989) (discussing the adverse consequences of an upbringing in a patriarchal "private" environment on the moral and political development of children).

11. Jean Piaget, *The Moral Judgment of the Child* (New York, 1965); Allen Buchanan and Dan W. Brock, *Deciding for Others: The Ethics of Surrogate Decision Making* (Cambridge, Mass., 1989), pp. 220–23.

12. Gary B. Melton, "Decision Making by Children: Psychological Risks and Benefits," in *Children's Competence to Consent*, ed. Gary B. Melton, Gerald B. Koocher, and Michael J. Saks (New York, 1983), pp. 21, 27; June Louin Tapp and Gary B. Melton, "Preparing Children for Decision Making: Implications of Legal Socialization Research," in *Children's Competence*, pp. 225–26.

13. Gerald Dworkin, *The Theory and Practice of Autonomy* (New York, 1988), p. 20.

14. See Harry Brighouse, "Egalitarian Liberals and School Choice," *Politics and Society* 24 (1996): 457–86, for a summary of and valuable contribution to the academic debate.

15. See Mary Beth Gehrman, "Reading, Writing, and Religion," *Free Inquiry* (fall 1987): 18.

16. Rawls, *A Theory of Justice*, pp. 396, 440.

17. See, e.g., John Exdell, "Feminism, Fundamentalism, and Liberal Legitimacy," *Canadian Journal of Philosophy* (Sept. 1994).

18. Rawls, *A Theory of Justice*, p. 84. See Brighouse, "Egalitarian Liberals and School Choice" for a discussion of equal educational opportunity based on assumptions about the value of autonomy for the broader goal of individuals' finding "worthy lives."

19. Rawls, *A Theory of Justice*, p. 84.
20. Ibid., p. 338. See also ibid., pp. 178, 430.
21. See Kymlicka, *Multicultural Citizenship*, p. 89.
22. Rawls, *Political Liberalism*, p. 199.
23. Ibid., p. 200.
24. Ibid., p. 199.

Index